EARLY COURT RECORDS OF PULASKI COUNTY, GEORGIA

1809-1825

by

Lee G. Barrow

The publication of this book was made possible by a grant from the R. J. Taylor, Jr. Foundation of Atlanta

Early Court Records of Pulaski County, Georgia, 1809-1825
by Lee G. Barrow

Published for the author by:
Southern Historical Press, Inc.
375 West Broad Street
Greenville, S.C. 29601

Copies of this book can be ordered from:
Lee G. Barrow
1530 S. W. 100 Terrace
Fort Lauderdale, FL 33324

ISBN 0-89308-502-2

Early Court Records of Pulaski County, Georgia, 1809-1825

by Lee G. Barrow

Contents

Foreword

Between 1805 and 1820 many pioneers settled the newly-opened lands of central Georgia, but the lack of surviving records makes learning about these people difficult. Many county records have been lost, and numerous families had come and gone before the first surviving federal census was taken in 1820. If a person did not participate in one of the land lotteries, there is often little information available to searchers.

Fortunately Pulaski County (which originally included most of present-day Dodge and Bleckley Counties) has not had a major loss of court records. There is a wealth of information in the early records, including thousands of names, hundreds of family relationships, where people lived, and even a few birth and death dates. Yet only a few isolated tax lists have been published and only the deed records and one minute book are indexed. The likelihood of finding information on someone who did not own land is rare without a tedious search.

This book is a transcription of all known extant court records, except deeds and tax lists, of Pulaski County from its formation in 1809 until 1817. Lists of jurors, administrators, executors, and guardians (which take up less space and usually provide more genealogical information) are included up until 1825. The index lists all references to persons by full name as well as cross-references for spelling variations.

Acknowledgements

This project was made possible in part by a generous grant from the R. J. Taylor, Jr. Foundation of Atlanta, which should be commended for its commitment to genealogical research in Georgia. The author would also like to thank the staffs of the Georgia Archives and the offices of the Pulaski County Clerk of Court and Probate Judge for their assistance. Most of all he would like to thank his talented wife Ingrid for her encouragement and for tolerating his many long research trips.

Formatting

Because of the varying styles of the different clerks, an attempt was made to standardize some elements for consistency and ease of reading. For example, certain punctuation marks have been added, such as commas between names and periods at ends of sentences, and many capitalizations have been changed to conform to modern practice.

Most misspellings and obvious mistakes are entered as they appear in the original with the mistake underlined. However, some old style spellings (authorised, shew) and misuse of double letters (Sherrif, stabing) are entered without comment. Text which was crossed out in the original but is still readable is included here, struck through with a single line.

Except in the jury lists, all last names have been capitalized to assist the reader in locating them.

The following symbols are used:

? Question marks indicate that the handwriting was difficult to read and that the word represents the editor's best guess.

[!] An exclamation point indicates an apparent incongruity, such as a statement which contradicts itself in some way.

\ / Slashes enclose text which was inserted in the original as an afterthought or a correction.

[ ] Brackets enclose text which was added by the editor, either as an assumption of missing text or as a comment (in italics).

) Right parentheses over one another are used to indicate wavy
) vertical lines.

{ } Braces enclose text which in the original is enclosed by a wavy circle.

JUROR LISTS
1809-1823

Note: This book was apparently copied from original lists, as loose originals were located for 1818, 1821, and 1823. For these years, some names differed or were not copied into the book, as indicated herein by notes.

Since the pages are not numbered in the original book, an attempt was made to emulate its layout in order to facilitate comparisons.

Georgia
Pulaski County

The following list contains the names of persons selected as Grand Juriors for said county agreeable to an act of the general assembly passed the seventh day of December, 1805:

1 George Walker
2 Joseph Reaves
3 William A. Harper Esqr.
4 Dickson Jelks
5 Samuel Jones Esqr.
6 Daniel Regan
7 James Adams
8 Joel Dauson
9 Mark Mason
10 Samuel Regan
11 David Snell
12 Sanders Bush
13 William Hall
14 Needham Stephens
15 Robirt Daniel
16 Sutton Truluck
17 Charles Mayo
18 Joseph Davison
19 William Brackin
20 James Bush
21 William McCormack
22 William Jelks
23 Theophilus Sutton
24 Michael Horn Junr.
25 Jacob Snell
26 Sanders Colson
27 James Ramsey
28 William S. Lancaster
29 Henry Fulgham Esqr.
30 Archibald Lassiter
31 James T. Thomas Esqr.
32 Joab Horn
33 Jessee Powel
34 Benjaman Brown
35 Benjaman Smith
36 Elisha Higgs
37 Abraham Vickers
38 Edmond Hogan Esqr.
39 Thomas McGriff
40 George G. Gaines
41 John Snelling
42 Sands Standley
43 Joseph Everitt
44 Philip Jones
45 Hardy Vickers
46 William Goodson
47 Needham Bryant
48 Gedion Mayo

49 Michael Horn Sr.

50 Joseph Barron

51 John Rosure

Pulaski

We the undersigned Justices of the Inferior Court for the County aforesaid having met agreeable to law for the purpose of selecting Grand Juriors from the best information that could be collected being no tax returns in the County – Do certify that the foregoing list is a true transcript of fit & proper persons to serve as Grand Juriors for the ensuing year.

Given under our hands this 5th day of June 1809.

Edmund Hogan, J.I.C.
H. Fulgham, J.I.C.
James T. Thomas, J.I.C.
Richd. H. Thomas, Clk.
Lewis Holland Sheriff

Georgia
Pulaski County

The following list contains the names of persons selected as Petitt Juriors for said county agreeable to an act of the general assembly passed the seventh day of December, 1805:

1 John Yon

2 John McCray

3 Nathaniel Harthhorn

4 Isham Jordin

5 Robirt Thompson

6 Moses Kirkland

7 William Wynn
8 John Scarborough
9 Joel Ellis
10 Thomas Coats
11 Leonard Stringer
12 Paskil Hammick
13 Joseph Stringer
14 William Hammick
15 John Lungino
16 Demsey Taylor
17 Charles Daniel
18 Jerimiah Gilstrap
19 Robert Sillivant
20 James Dyckes
21 Orenditus Watson
22 Abraham Bush
23 Hasil Holley
24 James Trull
25 Spiar Mills
26 Bigar Singleton
27 John Grinstid
28 Isaac Dyckes
29 John Gilstrap
30 William Grinstid
31 John Smith
32 William Taylor Sr.
33 Edward Lassitir
34 Henry Dewit
35 Arther Jones
36 Haywood Jones
37 Benjamin Robinson
38 Jacob Taylor
39 William Morris
40 James Raney
41 Henry Dorch
42 John Bennet
43 Benjamin Harrison
44 Drury Mayo
45 David Gartman
46 George Jemison
47 Laban Kent
48 Eley Ramsey
49 Holden Dunn
50 Jacob Dunn
51 John Barrow
52 William Taylor
53 John Swearingen
54 William Nobles
55 Elihu Heeth
56 William Roberts
57 James Tomberlin
58 Jordin Dees
59 Sanders McDaniel
60 Isham McDaniel
61 George Kelley
62 Maliciah Kelley
63 William Kelley

64 Edward Bryant
65 Bartholomew Lungino
66 William Johnson
67 Joseph Regan
68 Nathan Sowel
69 Lester Crafford
70 Jessee Lively
71 Thomas Adams
72 Thomas Bagget
73 Drewry Mims
74 John Coleman
75 John Vass
76 Stephen Mitchel
77 Abraham Hollady
78 Aaron Johnson
79 Joseph Spell
80 Marmaduke Kent
81 Sanders Spell
82 Robirt Mumfort
83 John Manning
84 Henry Senterfit
85 Samuel Senterfit
86 Drewry Dees
87 William Allin
88 Thomas Warren
89 William Hagans
90 Isham Hagans
91 Charles Stuart
92 Henry Stuart
93 John Stuart
94 Henry Hart
95 Isaac Bracken
96 Joshua Lee
97 Isaac Philips
98 Jonathan Peacock
99 Samuel Peacock
100 Samuel Hart
101 Barney Hart
102 Neale McAlpin
103 Archabal Thompson
104 Nimrod Smith
105 Benjaman Posey
106 William Dreadin
107 John Moses
108 Samuel King
109 Bolin Swearingen
110 Richd. Thomas
111 William Pearce
112 Wilson Bass
113 Archibald Jones
114 Thomas Franklin
115 Amos Wheelar
116 Ebo John Smith
117 William Smith
118 Mark Wheelar
119 Reubin Wheelar
120 John Bryant
121 Turner Everitt
122 Charles Everitt

123 James Everitt

124 Robirt Dewit

125 Daniel Coats

Pulaski

We the undersigned justises of the
Inferior court for the county aforesaid
having met agreeable to law for the
purpose of selecting pettit juriors
from the best information that could
be collected being no tax returns in the county
do sertify that the foregoing list is a true
transcript of fit and proper persons to
serve as Pettit Juriors for the ensuing year
Given under our hands this 5th day of June
1809.

Edmund Hogan, J.I.C.
H. Fulgham, J.I.C.
James T. Thomas, J.I.C.
Richd. H. Thomas, Clk.
Lewis Holland Sheriff

Entered this 10th day of June 1809.

Richd. H. Thomas, Clk.

[*Next page of book is blank*]

Georgia) The following list contains
Pulaski County) the names of persons selected as
Grand Jurors for said county agreeable
to an act of the general assembly passed
the seventh day of December 1805.

1 Daniel Regan
2 John Rozar
3 Nathaniel Mercer
4 James Odom
5 Archabald H. Odom
6 Leonard Stringer
7 Joseph Davison
8 Moses Tison
9 Joseph Barron
10 George Dykes
11 Mordock McLeod
12 William Brackin
13 Sutton Truluck
14 Benjaman Brown
15 William Johnson
16 Sands Standley
17 Hardy Vickers
18 Benjamin Smith
19 William Goodson
20 Abraham Vickers
21 William Hall
22 Edward Briant
23 Lester Crawford
24 John Snelling
25 George G. Gains
26 Edmund Hogan Esqr.
27 William S. Lancaster
28 Archibald Lassiter
29 William Jelkes
30 Thomas Sheppard
31 Joseph Sessions
32 Elisha Higgs
33 Orandatus Watson
34 Phillip Jones
35 Charles Cardin
36 John Grinstead
37 James T. Thomas Esqr.
38 Michael Horn Junr.
39 Hinche Warren
40 Daniel Snell
41 James Ramsey
42 Joel Dawson
43 Benjamin Harvey
44 Simon Bardin
45 Jacob Snell
46 David Snell
47 Jessee Powell

48 John Raney
49 Joseph Reaves
50 John Sheard [*Sherrard*]
51 Henry Fulgham Esqr.
52 Gedion Mayo
53 William A. Harper Esqr.
54 James Dees
55 Mark Mason
56 Shadrick Atkins
57 William Deshazo
58 Lewis Holland
59 Josiah Everitt
60 William Haney
61 George Walker
62 Samuel King
63 Sanders Colson
64 Bolin Swearingin
65 Daniel Cole
66 Needham Stephens
67 Allin Tooke
68 John Gilstrap
69 Samuel Jones Esqr.
70 Thomas McGriff
71 Rich^{d}. H. Thomas
72 Turner Averitt
73 Asa Pipkin
74 John Stegall
75 Isaac Dykes
76 Demsey Daughrity
77 John Stewart
78 Zion Davis
79 Robert Dewit

Hartford

We the undersigned Justises of the
Inferior court for the county aforesaid
having met agreeable to law for the pur
=pose of selecting Grand Juriors from the
books of the receiver of tax returns for the
county aforesaid; Do sertify that the fore
=going list contains a true transcript of fit
and proper persons to searve as Grand Juri
=ors for the ensuing year; given under our
hands this 4th day of June 1810) H. Fulgham, J.I.C.
) S. Jones, J.I.C.
Entered this 5th day of June 1810) Ja^{s}. T. Thomas, J.I.C.
) R. H. Thomas, Clk.
R. H. Thomas Clk.) Elisha Higgs, Sher[iff]

Georgia) The following contains
Pulaski County) the names of persons selected
as petit juriors for said county agreea
=ble to an act of the general assembly pass
=ed the seventh day of December 1805

1 Richard Wheelear
2 John Flowers
3 Thomas Rogers
4 Ferrel Belcher
5 Samuel Millar
6 Shadrick Lee
7 Thomas Hester
8 Edmund Hester
9 Henry Beatey
10 Abram Yearta
11 Needham Briant
12 Blakeley Edens
13 John Phillips
14 Evan Thomas
15 George Wright
16 Charles Mills
17 William Wynn
18 James McNorton
19 Reubin Wheelar
20 Joseph Stringer
21 Moses Giddons
22 John Briant
23 Moses Kirtlan
24 William Briant
25 George Warren
26 William Drawdy
27 John Smith
28 William Smith
29 Sherrod Phillips
30 Thomas Westley
31 Hezekiah Phillips
32 Wright Woodard
33 William Phillips Senr.
34 William Phillips
35 Jethro Phillips
36 Burrel Phillips
37 Benjaman Weeks
38 Ephram Phillips
39 Benjn. Stegall
40 James Denard
41 Robert Hodges
42 Adam Billings
43 Christopher Edwards
44 Isaac Phillips
45 James Dykes
46 Isaac Boyett

47 Joshua Lee
48 William Briant [#2]
49 Benjaman Harrison
50 Soloman Brewer
51 Jessee Briant
52 Felix Dykes
53 Drewry Mayo
54 Aaron Scarborough
55 Jessee Lee
56 James Beatey
57 Nimrod Phillips
58 Elias Phillips
59 John Lee Sn^r^.
60 John Dixon
61 Jonathan Miller
62 Archabald Odom
63 Baley Harral
64 John Lee Junr.
65 Ann Moses
66 Christopher Mercer
67 Richard Taylor
68 Edmund Giddons
69 Henry Stewart
70 Isham M^c^Daniel
71 James Temples
72 Jacob Singleton
73 Malica Kelley
74 George Kelley
75 Aner [*Abner?*] Singleton
76 Samuel Smith
77 William Kelley
78 Alexander Daniel
79 Augley Coward
80 Isham Shuffield
81 Marmaduke Kent
82 John Harrall
83 John Swearingin
84 Josiah Corthorn
85 Spire Mills
86 Charles Daniel
87 Amos Wheelar
88 Benjaman Posey
89 Arthor Jones
90 Biggars Singleton
91 John Jones
92 William Grinstead
93 Lewis Dewet
94 Humphrey Posey
95 Mark Wheeler
96 Christopher Boyce
97 Henry Dewet
98 Whashington Lancaster
99 William Hilyard
100 John Harvey
101 Aaron Johnson
102 William Morras
103 Burril Campbell
104 Marmaduke Kimborough
105 William Parker
106 Nimrod Smith
107 George Blare

108 Bartholomiew Lungino
109 Edward Lasseter
110 Holden Dunn
111 Daniel Cornwell
112 James Adams
113 John Bedingfield
114 James Bedingfield
115 Michael Horn Sr.
116 James Tomlinson
117 Charles Mayo
118 Paskel Hammack
119 John Manning
120 Thomas Loftin
121 Jacob Taylor
122 Thomas Warran
123 Silas Johnson
124 Jordin Dees
125 Demsey Taylor
126 Martin Horn
127 Abraham Bush
128 Richd. Wynn
129 Robert Munford
130 Jeffery Montford
131 James Raney
132 William Roberts
133 Martin Swearingen
134 William Hammack
135 Robert Sillivant
136 Barney Hart
137 Henry Hart
138 William Allen
139 Drewry Dees
140 Laban Kent
141 David Boyce
142 William Dryden
143 Reubin Rowland
144 William Mayo
145 William Taylor
146 Reubin Warran
147 Wilson Bass
148 Francis Harvey
149 Robert Matthews
150 Absolam Hopson
151 Joel Walker
152 James Williams
153 James Carmicael
154 Lewis Lee
155 Elihu Keith
156 John Barrow
157 Chesley Davis
158 James Bush Sr.
159 Charles Stewart
160 Levi Bush
161 William McCormack
162 Hardy Fulgham
163 Elisha Garbit
164 John Moses
165 Thomas Franklin
166 Henry Senterfeit
167 James Watson
168 Isham Hagan

169 Samuel Hart
170 William Hagan
171 Arthor Tooke
172 Jeremiah Gilstrap
173 Haywood Jones
174 Elijah Barker
175 Theophilus Sutton
176 John Dees
177 David Gartman
178 Samuel Regan
179 William Smedley
180 Joab Horn

Heartford Pulaski County

We the undersigned justises of the superior court for the county aforesaid having met agreeable to law for the purpose of selecting pettit jurors from the books of the receiver of tax returns for the County of Pulaski do sertify that the foregoing list is a treu transcript of fit and proper persons to serve as pettit jurors for the ensuing years.

Given under our hands ~~and seals~~
this 4th day of June 1810

H. Fulgham, J.I.C.
S. Jones, J.I.C.
Jas. T. Thomas, J.I.C.
R. H. Thomas, Clk.
Elisha Higgs, Sheriff

Entered this 5th day of June in the year 1810.

Richd. H. Thomas, Clk.

Georgia) The following contains the
Pulaski County) names of persons selected as
grand jurors for said county agreeable to an
act of the general assembly passed the seventh day
of December 1805.

1 Doct^{r}. M. H. Powell
2 Clement Lanier
3 William Jelks
4 Daniel Cole
5 Joab Horn
6 James T. Thomas
7 James L. Perry
8 Isaac Burkhalter
9 Ja^{s}. M. Taylor
10 W^{m}. S. Lancaster
11 Michael Horn
12 George G. Gaines
13 Jacob Snell
14 Neil McAlpin
15 Gideon Mayo
16 Zion Davis
17 Benjamin Bruton
18 Sands Standley
19 Shadrick Atkins
20 Joseph Reeves
21 Joel Dawson
22 Benjamin Smith
23 Charles Mayo
24 Thomas McDaniel
25 Elijah Wallis
26 Jesse Powell
27 James Clark
28 Ja^{s}. Braswell
29 William Isler
30 John Snelling
31 Allen Tooke
32 Hinche Warren

33 Murdoch McLeod

34 James Dees

35 Sanders Colson

36 Neidham Stephens

37 Wm. H. Gross

38 Benjamin Harvey

39 Samuel Jones

40 Turner Everett

41 Drury May

42 Mark Mason

43 Lewis Holland

44 David Snell

45 Daniel Snell

46 George Walker

47 Joseph Barron

48 Thomas McGriff

49 Henry Fulgham

50 Christopher Rodes

51 Blakely Edins

52 R. H. Thomas

53 Jas. McNorton

54 Asa Pipkin

55 John Shearard

56 Wm. Mehaffee

57 Nathaniel Mercer

58 Simon Barden

59 Archibald Odam

60 Hardy Vickers

61 Abraham Vickers

62 Lester Crofford

63 Ferrel Belcher

64 John Crofford

65 Archibald H. Odam

66 Stephen Mitchell

67 James Roundtree

68 John Wilcox

69 John Rozier

70 John Lee Jn[r].

71 Edward Bryan

72 John Lester

73 Benjamin Brown

74 William Hall

75 Daniel Regan

76 James Everett

77 Robert Daniel

78 Dixon Jelks

79 James Tomberlin

80 Robert Thompson

81 Charles Cardin

82 James Ramsey

83 William Goodson

84 Samuel Regan

85 John Harvey

86 Robert Dewitt

87 Orandatis Watson

88 Archibald Lasiter

89 Thomas A. Hill

90 John Ramsey

91 Archibald Thompson

92 William Johnson

93 John Grinstead

94 William Deshazo

95 Joab Crutchfield

96 Drury Dees

97 Robert Mathis

98 John Gilstrap

99 Samuel Hart

100 William Mayo

101 Chesley Davis

102 William Yarbrough

103 Sutton Truluck

104 John Moses

105 Colson Adams

106 Philip Jones

107 William Haney

108 Robert Hodges

109 Jeffrey Montford

110 David Gartman

111 William Burnam

112 John Stewart

113 Josiah Everett

114 William Wood
115 John Grace
116 William Lyon
117 Reuben Warren
118 John Swearingen
119 John Rainey

Pulaski

We the undersigned justices
of the inferior court for the county aforesaid
having met agreeable to law for the purpose
of selecting grand jurors from the books of the
Receiver of Tax Returns - do certify that the
foregoing list is a true transcript of fit &
proper persons to serve as Grand Jurors for the ensu
=ing years - given under our hands this
first day of June 1812 -

Henry Fuglham J.I.C.
James T. Thomas J.I.C.
James M. Taylor J.I.C.
Richard H. Thomas Clk.
Allen Tooke Shff.

Entered this 4th day of August in the year
1812.

Richard H. Thomas Clk.

Georgia) The following contains the names
Pulaski County) of persons selected as petit jurors for
said county agreeable to an act of the general
assembly passed the seventh day of December
1805.

1 Edmund Burke

2 John Maning

3 Elisha Hanks

4 Joseph Regan

5 Henry Beaty

6 Moses Kirkland

7 Elias Philips

8 Nathan Mattox

9 Isaac Blount

10 Isham Shuffield

11 James Temples

12 William Kelley

13 Malica Kelley

14 Isham Carr

15 John Hagan

16 Starling Sanders

17 Benja. Mewborn

18 William Ward

19 Archd. McMillan

20 Marideth Mercer

21 Jesse Williams

22 Joshua Harris

23 William Moore

24 Wm. Yarbrough Jnr.

25 Isham Hagan

26 Hugh Ingram

27 John Maning [#2]

28 Martin Horn

29 John Stegall

30 Henry Hart

31 Barney Hart

32 John Smedley

33 John A. Williams

34 Wm. T. Reneau

35 Wm. D. Rice

36 Nathan Posey

37 Joel Williams

38 Thomas H. Davis

39 Thomas Hatton

40 John Jones

41 James Cardin

42 John Bradshaw

43 Henry Dewitt

44 John Yon

45 Biggers Singleton

46 John Cardin

47 John J. Ford

48 Holden Dunn

49 Thomas Howell

50 Bartley C. Williams

51 William Hammock

52 Thomas Morrow

53 Laban Kent

54 Robert Monfort

55 James Barrow

56 John Barrow

57 Jesse Pennington

58 Joel Reeves

59 William Cardin

60 Theophilus Sutton

61 Jordan Dees

62 Daniel Shine

63 William Taylor Jr.

64 Jacob Taylor

65 James W. Shine

66 Dempsey Layton

67 Grantham Horn

68 James Rainey

69 Philip Whitchard

70 William McCormick

71 John Yarbrough

72 Josiah Winbern

73 Nelson Chace

74 Francis Cody

75 John Nelson

76 Jacob Joiner

77 Abram Nipper

78 John Blackbourn

79 Alexander Shaw

80 Elisha Brannon

81 Archd. Jones

82 Jeremiah Bell

83 Stephen Hagan

84 Etheldred Howell

85 Theophilus Rogers

86 Thomas Temples

87 Moses Harrell

88 Levi Brown

89 Jordan Leppard

90 Benja. Johnson

Petit Juror list, June 1812

91 John Kelley
92 Andrew Faulk
93 John Temples
94 Baptist Brumley
95 Frederick Temples
96 Charles Covinah
97 Jesse Jump
98 Richard Gainey
99 Thomas Philips
100 John Vass
101 Baley Harrill
102 Arthur Shuffield
103 Levi Harrell
104 West Shuffield
105 Conrod Augley
106 John Harrell
107 Briant Shuffield
108 Silas Johnson
109 Wm. Burkhalter Jnr.
110 Wm. Burkhalter Snr.
111 Jacob Harrell
112 Asa Harrell
113 Jesse Harrell
114 Etheldred Harrell
115 Henry Evans
116 Levi Harrell [#2]
117 William Harrell
118 Samuel Smith
119 Lewis Thomas
120 William Bolin
121 Aaron Scarbrough
122 Samuel Miller
123 William Barrow
124 Jonathan Miller
125 Henry Cooper
126 Alexander Smith
127 John Smith
128 Thomas Rogers
129 Needham Bryan
130 Jesse Bryan
131 Jesse Pipkin
132 Christopher Edwards
133 James Bush
134 William Smith
135 Moses Cherklin
136 John Bryan
137 William Long
138 Thomas Taylor
139 Richard Taylor
140 Edward Giddins
141 John Dixon
142 Thomas Westley
143 Joshua Lee
144 Soloman Brown
145 Moses Giddins
146 Benjamin Stegall
147 Warren Hart
148 Stephen Pipkin
149 Abraham Yarter
150 Jacob Yartey
151 Ephram Philips
152 Sharrard Philips
153 Ephram Philips [#2]
154 James Miller
155 Jonathan Vickers
156 John Miller
157 John Bird
158 Jas. Bedingfield
159 George Armstrong
160 William Hilliard
161 Washington Lancaster
162 Charles Daniel
163 Amos Wheeler
164 William Grinstead
165 Richd. Wheeler
166 Haywood Jones
167 Jacob McCuller
168 Reubin Rolin
169 Richard Winn
170 John Clark
171 Joel Walker
172 Thomas Franklin
173 Wilson Bass
174 Patrick McGriff
175 Fedk. Swearingen
176 Daniel Mercer
177 William Smith [#2]
178 Jeremiah Gilstrap
179 Samuel Stewart
180 Charles Stewart
181 Charles Creech
182 Lewis Baggot
183 Nicholas Baggot
184 Benja. Smith Jnr.
185 Little J. Smith
186 Samuel Hutson
187 John Daniel
188 John Baggot
189 Elisha Evans
190 Reubin Roundtree
191 Laurence Folsom
192 Marmaduke Kent
193 Ezekiel Jornican
194 Dennis Adams
195 Isaac Foreman
196 William Taylor Snr.
197 Hugh Taylor
198 Thomas Rogers [#2]
199 Thos. Averitt
200 Elisha Garbitt
201 Samuel King
202 Wm. Roberts
203 John Dees
204 Elisha Barker

205 William Hagan
206 Robert Deshazo
207 Gillis Ryals
208 William Little
209 Jason Brinson
210 Thomas Paramore
211 Jesse Lively
212 Noah Calhoon
213 Thomas Adams
214 Solomon Lamb
215 William Hamilton
216 John Silvester
217 Josiah Taylor
218 Larrey Jiner [*Joiner*]
219 Thomas Cuningham
220 Benjamin Posey
221 John Ratliff
222 James Ratliff
223 John Coleman
224 Edward Runnels
225 Nathan Sowell
226 Jacob Spickard
227 Philemon Terrell
228 Christopher McCray
229 William Lester
230 William Philips Snr.
231 Aaron Johnson
232 Fort Alford
233 Mark Wheeler
234 Umphrey Posey
235 John Jones [#2]
236 Francis Harvey
237 Daniel Conwell
238 James Jones
239 John Bennett
240 John Hawthorn
241 Spire Mills
242 Moses Sutton
243 Ezekiel Philips
244 Thomas Hester
245 Edward Hester
246 Lennerl Brown
247 Phelix Dykes
248 Benjamin Weecks
249 Thomas Tamley
250 Daniel Thompson
251 Shadrach Lee
252 Nimrod Philips
253 Neal McCormack
254 James Beaty
255 John Lee Snr.
256 William Smith [#3]
257 John Lee Yr.
258 Jesse Lee
259 William Bryan
260 Jas. Deikes
261 William Smith [#4]
262 Henry Mills
263 Fredk. Wolf
264 Nimrod Smith
265 Danl. Sparrow
266 William Coon
267 Saml. Coleman
268 Abram Holliday
269 William Ray
270 Soloman Sutton
271 Peter Hagan
272 Henry Hagan
273 Philemon Bryan
274 Thos. Shepherd
275 Edward Lasiter
276 Henry Senterfeit
277 John Parish
278 Arthur Tooke
279 Jonathan Taylor
280 Noah Wheeler
281 Adams Billings
282 Josiah Singletary
283 George Kelley
284 James Odam
285 Benja. Harrison
286 Willis Bryan
287 Isaac Philips
288 Burrell Philips
289 Wm. Winn
290 Aaron Singletary

291 Daniel Dyckes)
292 Isaac Harrell)
293 Samuel Perkins)
294 Dan[l]. Henderson) We the undersigned justices of the inferior court for the County aforesaid having met agreeable to law for the purpose of selecting Pettit Jurors from the books of the Receiver of Tax Returns - do certify that the foregoing list is a true transcript of fit and proper persons to serve as Pettit Jurors for the ensuing years.

Given under our hands this first day of June 1812.

Henry Fulgham J.I.C.
James T. Thomas J.I.C.
James M. Taylor J.I.C.
Richard H. Thomas Clk.
Allen Tooke Shff.

Entered this 4 day August in the year 1812 –

Richard H. Thomas Clk.

Selection of Grand and Petit Jurors made 17 October 1818

Grand Jurors

Oran D. Watson Senr.
Furney F. Gatlin
James S. Ivey
William Jelks
Thomas Clayton
Uriah Yarborough
Jacob Watson
Daniel Cornwall
Burton H. Pitts
Henry Hagan
Allen Tooke
Arthur Tooke
Allen Scarborough
Edward Blackshear
Thomas J. Johnson
William Yarborough Senr.
Needham Stephens
Sands Stanley
William McCormick

Petit Jurors

Daniel Sparrow
Arche Daniel
Wiley Williams
Dennis Adams
John Cardin
Robert Dewitt
Ulysses Crutchfield
Charles Cardin
Samuel Hart
William Pratt
John Bradshaw
Jeffrey Montfort
William Grinstead
Daniel McNair
Elias Ballard
James Hayes
Levi Timmons
John McLenan
Daniel McLenan
John Bird
Aquilla McNair
Amos Wheeler
Samuel Jones J^{r}.
John Hagan
David Hagan
Isham Hagan
Sterling Tooke
Robert Thompson
Kinchen Dawson
John Jones
Robert Lee
Dixon Jelks

Grand Jurors	Petit Jurors
Josiah Everitt	Biggars Singleton
James M. Taylor	John Nelson
John Carruthers	Seth Watson
Jessee Cannon	Charles Williams
Jos. W. Denson	Burton Ferrel
James Roach	William Barefoot
Thomas Howell	John McCormick
David Girtman	Mathew McCormick
Joab Horne [*orig. only*]	Nelson Clayton
Jessee Senterfit	Wesley Yarboro
Sanders Coalson	Neel Ard
Isaac Buckhalter	Hugh Carr
John Gillstrap	George Cherry
Jessee Powell	John Howell
William Horne	Wright Howell
Thomas Johnson Senr.	Francis Faircloth
Zelah Pullin	John Pollun
George Walker Senr.	John Haddock
Joseph B. Bryan	Fred^{k}. Wolf
Joel Walker	Spier Mills
Ezekiel Taylor	Ethel^{d}. Howell
Robert Mathews	Henry Senterfit
Daniel Rhodes	Charles Seabert
Bartlett Barker	Edward Herrin
Bolin Swearingame	John W. Turner
W^{m}. Mayo	Thos. Smith S^{r}.
John Dees	John O. Grant
Simon Bardin	Willis Reeves
William Garbitt	Eli Horne
	Burwell Howell
	John Little
	John Donaldson
	Eliphlet King

Grand Jurors	Petit Jurors
Gideon Kellam	William Whiggam
Thomas McGriff	Henry Smith
Jordan Anderson	Thomas Smith Junr.
Blakely Edins	Thos. Atkinson
Turner Everett	Wm. Donaldson
Christopher McRae	John Cofield
James Phillips	Hardy Powers
Samuel Jimison	James Pratt
Moses Bryant	Phineas Oliver
Turner Coley	James Mayo
Aaron Scarborough	Reuben Boreland
Joseph Barren	Benja. Mayo
Drewery May	Elisha Garbett
Richd. H. Thomas	Josiah Roberts
Lewis Holland	Thomas Burnam
Gin. John Lee	Elijah Barker
	John Parramore
	Phillip Hudgins
	Abram Simmons
	Richd. H. Davis
	Kern Branham [*orig. Branam*]
	Wiley Brannam
	Henry Moses
	William Burnam
	James Burnam
	Joel Burnam
	Thomas Simpson
	James Ricks
	Benjn. Burnam
	Ransom Golightly
	Redmond Mason
	John Hodgers
	Asa Johnson
	John Lamb
	Thomas Scott

Grand Jurors	Petit Jurors
James Dykes	Jessee Sutton
Abraham Yerta	Yancey Griffin
	Pressley Tharp
	Richard Thomas
	Joseph Rouse
	Samuel Walden
	Major Cutts
	Needham Briant
	Harbert Taylor
	Jesse Briant
	Solomon Bruer
	Bush Defnal
	Jessee Lee
	Green Brown
	James Lee
	Alexander Peacock
	Josiah Dykes
	W^{m}. Bolling
	W^{m}. Long
	Henry Dykes
	Josiah Nicolas
	Nathaniel Dykes
	William Bryant
	John Parris
	George Varner
	Fred^{k}. Floyd
	Benjn. Daniel
	W^{m}. Harrell
	John Horton
	John Cocks
	Harbert Hill
	Orren Tucker

Grand Jurors	Petit Jurors
[*none on this page*]	John Powers
	Pressley Tharp Senr.
	Riu Watson
	Wiley Horne
	Levi Bush
	W. M. Griffin
	Stephen Williamson
	George Johnson
	Stephen Bryan
	Reubin Ellis
	Branson Bardin
	Jos. Harrell
	Arthur Bardin
	Jno. Moses
	Adam Billings
	David Pipkin
	Martin Pipkin
	Sherrod Allen
	Elias Phillips
	Elijah Harrell
	William A. Hendley
	Elijah Tilman
	John Chastain
	Jos. Butler
	Isaac Foreman
	Arch^{d}. B. Graham
	Wilkes Pitts
	John Williams
	Benjn. Crum
	James D. Shanks
	Jno. R. McCoy
	Christ^{r}. Simpson
	Thos. Boyd
	George Graham
	Thos. Hendley

Grand Jurors	Petit Jurors
William Hawthorn	Moses Odom
Saml. Roberson	Robert Jones
Abraham Wood	John Yon
George G. Gaines	Malliki Kelly
Benjamin Chairs	John H. Davis
John McGriff	William Kelly
Martin Wood	Wiley Herren
Caswell Ball	James Holmes
Rich^{d}. McGriff	Lewis Wood
Marmaduke Kent	W^{m}. J. Murrell
Jordan Dykes	Henry Hart
John Jane	James Nobles
Jos. B. Coalson	John Wormack
Ralph Kirkland	Benj. Hayes
Whitmel D. Horne	Jessee Yates
Theophilus Sutton	James James
Daniel Magee	Nathl. McCall
George Walker Junr.	Henry King
Isaac H. Horne	W^{m}. Ramsey
Benjn. Mewborn	James Odom
Robert Winn	Elisha Cain
Archibald Odom	John Stegall
Moses Kirklin	John Turner
Murdock McLeod	John Spikes
Robert Hogen	Averl Scarborough
	Warren Hart
	Ishariah Siry
	Moses Giddins
	Benja. Stegall
	Edwin Giddins
	Jessee May
	William Crate
	John Lee
	Edward Briant
	William Brown
	Elias Brown
	Linale Brown
	John Rogers
	Thomas Wesley

Grand Jurors	Petit Jurors
Patrick McGriff	John Stewart
Shadk Atkinson	Shadrack Sutton
William Hall	Charles Long
	James King
	James Bernhill
	Thos. Tomberlin
	Isaac Blunt
	Isham Garrit
	John Roseil [*Rozier?*]
	Thomas Gey
	Moses Pipkin
	William Phillips
	Jacob Taylor
	John Hays
	Alexander Simpson
	Asa Bradley
	Charles Ballard
	Irby Brown
	Wm. Norwood
	Joab Oswell
	Wm. Holland
	James Trull
	David Smith
	John Brown
	Wm. Smith
	Jno. Briant
	Asa Brown
	Albert Bishop
	Nathan Sowell
	George Folsom
	Farmer R. Carragan
	Humphrey Posey
	Kindred Hall
	William Wilson
	John Taylor
	John Hodges
	George Little
	James Smith
	Charles Long [#2]

Grand Jurors	Petit Jurors
Edward Bryant	James Bush
Michael Horne	Elias Dykes
Lawrence Folsom	Josiah Bush
Sutton Truluck	William Barron
Coalson Adams	Lewis Thomas
Hardy Vickers	Littleberry Waters
James Powell	Harmon Barron
William Lester	John Varner
James T. Thomas	John Swearingame
	George Tharpe
	John Rogers
	Richard Gainey
	Jesse Jump
	Isaac Kirksey
	Thos. Steptoe
	James Pormor [*Parramore?*]
	W^{m}. Folsom
	W^{m}. Curenton
	Arthur Williams
	Barna Williams
	James Roundtree
	Reuben Roundtree
	William Taylor
	Batts Newsome
	John Daniel
	Mathew Daniel
	David Harrell
	John McCormick
	Dimpsey Gregory
	Dennis Adams
	Benjn. Hynes
	Thomas Coleman
	John Coleman
	John Gregory
	Benjn. Posey
	Josiah [*no last name*]
	W^{m}. Winburn

Grand Jurors	Petit Jurors
Robert Moreland Senr.	W^{m}. Phelps
Tuttle H. Moreland	Thomas Everett
Elisha Farnell	Ja^{s}. Chastain
Benjn. Smith	Hugh Taylor
William Hilliard	John McRay
John Rawls	Isham Adams
Gray B. Gardner	William Tyner
Edward Smith	Francis J. Hobby
Thomas Hatton	George Mansel
Joseph Wood	Thomas Adams
Stephen Gatlin	W^{m}. Hendley
Saml. Jones S^{r}.	Rolland Tait
Lewis Yarborough	Elisha Evans
James A. Everett	James Crawford
Thos. Mills	Horton Hendley
Ambrose Baber	Jessee Williams
Jas. Bracewell	Jesse Fann
W^{m}. Williams	Nathl. Folsom
R. Mitchell	W^{m}. Pate
D. Ray	Ab^{m}. Nipper
Jno. A. Williams	Martin Johnson
Washington Lancaster	Jno. Boon
William Johnson	Charles Daniel
	Lewis Dewett
	Charles Bush
	Aaron B. Puckett
	Henry Dewett
	Arthur Graddy
	Joseph Regan
	John Kelly
	Aaron Johnson
	Patrick Robinson
	Jacob Spikard
	Aaron Cox
	Sampson Culpepper
	John Sparrow
	Wright Lancaster
	Allen Carr
	Saml. Fowle
	Rich^{d}. Johnson
	W^{m}. Kinchen

Grand Jurors	Petit Jurors
Nathl. Mercer	Mitchell Towerling
Stephen Pipkin	Lewis Pipkin
Thomas Rogers	Barnabus Pipkin
Ja^{s}. McNorton	Silas Mercer
Thomas Paxton	Ephriam Philips
George Kornega	Jesse Mercer
Benja. S. Lanier	Arch^{d}. Cain
Zion Davis S^{r}.	W^{m}. Pipkin
	Edwd. Cobb
	Burwell Philips
	John Dixon
	Amos Pipkin
	Shad^{k}. Allen
	Allen Perry
	Neil Culbreath
	Jesse Snow
	Sterling Sanders
	Ja^{s}. McBeth
	John R. Hardee
	O. D. Watson J^{r}.
	Young Johnson
	Hardy Mills
	Fred^{k}. Mills
	Abram Mills
	Council Mills
	Dugald McPhail
	Mich^{l}. K. Singletary
	Randal Yarborough
	John B. Howard
	Benjamin Turner
	B. M. Collins
	R. Moreland J^{r}.
	W^{m}. Arthur
	Thos. Wilton
	Gilbert McNair
	Silas Williams
	John Harrell
	Richard Brown
	George Evans
	Henry Evans

Grand Jurors	Petit Jurors
	Daniel Henderson
	Conrad Augley
	Ethel^{d}. Howell Senr.
	Levi Harrall
	Asa Harrall
	Jesse Harrall
	James Goodrich
	Ja^{s}. Brown
	Jacob Harrall
	W^{m}. Hambleton
	Francis Harrall
	Ja^{s}. Cole
	Moses Harrall
	W^{m}. Kean
	Josiah Kean
	Isham Sheffield
	W^{m}. Owens
	Thos. Spears
	Jacob Parkerson
	Lawson Parkerson
	J. W. Spears
	W^{m}. Sheffield
	Chappel Bond
	Uriah Feagan
	W^{m}. Brock
	Randal Richardson
	Zachariah Davis
	George Livingston
	Evan Andrews
	John Valentine
	Hoziah Davis
	Jno. Rainey
	Bird J. Lanier
	Rinderson H. Tisdale
	Charles Creech
	James Psalter
	John Shirley
	Jacob D. Jump
	Hardy Lasly
	Isaac Dykes
	Saml. Storey

Allen Tooke J.I.C.
R. H. Thomas J.I.C.
Stephen Gatlin J.I.C.
Bartlett Barker D. Shff.
Gray B. Gardner Clk. Sup^{r}. Ct.

Done on the 17th October 1818
by us

Selection of Grand Jurors made this 24th February 1821

Conrad Augley
Jacob Harrall
William Hawthorne
Archibald Odom
Lewis Holland
Nathaniel Mercer
Murdoch McLeod
John Stewart
Nathan Maddox
William Norwood
Thomas Rogers
Patrick McGriff
James Holmes
William Lester
Lawrence Folsom
Caswell Ball
W^{m}. B. McGehee
Edward Bryan
Michael Horne
James Roundtree
W^{m}. Hall
Hardy Vickers
John Daniel
Stephen Mitchell
Abraham Wood
James T. Thomas
George Kornegay
Shadrach Atkinson
Hiram Atkinson
Thomas Mills
Ica Atkins
William Brock
James Dykes
Green Brown
Ralph Kirkland
Aaron Scarborough
Benjamin Harrison
John Lee (Gin) [*General?*]
Moses Bryan
Isaac Nichols
William Garbett
Saml. Robinson
Turner Coley
John Morris
Theophilus Sutton
Thomas Howell
Isaac Buckhalter
Jesse Powell
William Little
Needham Stevens
Saml. Hart
Sanders Coalson
Thomas Johnson
Richard Whitaker
Benjn. Howell
John Donaldson Senr.
John Gillstrap
Bruy [*orig. Bray*] Mayo
Joseph B. Coalson
Hardy Powers
Henry Senterfit
Stephen Roach
W^{m}. G. Dudley
Moses Willson
John Powell
David Girtman
R. W. W. Wynn
James Mayo
Redmon B. Mason
Jeremy Stone
John Dees
Jordan Anderson
Bolling Swearingame
George Walker Senr.
Blakely Edins
Joseph B. Bryan

Selection of Grand Jurors made this 24th February 1821

Joel Walker
W^{m}. Mayo
Gideon Kellam
Ezekiel Taylor
Chris^{r}. McRae
Reuben Warren
George Walker Junr.
Saml. Peace
James Phillips
Henry Fenn
Benjn. Chairs
Saml. Jamison [*orig. Jemison*]
Thos. McGriff
Robert Mathews
Simon Bardin
Rich^{d}. McGriff
William Jelks
Ja^{s}. S. Ivey
W^{m}. Yarborough
W^{m}. McCormick
John Cardin
John Carruthers
Edwd. Blackshear
Stephen Gatlin
Thomas J. Johnson
Furney F. Gatlin
Joel Sherrard
Burton H. Pitts
Nelson Clayton
Rich^{d}. H. Thomas
Allen Tooke
George G. Gaines
James M. Taylor
Arthur Tooke
Washington Lancaster
Abednego Wright
Uriah Yarborough
Lewis Yarborough
Gray B. Gardner
John A. Williams
Benjamin Smith
James Bracewell
Benjamin Mewborn
Jos. Wood
Edward Smith
Josiah Everett
Bartlet Barker
Elisha Farnell
Joseph W. Denson
John Rawls
Ja^{s}. A. Everett
Duncan Ray
Richard Mitchell
Thomas Hatton
Jacob Watson
A. [*orig. Adon*] Scarborough
George Norwood
Robert Hodges
Jordan Dykes
James Allen
Willis B. Reeves
Thomas Cole
Sterling Tooke
W^{m}. Johnson
Giles Shute
Abner Moore
O. D. Watson J^{r}.

Gray B. Gardner Clk. S.C.
B. Barker Shff.
Rich^{d}. H. Thomas J.I.C.
Allen Tooke J.I.C.

Selection of Petit Jurors made this 24th February 1821

Richd. Brown
Josiah Keen
Lewis Harrall
George Roan
Jesse Harrall
John Shirley
George Evans
Henry Evans
Francis Harrall
~~Jacob Harril~~ [2]
~~William Brock~~ [2]
John Brock
Jacob Parkerson
Moses Harrall
Wm. Sheffield
John Balentine
Chapel Boutwell
Thomas Spiers
William Pate
John W. L. W. Spiers
William Roberts
Benjn. Johnson
Wm. Hamilton
James Brockston
Joshua Dykes
Stephen Johnson
John Rollins
Silas Dean
~~Hozia L. Davis~~ [2]
Thomas Atkinson
Bird J. Lanier
John Dickinson
Thomas Oliver
James Goodrich
Martin Livingston
Abraham Nipper
William Kean
Edmond Herring
James Brown
William Brown
Mathew Nutt
Lawson Parkerson
Arthur Sheffield
Wm. Owen
Hezekia Wade
Asa Harrall
Wm. Sheffield Senr.
Evan Anders
Levi Harrall
James Cole
John Armstrong
John Harrall
Isaac Harrall
Martin G. Mims
John J. [*orig. S.*] Lanier
Jordon Bush
James Kelly
Joseph Clements
John Buchan
John Henderson
Wm. Hendly
Hardy Lashly
John Nipper
Wm. Nipper[1]
William Nix
John Owens
Joseph Parrot
Mack Wade
James Odom
William Brown [#2]
Sherwood Allen
~~Adam Scarbrough~~ [2]
~~John Turner~~ [2]
John Brown
Moses Gedions
Raymon Savage
Jesse Mercer
Benjn. Stegall
Avon Scarborough
Silas Mercer
~~John Sims~~ [2]
Edwd. Gideons
Moses Pipkin
Alexr. Simpson
John Haddon
Brinkley Brown
Thomas Irwin
Jas. Brown [#2]
Jacob Yerta
Charles Ballard
Henry Smith
Benjn. Craft
John Rozier Jr.
John Lee
Shadrach Sutton
James Tripp
Wright Manning
Irby Brown
John Powell Sr.
Asa Brown
Bryant Peacock
Edward Cobb
Robt. Jones
Kinsel Pipkin
~~William Pipkin~~ [2]
Adam Billings
John Ard
Robt. L. Savage
John Moore
John Gay
Burwell Phillips
Thos. Atkinson [#2]
John Bryan
John Rodgers
~~George Norwood~~ [2]
William Corkins
Seaborn Rozier
Reuben Gay
Moses Holland
Elisha Cain
James Cain
Wiley Cobb
William Rogers
Kinchen Peacock
James Stewart
Chappel Bond
Robert Hodges
William Morris
Hiram Pollard
Charnel Hightower
~~Jesse Jump~~ [2]

[1]*original only*
[2]*orig. only, crossed off*

Selection of Petit Jurors made this 24th February 1821

John McRae
John Crawford
Elisha Evans
Dempsey Gregory
William Folsom
John Folsom
W^{m}. Hendly [#2]
Kindred Hall
Randal Folsom
Thomas Adams
Mathew Daniel
W^{m}. Winborn
Charles Williams
Levi Posey
Horton Hendley
Thos. Coleman
Jordan Dees
Lewis Wood
Eben^{r}. Folsom
Benjn. Holloman
Thomas Gregory
Humphrey Posey
Benjn. Posey
John Little
Harbert Hill
Jesse Sutton
Henry Dykes
Josiah Bush
John Cox
W^{m}. Kelly
Richmon R. Watson
William Lang
Jonathan Miller
Martin Walden
Jesee Bryan
Larry O. Bryan
Charles Lang
Henry King
John Roland
Moses Manning

W^{m}. Bryan
George Little
Oren Tucker
Jordan Dykes
James Holland
Joshua Thomas
Thomas Harrison
Joshua Holland
Solomon Brewer
Yancy P. Griffin
Reuben Walden
Presley Tharp
Thomas Walden
Orin Stephens
Joseph Floyd
Lewis Thomas
Elias Dykes
John Thomas
Drury May
William Bolin
Willis Bryan
William Smith
Henry Land
Benjn. Manning
Daniel Sparrow
Elias Bryan
Benjn. Daniel
David Smith
W^{m}. Miller
John Miller
Malakiah Kelly
John Sweringen
John Sulivan
John Lee [#2]
Herbert Taylor
Hugh Carr
David Simpson
Major Cutts
Bricy Holly
Joel Bryan
Saml. Stephens
Jesse Kirkland

James Bryan
Baker Adams
Arthur Boyt
Stephen Bryan
Alex^{r}. Manning
John Morris
John Faircloth
Joseph Rouse
George Willis
William Faircloth
Moses Faircloth
Saml. Cherry
Ethel^{d}. Howell
William Thompson
John Deshaza
Elbert Bishop
Abner Moore
Fred^{k}. Howell
Eli Horn
Charles Seybert
John W. Wynne
~~John Howell~~ [2]
James Johnson J^{r}.
Henry Hart
James McCormick
John Shipp
Caswell Lassiter
William Harrall
George Cherry
John B. Bush
Fred^{k}. Wolf
John Hancock
John Foard
Littleberry Waters
James Williams
William Hand
James Yates
James Robuck
James Little
William Donaldson J^{r}.
John Donaldson J^{r}.
~~Willis B. Reeves~~ [2]
Burwell Howell
Lewis M. Loper
Philip Troy
John Parramore

[2]*orig. only, crossed off*

Selection of Petit Jurors made this 24th February 1821

William [S.[3]] Hadnot
Philip Whitchard
Fredk. Simpson
William Sulivan
Henry Senterfit Jr.
~~Thomas Cole~~ [2]
John Stegall
Fredk. Wood
Jesse Senterfit
Francis Faircloth
William Whigham
Wm. Ship
John Herrington
Philip Hudgins
William Herrington
Jacob Taylor
John Pierce
Wm. Burnam
Absolem Hopson
Nathan Womble
~~Sterling Tooke~~ [2]
John Hodge
Elisha Garbett
Washington McFarlane
William Quinerly
Micajah E. Davis
Counsel Wooten
Richd. H. Davis
Benjn. Burnam
James Burnam
Elijah Barker
Branson Bardin
Danl. Womble
Dugal [C.[1]] McPhail
George Tharp
Wm. H. Mathews
Eliphalet King
Wm. Simpson
Joseph Roberts
Wm. K. Hall
John McCoy
Hillery Henderson
Thomas Collins
John C. Weaver
James Simpson
Thomas Simpson
Jacob Simpson
Wright Howell
Mathias McCormick
John S. Lavender
Saml. Noble
Jeffry Montfort
Bush Defnal
John Bradshaw
Wm. Grinstead
Christopher Simpson
John McLennan
Henry Mancil
Ulysses Crutchfield
Jesse Cannon
Mathew Cannon
Francis Delamar
Robert Thompson
Robert Moreland Jr.
Elias Ballard
John Simon
John Bird
John Nelson
John Kinard
John Cofield
John Williford
John Caruthers Jr.
William Pratt
Saml. Jones
Neal Ard
Wm. Haddock
Bryant Bradley
James Hayes
Wiley Williams
Beverly A. Simmons
Joseph Simmons
Pinkney Yarborough
Silas Williams
Edwd. Murkinson
Lewis Dewitt
John McCormick
Levi E. Bish [*Bush?*]
John Jones
Darling Jones
John Wallace
Eppes Ivey
Allen Perry
Joseph Brinn
Hardy Mills
Thomas Boyd
Wright Lancaster
Thomas Folsom
~~Wm. Johnson~~ [2]
Arthur Graddy
Wm. Kinchen
Aaron Johnson
Jinatt Kingsley
John Coleman
Randal Yarborough
Thos. M. Golightly
Daniel Magee
James Jackson
Daniel Kelly
Grosvenor Titus
B. W. Bracewell
George Mansel Jr.
~~Giles Steale~~ [2]
Wesley Yarborough
Richd. Johnson
Edward Smith Jr.
Robert Lee
Moses Yarborough
Amos Wheeler
~~Oren D. Watson Jr.~~ [2]
Philip S. Paris
Frederick Floyd

G. B. Gardner, Clk.
Sup. Ct.
B. Barker, Shff.
Allen Tooke J.I.C.
Richd. H. Thomas J.I.C.

[1] *on original*
[2] *orig. only, crossed off*
[3] *in book*

Selection of Grand Jurors made on 11th October 1823

Sharrick Allen
James Cayn
Louis Holland
Robert Hodges
Nathan Matax
Nathaniel Mercer
Patrick McGriff
Archibald Odam
Thomas Rogers
Adin Scarborough
Robert Savage
Baker Adams
James Allen
William Byan [*Bryan?*]
Moses Bryan
Green Brown
John Bryan
Turner Colley
James Dykes
Yancy P. Griffin
Orrin Stephens
Benjn. Harrison
Henry King
John Little
William Miller
William Pace
Samuel Roberson
William Smith J^{r}.
Aaron Scarborough S^{r}.
Jesse Sutton
Reuben Waldin
Elijah Barker
Simon Bardin
Jos. W. Brantly
Henry W. Fenn
William Mayo
Thos. McGriff
James Philips
Bolin Swaringin
Ezekiel Taylor

Sterling Tooke
George Walker
Joel Walker
George Walker [#2]
Reuben Warren
~~John Bradshaw~~ [2]
George Cooper
Nelson Clayton
John Carruthers
Jesse Cannon
Joseph W. Denson
Stephen Gatlin
Ja^{s}. S. Ivey
William Jelks
Ralph Kirkland
Louis M. Loper
Mathias McCormick
Samuel Nobles
Lunceford C. Pitts
Burton H. Pitts
Allen Perry
Beverly A. Simmons
Joel Sherrard
Hardy Vickers
Isaac Buckhalter
John B. Bush
George Cherry
Sanders Coalson
William Garbitt
Burrel Howell
Benjn. Howell
James Mayo
Thomas Johnson
William Little
Willis B. Reeves
Stephen Roach
David Roach
Henry Senterfit
Giles Shute
Needham Stephens
R[obert[1]] W. W. Wynne
~~Conrad Augley~~ [2]
John Brown
Bird Lanier
William Hamilton
Ica Atkins

Hiram Atkinson
Shadrach Atkinson
Caswell Ball
Elisha Evans
William Henely
Charnel Hightower
William Hall
William Lester
William B. McGehee
Stephen Mitchell
Bats Newsom
James Roundtree
James H. Truluck
Louis Wood
Bartlett Barker
James Bracewell Senr.
Daniel Cornwall
Furney F. Gatlin
Francis Hobby
Aaron Johnson
Wright Lancaster
John J. Lanier
Washington Lancaster
Murdoch McLeod
Isaac W. Mitchell
Richard Mitchell
John Rawls
Michael K. Singletary
Joshua R. Wimberly
Green Chairs
John Dees
William Phelps
Sessums Perkin
John Bradshaw
Burrel Philips
John Rogers
Major Cutts
George Little
Arthur Bardin
William Herrington
~~Charles~~ [2] David Walker
Solomon Nelson
Joseph Simons
Wiley Williams

[1]*on original*
[2]*orig. only, crossed off*

Selection of Grand Jurors made on the 11th October 1823

William Holloman
Hardy Powers
Jesse Senterfit
Mathew W. Daniel
John McCray
Joseph J. Bracewell
James Yates
John J. Taylor
Amos Brown
Samuel Peace
James H. Warren
Ambruse Kellim
Andrew Carsin
Benjamin West
Freeman D. Cardin
John Crawford
James Phelps
Louis Dewitt
William Loveless
Thomas Cardin
John Wallace

Georgia) The foregoing is a true selection
Pulaski County) made by us on the 11th October 1823

Gray B. Gardner Clk. S. C.
W. Lancaster J.I.C.
Furney F. Gatlin Shff.
L. M. Loper J.I.C.
Moses Bryan J.I.C.

Selection of Petit Jurors made on the 11th October 1823

Benjn. Allen
Asa Brown
Pearson Brown
John Brown Senr.
James Brown
John Brown Junr.
Daniel Brown
Benony Brown
William Brown
Wiley Cobb
Benjn. Craft
Moses Giddins
Edward Giddins
Moses P. Giddins
John Gay
John Harrell
John Holland
Thos. McKigney
James Manning
Jno. Moore
James Odom
~~Burrell Phillips~~ [2]
Hiram Pollard
Jno. Powell
Jno. Pelt
Bryant Peacock
Wm. Pipkin
Elias Regan
Wm. Rogers
~~John Rozier Jr.~~ [2]
~~John Rozier Sr.~~ [2]
Seaborn Rozier
Benjn. Stegall
Wm. Smith
Henry Smith

~~Adon Sc~~ [2]
Jno. Steward
Jas. Smith
Jas. Trull
Wm. Trull
Jas. Tripp
Thos. Worsely
Jacob Yearty
Elias Bryant
Wm. Bolin
Larry O. Bryan
Jesse Bryan
Miles Barefoot
Joel Bryan[t[3]]
Joshua Bryan
George Boling
Jos. Bush
Jos. Bryan[t[3]]
Levi E. Bush
Solomon Brewer
Isaac Bush
John Holland [#2]
~~Majer Carr~~ [2]
Hugh Carr
Jacob H. Dykes
Elias Dykes
Isaac Dykes
Jacob Dykes
Fredk. Floyd
Jas. S. Holland
James J. Holland
Thos. Harrison
Moses Holland
John Holland [#3]

Joshua Holland
Archibald Jones
James Lee
Jonathan Miller
Wm. Nutt
Jno. Miller
Jno. Morris
Matthew Nutt
Moses Odom
David Smith
Jno. Swearingen
Aaron Scarborough [Jun.[1]]
James Smith [#2]
Jno. S. Smith
~~Presley Tharp~~ [2]
Harberd Taylor
Philip Tryo[1]/Troy[3]
Jno. Thomas
Lewis Thomas
Martin Walden
Zachariah Willis
Lemuel Walden
Richmond R. Watson
Benjn. Burnam
~~Arthur Barden~~ [2]
Wm. Burnam
~~Richard H. Davis~~ [2]
Elisha Garbitt
~~Wm. Herrington~~ [2]
Wm. Quinnerly
Wm. Sullivan
~~David Walker~~ [2]
Charles Walker
Neil Ard
~~John Bradshaw~~ [2]
Bryant Bradley
Wm. Barrow
James P. Carruthers

[1]*on original only*
[2]*on orig., crossed off*
[3]*in book*

Selection of Petit Jurors made on the 11th October 1823

John Carruthers Jr.
David Cardin
Francis Delamar
Bush Defnal
Wm. Grinstead
Jno. Hendley
Moses Kirkland
Jas. C. Lister
Jeffrey Montford
Bartholomew Murphy
Robt. Moreland [Jun.[1]]
Jeremiah McCormick
Noah Nelson
Solomon Nelson
Wm. Pratt
~~Joseph Simons~~? [2]
~~Christopher Simson~~ [2]
Chas. G. Williams
Wiley Williams
Jno. Barrow
Jno. Bynum
Sanders Bush
Saml. Cherry
Jno. Donaldson Jr.
Wm. Donaldson
Thos. Davis
Francis Faircloth
John Faircloth
Wm. Faircloth
Moses Faircloth
James Forchand
Eli Horn
Wright Howell
~~Wm. Tomblinson~~ [2]

James Little
Benjn. Mayo
Spire Mills
~~Hardy Powers~~ [2]
Allen Palmer
Wm. Robuck
James Robuck
Stephen Senterfit
~~Jessey Senterfit~~ [2]
Wm. Singletary
Jno. W. Wynn
Daniel Wamble
Jas. Armstrong
Evans Andrews
Thos. Atkinson
Ludwell Armstrong
James Brown [#2]
Stephen Boutwell
Danl. Brock
Wm. Brock
Jno. Valentine
Chappel Boutwell
James Broxton
Jos. Clements
George Evans
Henry Evans
James Goodrich
Lewis Harrell
Asa Harrell
Horton Hendley
Francis Harrell
Elisha Harrell
Jno. Harrell [#2]

Moses Harrell
Isaac Harrell
Levi Harrell
Jesse Harrell
~~Wm. Haney~~ [2]
Benjn. J. Johnson
Jacob D. Junk[1] [*Jump*]
Jacob DeJonk[3]
Wm. Kean
Josiah Kean
Wm. Kelly
Martin Livingston
Abm. Nipper
Thos. Oliver
~~Wm. Owin~~ [2]
Lawson Parkinson
Isham Philips
Jno. Rolinger[1]/Rawlings[3]
Seaborn Rainey
Richd. Storey
Thos. Spears
Purnel Summons
Hezekiah Wade
Jno. Carmichael
Alfred Belote
Jno. Bush
Jas. Daniel
~~Mathew W. Daniel~~ [2]
Ebn. Folsom
Thos. Gregory
James Hainy
Benjn. Hollamon
Eliphalit King
Bazel Kornegay
~~John McRae~~ [2]
David M. Spring

Selection of Petit Jurors made on this 11th October 1823

Chas. Williams
~~Joseph J. Bracewell~~ [2]
Jas. Bracewell Jr.
Elisha Copeland
Jno. Chastain
Thos. Folsom
Daniel Kelly
Jinnatt Kingsley
Jno. Nelson
Wm. Russel
Edwd. Smith
Chas. Kingsley
Francis L. Armstrong
Jos. Tooke
Levin Gillstrap
~~Jas. Yates~~ [2]
Jno. J. Taylor
Nicholas Taylor
Danl. Wamble [#2]
Ahaz Jones
~~Amos Brown~~ [2]
~~Samuel Peace~~ [2]
Littleberry Waters
Julius Robuck
~~Ambrose Kellam~~ [2]
James Williams
Henry Horne
Jno. Shipp
David Shipp
~~Andrew Carsson~~ [2]
Tuckel McNear[1]/ Terquil McNair[3]
Enoch Row
James Burnam
~~Benjamin Hinderson~~ [2]
Wm. West
Allen Wheeler
Wiley Kent

Taylor Montford
Robt. Lee
Freeman D. Cardin
Kornegay Stephens
Robt. Howell
James Travis
Jno. Mitchell
~~John Crawford~~ [2]
Elbert Crawford
James Phelps
Jno. T. Grainger
David Frazer
Jas. Johnston
[Abs.[1]/Aph.[3]] Whichard
Jno. Cofield
Thos. Hanks
Silas Williams
Jno. Hancock
Wm. Hancock
Thos. Sutton
Patrick Thomas
Nathan Sowell
Alexander Banister
Henry Dewitt
~~Lewis Dewit~~ [2]
Calvin Pratt
Danl. Sparrow
Jno. Price
~~Wm. Loveless~~ [2]
Jno. Sherrard[1]/Sherrod[3]
Seaborn Sherrard[1]/ Sherrod[3]
Asa Edins
Edwd. Gatlin

Sampson McGill
~~Thomas Cardin~~ [2]
Philip S. Parris
Nathan Parris
Wm. Swain
~~John Wallis~~ [2]
Epps. Wallis[1]/Wallace[3]

[1]*on original*
[2]*on orig., crossed off*
[3]*in book*

Georgia) The foregoing is a true selection
Pulaski County) made by us on the 11th October
1823 —

Gray B. Gardner Clk. S. C.
W. Lancaster J.I.C.
L. M. Loper J.I.C.
Furney F. Gatlin Shff.
Moses Bryan J.I.C.

Entered by Gray B. Gardner Clk.

[*end of transcript; book continues with juror lists for 1827*]

SUPERIOR COURT
MINUTES, BOOK 1
1809-1812

I Lewis HOLLAND do solemnly swear that I will faithfully execute all writs, warrents, precepts and processes directed to me as sheriff of the county of Pulaski and true returns make and in all things well and truly and without malice or parçiality perform the duties of the office of Sheriff of the county aforesaid during my continuance in office and take only my lawful fees so help me God.

James T. THOMAS J.I.C.)
Edmund HOGAN J.I.C.) Lewis HOLLAND
H. FULGHAM J.I.C.)

Entered this 6th day of June in the year of our Lord 1809.
Rich^{d}. H. THOMAS Clk.

I Elisha HIGGS do solemnly swear... [*continues exactly as above*]

Edmund HOGAN J.I.C.)
W^{m}. A. HARPER J.I.C.) Elisha HIGGS {LS}
S. JONES J.I.C.)

Entered this 2nd day of January 1810. Rich^{d}. H. THOMAS Clk.

Page 2 blank; Page 3, April 1810

Hartford Pulaski County. Monday 23^{d} day of April 1810. The Clerk of this Court having received a notice in writing from his Honor Judge CARNES now presiding in this court directing the Superior Court of this county to be opened according to law & adjourned untill the fourth Monday in July next, as the Jury lists were not made out & prepared for being drawn at this term & requesting that the said Jury lists both Grand and Petitt might be in readiness on the fourth Monday being the 23^{d}. day of July next of which proceding all persons concerned were desired to take notice. Attest R. H. THOMAS Clk.

July 1810

Hartford Monday 23^{d}. day of July 1810. The Court met agreeably to adjournment. Present Honble. Thomas P. CARNES

The court having ordered the Jury box to be produced, the following persons were drawn in open court to serve as Grand and Petitt Jurors at the next term of the Superior Court:

Page 4

Grand Jurors to wit

1 Leonard STRINGER
2 W^{m}. GOODSON
3 W^{m}. JELKS
4 Archibald LASSITER
5 John RAINEY
6 Joel DAWSON
7 John GRINSTEAD
8 Zion DAVIS
9 Joseph REEVES
10 Isaac DEIKS
11 James ODAM
12 Thomas SHEPHERD
13 Charles CARDIN
14 William JOHNSON
15 William BRACKEN
16 Benjamin HARVEY
17 Michael HORN Jn^{r}.
18 Samuel KING
19 Hardy VICKERS
20 John SHERROD

21 Sutton TRUELUCK
22 James DEES
23 Mark MASON
24 Shadrick ATKINS
25 Robert DUET
26 Edward BRYANT
27 John STEGALL
28 Daniel SNELL
29 Benjamin BROWN
30 Joseph BARRON

Petitt Jurors

1 Haywood JONES
2 John DEES
3 Joab HORN
4 Elijah BARKER
5 Arther TOOKE
6 Jeremiah GILSTRAP
7 William TAYLOR
8 Hardy FULGHAM
9 Samuel REGAN
10 Thomas FRANKLIN
11 John MOSES
12 Reubin WARREN
13 Drury DEES
14 David BOYCE
15 W^{m}. M^{c}CORMICK
16 James WATSON
17 Robert MATHEWS
18 Absolom HOPSON
19 Theophilus SUTTON
20 James DYKES
21 Archibald ODOM
22 William SMEDLEY
23 David GARTMAN
24 W^{m}. HAMMOCK
25 Charles STEWART
26 James BUSH
27 Levi BUSH
28 Elisha GARBERT

Page 5

29 Joel WALKER
30 Reubin ROLAND
31 Martin SWEARINGIN
32 Henry SENTERFIT
33 Daniel CORNWALL
34 John BARROW
35 Charles DANIEL
36 John HARRELL
37 Jefrey MONFORD
38 Wilson BASS
39 Chesley DAVIS
40 James CARMICAL
41 Isham HAGAN
42 Henry HART
43 Elihu KEITH
44 Labin KENT
45 Marmaduke KENT
46 Michael HORN Sn^{r}.
47 William ALLEN
48 Francis HARVY
49 Augly COWARD
50 William MAYO

Examined Thos. P. CARNES

The Court then adjourned till court in course. Attest Rich^{d}. H. THOMAS Clk.

I do solemnly swear that I will faithfully execute all writs, warrants, precepts and processes directed to me as Deputy Sheriff of the county of Pulaski and true returns make and in all things well and truly and without malice or partiality perform the duties of the office of Sheriff of the County aforesaid during my continuance in office, and take only my lawful fees, so help me God.

James T. THOMAS J.I.C.)
Edmund HOGAN J.I.C.) Allen TOOKE
H. FULGHAM J.I.C.)

Entered this 21st day ~~day~~ of August 1810. Attest R. H. THOMAS Clk.

Hartford Monday 22nd day October 1810. The Court met agreeably to adjournment - the Judge failing to attend, Court then adjourned till tomorrow ten Oclock. Attest R. H. THOMAS Clk.

Tuesday 23rd day Octr. 1810. The Court met agreeable to adjournment - the Judge failing to attend the Court then adjourned till court in course.

Attest R. H. THOMAS Clk.

February 1811

Hartford Monday 18th day February 1811. Agreeable to an act of the General Assembly passed the thirteenth day of December 1810 - authorising the Justises of the Inferior Court of Pulaski County to draw Grand & Pettit Jurors for the next term of the Superior Court Presents their Honors W^{m}. A. HARPER, Ja^{s}. T. THOMAS, Samuel JONES Esquires, the Justises of the Inferior Court of s^{d}. County.

Page 7

Grand Juriors to wit:

1 Daniel REGAN
2 Jessee POWEL
3 Asa PIPKIN
4 Abraham VICKERS
5 Hinchey WARREN
6 Orandatus WATSON
7 Joseph SESSONS
8 Edmond HOGAN
9 Daniel COLE
10 Nathan[iel] MERSER
11 James RAMSEY
12 Bolin SWEARINGIN
13 John ROSIER
14 Asa TISON
15 Turner AVERIT
16 Needham STEPHENS
17 Joseph DAVISON
18 George G. GAINS
19 W^{m}. A. HARPER
20 Josiah EVERETT
21 Henry FULGHAM
22 George DYKES
23 Morduck M^{c}LEOD
24 Lewis HOLLAND
25 Sanders COLSON
26 John GILSTRAP
27 Jacob SNELL
28 Thos. McGRIFF
29 Samuel JONES
30 Simon BARDIN

Petitt Juriors

1 William DRYDEN
2 John MANING
3 Spiar MILLS
4 Lewis LEE
5 Jacob SINGLETON
6 Samuel HART
7 William PHILIPS S^{r}.
8 William HAGAN
9 John SMITH
10 William DRAWDY
11 Henry STUART
12 James RANEY
13 Joseph STRINGER
14 Alexander DANIEL
15 Charles MAYO
16 Elias PHILLIPS
17 John SWEARINGAN
18 John BRYANT
19 Jacob TAYLOR
20 Jessee BRYANT
21 John LEE S^{r}.
22 Baley HARREL

23 John DIXON
24 Pascal HAMMACK
25 Banjamin POSEY
26 Drury MAYO
27 Christopher MERCER
28 Jno. LEE Jn^r^.
29 William BRYAN
30 Isham BOYET
31 Jonathan MILLER
32 James BATY
33 William ROBERTS
34 Isham PHILIPS
35 George WARREN
36 William PHILIPS Jn^r^.
37 Adam BILLINGS
38 Philex DYKES
39 Sherrod PHILIPS
40 Aaron SCARBROUGH
41 Moses GIDDINGS
42 Solomon BREWER
43 William SMITH
44 Burwell PHILIPS
45 Wright WOODWARD
46 Martin HORN
47 Benjamin HARRISON
48 William BRYAN [#2]
49 Joshua LEE
50 Jethro PHILIPS

Examined

Attest R. H. THOMAS Clk.

William A. HARPER J.I.C.
James T. THOMAS J.I.C.
Saml. JONES J.I.C.

Page 9, April 1811

April 22^d^. 1811. The Superior Court for the county of Pulaski met agreeably to law - Present his Honor Judge EARLY.

The following persons appear'd and were sworn on the Grand Jury at the present term:

1 Edmund HOGAN form^n^.
2 Daniel REGAN
3 Jessee POWELL
4 Abraham VICKERS
5 Hinche WARREN
6 Orandatus WATSON
7 Joseph SESSIONS
8 Daniel COLE
9 Saml. JONES
10 James RAMSEY
11 Bolin SWEARINGEN
12 John ROSIER
13 Needham STEPHENS
14 George G. GAINES
15 Henry FULGHAM
16 George DYKES
17 Murdoch M^c^LEOD
18 Sanders COLSON
19 John GILSTRAP
20 Jacob SNELL
21 Thomas M^c^GRIFF
22 Simon BARDIN
23 Asa PIPKIN

The following persons appeared and were sworn in the Petitt Jury:

1 William DRIDING
2 John MANNING
3 Spire MILLS
4 Lewis LEE
5 Jacob SINGLETARY
6 Saml. HART
7 William PHILIPS Sn^r^.
8 James RAINEY
9 Joseph STRINGER
10 Charles MAYO
11 Elias PHILIPS
12 John SWEARINGEN

A. & S. RICHARDS)
vs.) Debt
Wm. BRACKEN) We the Jury find for the plantiff the sum of one hundred & eleven dollars and eighty seven cents with interest & cost.
Lewis LEE foreman

Sampson SMITH)
vs. bearer) Case
Joel DAWSON) Settled

Seaborn JONES)
vs.) Case
DAVIS & WHEELER) We the Jury find for the plantiff the sum of fifty dollars, with interest & cost. Lewis LEE foreman

Thomas FITCH)
vs.) Debt
Levi E. BUSH, James)
BUSH & John BUSH) We the Jury find for the plantiff against Levi E. BUSH fifty dollars with interest & cost. Lewis LEE foreman

Page 11

~~The State)~~
~~vs.) Indictment Cattle Stealing~~
~~Jacob DUNN, Holden DUNN)~~
~~& William GRINSTEAD)~~

[*large blank space*]

The Grand Jury came into court & returned the following bills:

The State)
vs.) Indt. Misdemeanor
Archibald LASSITER)
& Jas. LANIER) True Bill Edmund HOGAN foreman

The State)
vs.) Indt. Assault
Spire MILLS &)
Abraham HOLLIDAY) True Bill Edmund HOGAN foreman

Page 12

The State)
vs.)
Robert DANIEL) Indt. Misdemeanor
Cader HAWTHORN)
& John HAWTHORN) No Bill Edmund HOGAN foreman

The State)
vs.) Ind^{t}. Misdemeanor
Archibald LASSITTER) Archibald LASSITTER principal John GRINSTEAD & Robert DANIEL securities come into court & acknowledged themselves bound to his Excellency the Governor & his successors in office in the penal sum of one thousand dollars ~~for~~ Conditioned to be void if the said Archibald LASSITER do appear at the next Superior Court in this County and not to depart thence without the leave of said court. Signed sealed & acknowledged in open court April 22^{d} 1811.

A^{d}. LASSITER {Seal}
Attest R. H. THOMAS Clk. John GRINSTEAD {Seal}
Robert DANIEL {Seal}

Page 13

The State)
vs.) Ind^{t}. Misdemeanor
James LANIER) James LANIER principal & William S. LANCASTER & Clement LANIER securities come into court & acknowledged themselves bound to his Excellency the Governor or his successors in office in the penal sum of one thousand dollars - Conditioned to be void if the said James LANIER do appear at the next Superior Court in this County & not to depart thence without the leave of said court. Signed sealed & acknowledged in open court this 22^{d} April 1811.

James LANIER {Seal}
Attest R. H. THOMAS Clk. William S. LANCASTER {Seal}
Clement LANIER {Seal}

The State)
vs.) Ind^{t}. Cattle Stealing
William GRINSTEAD) William GRINSTEAD principal & George G. GAINES & Murdoch M^{c}LEOD securities come into court & acknowledged themselves bound to his Excellency the Governor or his successors in office in the penal sum of two thousand dollars - Conditioned to be void if the said William GRINSTEAD do appear at the next Superior Court in this County & not to depart thence without the leave of said court. Signed sealed & acknowledged in open court April 22^{d} 1811.

his
William x GRINSTEAD {Seal}
mark
Attest R. H. THOMAS Clk. G. G. GAINES {Seal}
M. M^{c}LEOD {Seal}

Page 14

The following persons were drawn to serve as Grand Jurors at the next term:

1 ~~Dempsey DOHERTY~~
Benjamin SMITH
2 William HALL
3 Philip JONES
4 Thomas WARREN
5 George WALKER
6 Jno. SNELLING
7 Gideon MAYO
8 Lester CROFORD
9 David SNELL
10 Archibald H. ODAM
11 William DESHAZO

12 William HANEY
13 Wm. S. LANCASTER
14 Sands STANDLEY
15 Jas. T. THOMAS
16 Jno. STEWART
17 Jno. SHERROD
18 Thomas SHEPHERD
19 Joel DAWSON
20 James ODAM
21 Charles CARDIN
22 Samuel KING
23 Edward BRYAN
24 Joseph REEVES
25 Mark MASON
26 ~~Isaac D~~
William JELKS
27 Jno. STEGALL
28 Joseph DAVIDSON
29 Josiah EVERETT
30 William JOHNSON

The following persons were drawn to serve as Petit Jurors at the next term:

1 Jesse LEE
2 Thos. WESLEY
3 Nimrod PHILIPS
4 Hesekiah PHILIPS
5 Benjamin STEGALL
6 Christopher EDWARDS
7 Robert HODGES
8 Benjamin WEEKS
9 Reubin WHEELER
10 Ephram PHILIPS
11 Jas. TEMPLES
12 Amos WHEELER
13 Wm. KELLEY
14 Silas JOHNSON
15 Jno. BEDINGFIELD
16 Richard TAYLOR
17 Holden DUNN
18 Edmund GIDINS
19 Maliki KELLY
20 Abner SINGLETON

Page 15

21 Samuel SMITH
22 Moses KIRKLIN
23 Jas. BEDINGFIELD
24 George WRIGHT
25 William WINN
26 Jas. TOMLINSON
27 Jordan DEES
28 Robert MONFORD
29 Abram YEARTY
30 Charles MILES [*Mills?*]
31 Richd. WINN
32 Jas. McNORTON
33 Nedham BRYAN
34 Jno. PHILIPS
35 Evan THOMAS
36 George KELLEY
37 Blakely EDINS
38 Shadrick LEE
39 Isham SHUFFIELD
40 Aaron JOHNSON
41 Henry BATY
42 Saml. MILLER
43 Isham McDANIEL
44 Bigins SINGLETON
45 Thos. ROGERS
46 Thomas HESTER
47 Richard WHEELER
48 Edmund HESTER
49 Edward LASSITTIR
50 Lewis DEWETT

The State)
vs.) Indt. Assault
Spire MILLS) Spire MILLS principal & Thomas D. PORTER \Samuel HART/ securities come into court & acknowledged themselves bound to his Excellency the Governor or his successors in office in the penal sum of two ~~thousand dollars~~ hundred dollars -

Conditioned to be void if the said Spire MILLS do appear at the next Superior Court in this County & not to depart thence without the leave of said court.

April 22d 1811.

Spire x MILLS {Seal}
his / mark

Attest R. H. THOMAS Clk.

Thos. D. PORTER {Seal}

Samuel x HART {Seal}
his / mark

Page 16

The State)
vs.) Indt. Assault
Abram HOLLIDAY) Abram HOLLIDAY \principal/ & John PARIS, William T. RENEAU securities come into court and acknowledged themselves bound to his Excellency the Governor or his successors in office in the penal sum of two hundred dollars - Conditioned to be void if the said Abram HOLLIDAY do appear at the next Superior Court in this County & not to depart thence without the leave of said court.

April 22d 1811.

Abram x HOLLIDAY {Seal}
his / mark

Attest R. H. THOMAS Clk.

John x PARIS {Seal}
his / mark

Wm. T. RENEAU {Seal}

The State)
vs.) Indt. Cattle Stealing
Jacob DUNN) Jacob DUNN, William HILLIARD, Samuel HART securities come into court & acknowledged themselves bound to his Excellency the Governor or his successors in office in the penal sum of two thousand dollars

Conditioned to be void if the said Jacob DUNN do appear at the next Superior Court in this County & not to depart thence without the leave of the said court. April 22d 1811.

Jacob x DUNN {Seal}
his / mark

Attest R. H. THOMAS Clk.

William HILLARD {Seal}

Samuel x HART {Seal}
his / mark

Page 17

The State)
vs.) Indt. Cattle Stealing
Holden DUNN) Holden DUNN, Joseph SESSIONS, James SANDERS securities come into court and acknowledged themselves bound to his Excellency the Governor or his successor in office in the penal sum of two thousand dollars-

Conditioned to be void if the said Holden DUNN do appear at the next Superior Court in this County & not to depart thence without the leave of the said court.

	Holden DUNN {Seal}
April 22d 1811.	Jos. SESSIONS {Seal}
Attest R. H. THOMAS Clk.	James SANDERS {Seal}

The Grand Jury came into court & made the following presentments:

We the Grand Inquest for the County of Pulaski highly appreciate the opinions of his Honor Judge EARLY on the state of public roads and are fully opinion that nothing can add more to the respectibility of a county than to have public roads & bridges in complete order. But considering the situation of the county and the peculiar disadvantages under which...

Page 18

a number of its inhabitants labour, some of whom having removed from the most remote part of the union with large families and no other means of procuring a subsistance but by their own manuel labor, and only hope that as early as the situation of the people, and their circumstances will admit, the roads will be put in a more complete state of repair.

We congratulate his Honor the Judge on his first appearance into the County, and seriously hope that his labours may be lessoned by the virtues of the people.

Edmund HOGAN foreman

Daniel REGAN	George G. GAINES
Jesse POWELL	Henry FULGHAM
Abraham VICKERS	George DYKES
Orandatus WATSON	Murdoch McLEOD
Hinche WARREN	Sanders COLSON
Samuel JONES	Jacob SNELL
James RAMSEY	Thomas McGRIFF
Daniel COLE	Simon BARDEN
John ROSIER	Asa PIPKIN

Page 19

Examined Peter EARLY

The Court then adjourned till court in course. Attest R. H. THOMAS Clk.

October 1811

October 28th 1811. The Superior Court for the County of Pulaski met agreeable to law Present his Honor Judge EARLY.

The following persons appeared and were sworn on the Grand Jury at the present term:

1 \Jas./ THOMAS ~~Warren~~ fo<u>ur</u>man
2 John SNELLING
3 Benjaman SMITH
4 Giddeon MAYO
5 Lester CRAWFORD
6 David SNELL
7 William DESHAZO
8 William S. LANCASTER
9 Thomas WARREN
10 John STEWART
11 John SHERRARD
12 Joel DAWSON
13 Samuel KING
14 Joseph REEVES
15 Mark MASON
16 Joseph DAVISON
17 Josiah EVERETT
18 William JOHNSON
19 William HAYNIE
20 Thomas SHEPHERD
21 George WALKER
22 William HALL
23 Charles CARDEN

Page 20

The following persons appeared & were sworn as Petitt Jurors:

No. 1

1 Jesse LEE
2 Nimrod PHILIPS
3 Benjamin STEGALL
4 Hesekiah PHILIPS
5 Robert HODGES
6 Ephram PHILIPS
7 James TOMLINSON
8 Amos WHEELER
9 William KELLEY
10 Silas JOHNSTON
11 Holden DUNN
12 Moses KIRKLAND

No. 2 Petitt Jurors

1 James BEDDINGFIELD
2 William WINN
3 James TEMPLES
4 Abram YARTY
5 James McNORTON
6 Nedham BRYAN
7 George KELLEY
8 Blakely EDINGS
9 Shadrick LEE
10 Aaron JOHNSON
11 Samuel MILLER
12 Isham McDANIEL

Amos WHEELER) (Jury No. 2)
vs.)
John HAWTHORN) Trespass
John BLAKE) We the Jury find for the defendants.
Isham JORDAN) Blakely EDINGS, fo<u>ur</u>man

Page 21

William BRACKEN)
vs.) Tresp. vi et armis
John FORD) Settled at the plaintiffs cost.

William BRACKEN)
vs.) Case forward
John FORD) Settled at the plaintiffs cost.

Benjamin BROWN) (Jury N°. 2)
vs.) False Imprisonment
William TAYLOR) We the Jurors do find for the plaintiff one thousand dollars and cost.
Blakely EDINS, form^{n}.

The Grand Jury came into Court & returned the following bill:
The State)
vs.) Assault
Christopher EDWARDS) True Bill James T. THOMAS fourman

Joseph DENSON)
vs.) Case
William PHILIPS) Dissmission ~~by~~ at mutual ~~consent~~ cost.

William M^{c}GIBONY)
vs.) Case
William JELKS) Judgement confessed.

Page 22

The Grand Jury came into Court & returned the following bill:

The State)
vs.) Ind^{t}. forceable entry & detainer
Amos WHEELER) True Bill James T. THOMAS fourman

The Grand Jury came into Court & returned the following presentment:

We the Grand Jury for the County of Pulaski present that John A. WILLIAMS late of the county aforesaid Yeoman on the ninth day of June in the year of our Lord one thousand eight hundred & eleven, the same being on the Sabbath, with fource & arms at Hartford in the county aforesaid in & upon one Francis HARVEY in the peace of God & the said State then & there being, did make an assault & him the said Francis HARVEY then did beat, wound, & threat.

Ja^{s}. T. THOMAS

Josiah EVERITT, William HALL, William S. LANCASTER, Lester CRAWFORD, George WALKER, Charles CARDIN, John SHERROD, William JOHNSON, Gideon MAYO, David SNELL, Thomas SHEPHERD, Benjamin SMITH, Joel DAWSON, Joseph REEVES, Mark MASON, John STEWART, John SNELLING, William DESHAZO, Thos. WARREN, Saml. KING, Joseph DAVISON, William HAYNIE.

Page 23

John STOKES)
vs.) Case
John RAINEY) Settled at the ~~plaintiffs~~ \defendants/ cost.

William CLEMENTS)
vs.) Attachm^{t}.
Sanders SPELL) Settled.

Ex^{d}. Peter EARLY
The Court then adjourned till tomorrow nine Oclock. R. H. THOMAS Clk.

Tuesday 29th Octr. 1811. The Court then met agreeable to adjournment- William KELLEY being excused by the Court who belonged to the Petitt Jury N°. 1 and Lewis DEWIT sworn in his place.

The State)
vs.) Ind^{t}. Challinging
Benjamin BROWN) No Bill. James T. THOMAS fourman

Page 24

Samuel KING) (Jury N°. 1)
vs.) Case in nature of deceit
Thomas M^{c}GRIFF) We the Jurors find for the defendant with cost of suit.
Robert HODGES fourman

The State of Georgia) (Jury N°. 2)
vs.) Ind^{t}. Misdemeanor
Archibald LASSITTER) We the Jurors find the travisor \Archibald LASSITTER/ guilty. Blakely EDINS forman

The State)
vs.)
Abram HOLLIDAY) W^{m}. T. RENO came into court & surrendered his principal - Abram HOLLIDAY in discharge of himself and prays an exoneration. It is therefore ordered on motion of counsel that the said William T. RENO be discharged from his said securityship.

The Grand Jury came into Court and returned the following bill:

The State)
vs.) Ind^{t}. Assault &c.
Charles COLEY) No Bill Ja^{s}. T. THOMAS fourman

Page 25

The State) (Jury N°. 2)
vs.)
Spire MILLS &) Ind^{t}. Assault
Abram HOLLIDAY) We the Jury find the travisors \Spire MILLS & Abram HOLLIDAY/ guilty. Blakely EDINS fourman

William BROWN)
vs.) Debt
Elisha HIGGS) Settled at defts. cost.

The State)
vs.)
Jacob DUNN, Holden DUNN) Ind^{t}. Cattle Stealing
& William GRINSTEAD) Jacob DUNN acknowledged himself bound to his Excellency the Governor in the sum of one thousand dollars and George G. GAINES & John J. FORD acknowledge themselves bound in the sum of five hundred dollars each conditioned to be void if the said Jacob DUNN do appear at the next Superior Court in this County and not depart thence with out the leave of said Court otherwise to remain in full force & virtue.

his
Jacob ł DUNN {Seal}
mark

Attest
T. AVERETT D.Clk.

G. G. GAINES {Seal}
John J. FORD {Seal}

Page 26

The State)
vs.) Recognizance
James LANIER)
W^{m}. S. LANCASTER*)
& Clement LANIER) James LANIER being three times solemnly called by the sheriff and failing to appear and W^{m}. T. RINNEAU and Clement LANIER being also three times severally called by the sheriff and failing to produce the body of James LANIER their recognizance were forfeited. [**Note: Originally read Wm. T. RINNEAU ; changed to Wm. S. LANCASTER here, but not in body of paragraph*]

Benjamin BROWN)
vs.) False Imprisonment
William TAYLOR) In this case the defendant being dissatisfied with the verdict of the Jury comes into Court pays all cost & prays an appeal and Daniel COLE enters himself security in terms of the law.

Wm. TAYLOR {Seal}
Daniel COLE {Seal}

Attest R. H. THOMAS Clk.
T. AVERETT D.Clk.

The State)
vs.) Ind^{t}. Assault
John A. WILLIAMS) John A. WILLIAMS acknowledges himself bound to his Excellency the Governor in the sum of two hundred dollars and [*blank*] acknowledges themselves bound in the sum of one hundred dollars each conditioned to be void if the said John A. WILLIAMS do appear at the next Superior Court in this County and not to depart thence without leave of the court otherwise to remain in full force & virtue.

{Seal}
{Seal}
{Seal}

The State)
vs.) Ind[t]. Forceable entry & detainer
Amos WHEELER) Amos WHEELER acknowledges himself bound to his Excellency the Governor in the sum of two hundred dollars and Mark WHEELER & Christopher EDWARDS acknowledge themselves bound in the sum of one hundred dollars each conditioned to be void if the said Amos WHEELER do appear at the next Superior Court \in this/ County and not depart \thence/ without leave of the court otherwise to remain in full fource & virtue.

Amos x WHEELER {Seal}
Rich[d]. H. THOMAS Clk. Mark WHEELER {Seal}
T. AVERETT D.Clk. Christopher EDWARDS {Seal}

The State)
vs.) Assault
Christopher EDWARDS) Christopher EDWARDS acknowledges himself bound to his Excellency the Governor in the sum of two hundred dollars and Spire MILLS & Samuel HART acknowledge themselves bound in the sum of one hundred dollars each conditioned to be void if the said Christopher EDWARDS do appear at the next Superior Court in this County and not depart thence without leave of the court otherwise to remain in full fource & virtue.

Christopher EDWARDS {Seal}
his
Attest Rich[d]. H. THOMAS Clk. Spire x MILLS {Seal}
mark
his
T. AVERETT D.Clk. Samuel x HART {Seal}
mark

Page 28

We the Grand Jury for the County of Pulaski present that John A. WILLIAMS late of the County aforesaid Yeoman, on or about the twenty fourth day of February one thousand eight hundred & eleven with force & arms at Hartford in the county aforesaid in and upon William HALL one of the Justices of the Peace for the county aforesaid in the peace of God and the said State then & there being did make an assault on him the said William HALL then & there did beat, hurt, wound & ill treat.

We also report to the Honorable Court, we have exonerated Daniel COLE Tax Collector from the sum of seventeen dollars & ninety cents on insolvent list for the County of Pulaski for the year one thousand eight hundred & ten.

Also Elisha FARNEL for that part of Pulaski County formerly Laurens for the year of our Lord one thousand eight hundred & eight in the sum of thirty one dollars fifty eight 1/2 cents as an insolvent list.

We also return our thanks to his Honor Judge EARLY for his charge delivered at the commencement of the Court & take the liberty to express our full approbation of his conduct in discharging the functions of the important office which he fills.

Having gone through the business of Court sofar as we conceive it our duty wish his Honor the Judge a safe return to his family.

James T. THOMAS fourman	Benjamin SMITH
Josiah EVERETT	Joel DAWSON
William HALL	Joseph REEVES
Wm. S. LANCASTER	Mark MASON
George WALKER	John STEWART
Charles CARDEN	John SNELLING
John SHERROD	William DESHAZO
William JOHNSON	Thomas WARREN
Giddeon MAYO	Samuel KING
David SNELL	Joseph DAVISON
Thomas SHEPHERD	William HAYNIE

Exd. Peter EARLY

The Court then adjourned till tomorrow nine Oclock. Richd. H. THOMAS Clk.

Wednesday 30th Octr. 1811. The Court met agreeable to adjournment.

Page 30

Benjamin Hicks STURGES having made application for admission to he practice of the law in the courts of this State, & having undergone a satisfactory examination as required by the act of assembly; the usual oath was thereupon administred to the said Benjamin Hicks STURGES & he admitted ~~to~~ to practice as an attorney & solicitor in the several courts of law & equity in this State.

The State)
vs.) Indictment for assault
Spire MILLS &) Verdict of Guilty
Abram HOLLIDAY) Ordered that the defendants Spire MILLS & Abram HOLLIDAY do each pay a fine of ten [*changed from twenty*] dollars \& be discharged upon payment of cash/ ~~& stand each committed to the custody of the Sheriff untill their fines & costs be severally paid.~~

Page 31

The following persons were drawn to serve as Grand Jurors at the next term:

1 Hardy VICKERS	13 Sion DAVIS
2 George DYKES	14 Archibald LASSITTER
3 John RAINEY	15 Michael HORN Jnr.
4 James RAMSEY	16 Benja. HARVEY
5 John GRINSTEAD	17 Jesse POWELL
6 Shadrick ATKINS	18 Sutton TRUELUCK
7 ~~Wm. BR~~ Wm. GOODSON	19 Benjn. BROWN
8 Henry FULGHAM	20 Leonard STRINGER
9 Lewis HOLLAND	21 John ROZIER
10 Danl. SNELL	22 Abram VICKERS
11 Danl. COLE	23 Nathl. MERCER
12 Danl. REGAN	24 Jacob SNELL

25 Joseph BARRON
26 Robert DEWET
27 John GILSTRAP
28 James DEES
29 Simon BARDIN
30 Bolin SWEARINGEN

Page 32

The following persons were drawn to serve as Petitt Jurors at the next term:

1 Bartholomew LUNGINO
2 Abraham BUSH
3 George BLAIR
4 Nimrod SMITH
5 William GRINSTEAD
6 Arthur JONES
7 Jno. FLOWERS
8 W^{m}. HILLIARD
9 Mark WHEELER
10 Dempsey TAYLOR
11 Umphrey POSEY
12 Christopher BOICE
13 Washington LANCASTER
14 Jno. HARVEY
15 Jno. JONES
16 Henry DEWET
17 Ferrel BELCHER
18 Elijah BARKER
19 Haywood JONES
20 John DEES
21 ~~Henry ST Reuben WHEELER~~
Henry SENTERFIT
22 Joab HORN
23 Thos. FRANKLIN
24 John LEE Sn^{r}.
25 Saml. REGAN
26 Hardy FULGHAM
27 Drury DEES
28 Rich^{d}. WHEELER
29 Arthur TOOKE
30 William TAYLOR
31 Jno. MOSES
32 William M^{c}CORMICK
33 Theophilus SUTTON
34 Reubin WARREN
35 Jeremiah GILSTRAP
36 David GARTMAN
37 Jefry MONTFORD
38 James DYKES
39 William HAGAN
40 Charles STEWART
41 William MAYO
42 Wilson BASS
43 Robert MATHEWS
44 Francis HARVEY
45 Spire MILLS
46 Reubin HART
47 Ja^{s}. WILLIAMS
48 Elias PHILIPS
49 Charles MAYO
50 Marmaduke KENT

Page 33

The State)
vs.) Ind^{t}. Misdemeanor
Archibald LASITTER) Archibald LASITTER came into court & acknowledged himself bound to his Excellency the Governor in the sum of four hundred dollars & William WOOD and James CLARK in the same sum each conditioned to be void if the said Archibald LASITTER do appear at the next Superior Court in this County and not depart thence without leave of said court otherwise to remain in full force & virtue.

Ar^{d}. LASSETER {Seal}
William WOOD {Seal}
his
James x CLARK {Seal}
mark

Attest T. AVERETT D.Clk.

Examined Peter EARLY

The Court then adjourned till Court in course. Attest R. H. THOMAS Clk.

Page 34

I Allen TOOKE do solmnly swear that I will faithfully execute all writs, warrents, precepts and processes directed to me as sheriff of the county of Pulaski and true returns make and in all things well and truly, and without malice or partiality perform the duties of the office of Sheriff of the county aforesaid during my continuance in office, and take only my lawful fees, so help me God.

Sworn to and subscribed in presence of us Allen TOOKE
This 6th day of January 1812
H. FULGHAM J.I.C.)
Jas. M. TAYLOR J.I.C.)
M. McLEOD J.I.C.)

Entered the 7th day
of January 1812 –
R. H. THOMAS Clk.

Page 35, April 1812

April 27th 1812. The Superior Court for the County of Pulaski met agreeable to law, present His Honor Judge EARLY

The following persons appeared and were sworn on the Grand Jury at the present term:

1 Henry FULGHAM fourman
2 Hardy VICKERS
3 George DYKES
4 John RAINEY
5 John GRINSTEAD
6 Shadrick ATKINS
7 William GOODSON
8 Lewis HOLLAND
9 Daniel SNELL
10 Daniel COLE
11 Daniel REGAN
12 Archibald LASETER
13 Michael HORN Jnr.
14 Benjamin HARVEY
15 Jesse POWELL
16 Sion DAVIS
17 Sutton TRUELUCK
18 Benjamin BROWN
19 John ROSIER
20 Abram VICKERS
21 Jacob SNELL
22 Joseph BARRON
23 Robert DEWETT

Page 36

The following persons appeared and were sworn as Petitt Jurors:

No. 1

1 Bartholomew LUNGINO
2 Abram BUSH
3 William GRINSTEAD
4 William HILLIARD
5 Mark WHEELER
6 Dempsey TAYLOR
7 Umphrey POSEY
8 John HARVEY
9 John JONES
10 Henry DEWITT
11 Elijah BARKER
12 Haywood JONES

N°. 2 Petitt Jurors

1 John DEES
2 Henry CENTERFEIT
3 Thomas FRANKLIN
4 John LEE Sn^r^.
5 Saml. REGAN
6 Drury DEES
7 Arthur TOOKE
8 Theophilus SUTTON
9 William M^c^CORMICK
10 Reubin WARREN
11 Jeremiah GILSTRAP
12 James DYKES

Page 37

William ONEAL)
vs.) Fi fa
Leonard STRINGER)
& Edmond HOGAN) On motion of Seabourn JONES Jn^r^. Atto. for Plaintiff it is ordered that the Sheriff do produce the above fi fa into Court tomorrow morning nine oclock with his actings & doings thereon shew cause at that time to the contrary.

William MILTON)
vs.) Debt)
Leonard STRINGER) & Bail) In this case it ~~& bail~~ being stated to the Court that the Shff. has taken insufficient bail, On motion of Thomas W. HARRIS it is ordered that the Shff. shew cause, on tomorrow morning 9 oclock why he should not stand be held and considered as bail for the said Leonard STRINGER in terms of the act in such cases made & provided.

Edward WADE)
vs.) Special case
Samuel KING) Dismissed at plantiffs cost

Page 38

Hasle HOLLEY for the) Jury N°. 2.
use of Hamlin LEWIS)
vs.) Case
Edmund HOGAN) We find for the plantiff fifty seven dollars, with interest & cost. Samuel REGAN foreman

Jett THOMAS &) Jury N°. 2.
Richardson O. SEURRÝ?)
vs.) Debt
Edmund HOGAN) We find for the plaintiffs thirty four dollars six & a quarter cents with interest and cost. Samuel REGAN foreman

Abner DAVIS) Jury N°. 2.
vs.) Debt
Edmund HOGAN) We find for the plaintiff the sum of four hundred dollars, with interest & cost of suit. Saml. REGAN fourman

Abner DAVIS) Jury N°. 2.
vs.) Case
Edmund HOGAN) We find for the plaintiff the sum of fifty dollars with interest & costs.
Saml. REGAN foreman

Page 39

Jabez LONGWORTH) ~~No. 2~~
vs.) Debt
Archibald LASETER) I confess judgement to the plantiff for the sum of three hundred & seventy nine dollars and seventy nine cents with interest according to the notes declared on & costs. 27th April 1812.
Sanders DONOHO Def^{t}. Atto.

J. W. WILLIAMS) Jury N°. 1
vs.) In debitatus assumpsit
Noah WHEELER) We the Jury find for the plantiff the sum of thirty seven dollars and one cent with cost of suit. April 27th 1812.
John HARVEY foreman

James HILL and) Jury N°. 2
Isaac HILL)
vs.) Debt
Edmund HOGAN) We find for the plantiffs thirty five dollars with interest and cost.
Samuel REGAN foreman

Page 40

Roger OLMSTEAD for the) Jury N°. 2
use of West WHITAKER)
vs.) Debt
Edmund HOGAN) We find for the plantiff the sum of ninety seven dollars, with interest and costs.
Samuel REGAN foreman

John MAINER for the) Jury N°. 2
use of West WHITAKER)
vs.) Debt
Samuel SMITH) We find for the plantiff the sum of thirty dollars with interest and costs.
Samuel REGAN foreman

BENNETT & HILL)
vs.) Debt
Robert MATHIS) In open court I confess judgement to plaintiffs for forty one dollars sixty eight and three fourth cents with interest and cost.
Robert MATHIS

Joab HORN) Jury N°. 2
vs.) Case &c.
Mark MASON) We find for the plantiff fifty dollars with cost of suit.
Samuel REGAN foreman

John PEARCE)
vs.) Slander
James WHEELER) Settled at mutual cost.

Theodrick MONTFORD)
vs.) Case
William T. RENEAU) Settled at mutual cost.

The State)
vs.) Ind^{t}. Cattle Stealing
Holden DUNN) Joseph SESSIONS bail in the above case surrendered his principal into court. It is ordered that the said Joseph SESSIONS be henceforth discharged from his recognizance and it is further ordered that the sheriff take the said Holden DUNN into his custody and safe keeping untill discharged by leave of the court.

James L. PERRY) Jury N°. 1
vs.) Slander
William T. RENEAU) We find for the plantiff fifty dollars and cost of suit.
John HARVEY foreman

Retison DAVIS Indee) Jury N°. 1
vs.)
Sampson BRASWELL) Case
& James BRASWELL) April 27th 1812. We find for the plantiff six hundred dollars with interest & cost. John HARVEY foreman

Page 42

S. JONES) Jury N°. 1
vs.) Case
R. HODGES) We find for the plantiff thirty five dollars with interest & cost.
John HARVEY foreman

Robert SHARROD) Jury N°. 2
vs.) Trespass vi et armis
Christopher EDWARDS) We find for the plantiff thirty five dollars with cost of suit. Samuel REGAN foreman

S. JONES)
vs.) Case
Robert HODGES) In this case the defendant being dissatisfied with the verdict of the jury comes into court pays all cost & prays an appeal and Joseph SESSIONS enters himself security in terms of the law.
Attest Rich^{d}. H. THOMAS Clk. Robert HODGES

BENNETT & HILL)
vs.) Debt
Robert MATHIS) In this case the defendant comes forward pays all cost & prays a stay of execution & enters Elijah BARKER \as/ security in terms of the law.

Robert MATHIS
his
Attest Rich^{d}. H. THOMAS Clk. Elijah o BARKER
mark

Page 43

And the court adjourned 'till tomorrow morning eight oclock.
Ex^{d}. Peter EARLY

Tuesday 28th April 1812. The court then met agreeable to adjournment.

John A. WILLIAMS)
vs.) Divorce
Hester WILLIAMS) In this case it appearing to the court the defendant is not to be found; On motion of counsel it is ordered that judgement be taken as in cases of default unless cause be shewn to the contrary at the next term of this court; & that a copy of this order be published once a month for four months in one of the gazettes of this state.

W^{m}. ONEAL)
vs.) Fi fa
STRINGER & HOGAN) The sheriff having returned, in obedience to a rule obtained on Monday, the above fi fa with a levy indorsed on the same–

Page 44

It is therefore ordered that the sheriff do pay to the plantiff or his attorney the amount of the above execution, on or before the first Tuesday in August.

The State)
vs.) Ind^{t}. Cattle Stealing
Holden DUNN) Holden DUNN acknowledged himself bound to his Excellency the Governor in the sum of one thousand dollars and William GRINSTEAD and Rolling DUN \acknowledged themselves bound ~~in the sum of~~/ in the sum of five hundred dollars each conditioned to be void if the said Holden DUNN do appear at the next Superior Court in this county and not depart thence without the leave of said Court otherwise to remain in full force and virtue.

Holden DUNN {Seal}
his
Attest Rich^{d}. H. THOMAS Clk. W^{m}. x GRINSTEAD {Seal}
mark
his
Rolling x DUNN {Seal}
mark

W^{m}. MILTON)
vs.) Debt & Bail
Leonard STRINGER) Rule for the Sheriff to shew cause why he should not be held and considered special bail - The Sheriff having shewn sufficient cause it is ordered that the said rule be discharged.

Page 45

The following persons were drawn to serve as Grand Jurors at the next term:

1 William JOHNSON
2 David SNELL
3 Charles CARDIN
4 Edward BRYAN
5 Murdoch M^{c}LEOD
6 John SNELLING
7 Samuel KING
8 Philip JONES
9 James T. THOMAS
10 John STEGALL
11 W^{m}. S. LANCASTER
12 William HALL
13 John STEWART
14 Lester CRAWFORD
15 Joseph REEVES
16 Benjamin SMITH
17 Josiah EVERETT
18 William DESHAZO
19 John SHERROD
20 James ODAM
21 Thomas WARREN
22 Joseph SESSIONS
23 W^{m}. HAINIE
24 Orandatus WATSON
25 Mark MASON
26 Joel DAWSON
27 George G. GAINES
28 William JELKS
29 Thomas M^{c}GRIFF
30 Nedham STEPHENS

The following persons were drawn to serve as Petitt Jurors at the next term:

1 William SMITH
2 Benjamin POSEY
3 John SWEARINGEN
4 John BARROW
5 Lewis LEE
6 Daniel CORNWALL
7 Absolim HOPSON
8 Burwell PHILLIPS
9 Sherrod PHILLIPS
10 Phelix DYKES
11 Pascal HAMMACK
12 Drury MAYO
13 Richard WINN
14 Jacob TAYLOR
15 William ALLEN
16 Samuel HART

Page 46

17 Elisha GARBIT
18 John LEE J^{r}.
19 Charles DANIEL
20 Martin SWEARINGEN
21 ~~Elihu KENT~~ Archibald ODAM
22 John MANNING
23 ~~Levy BUSH~~ Jordan DEES
24 Reubin ROLEN
25 Joel WALKER
26 William ROBERTS
27 William PHILLIPS J^{r}.
28 William PHILLIPS S^{r}.
29 Chesley DAVIS
30 Christopher MERCER
31 Johnathan MILLER
32 William BRYANT
33 Benjamin HARRISON
34 William HAMMACK
35 Sol. BREWER
36 Jno. BEDINGFIELD
37 Isham HAGAN
38 Moses GIDDENS
39 Mich^{l}. HORN S^{r}.
40 Jesse LEE?

41 Jno. BRYANT
42 Henry HART
43 Jno. DIXON
44 Nimrod PHILLIPS
45 Jethro PHILLIPS
46 Bailey HARRELL
47 Edmond GIDDENS
48 James BAITY
49 Robert HODGES
50 Joshua LEE

The State)
vs.)
Amos WHEELER,)
Mark WHEELER &) Recognizance forfeited and
Christopher EDWARDS) sci fa ordered to issue

Page 47

The State)
vs.) Ind^{t}. Asault &c.
Colson ADAMS) True Bill Henry FULGHAM foreman

The State)
vs.) Ind^{t}. Larceny
W^{m}. PROCTOR) True Bill Henry FULGHAM foreman

The State)
vs.) Misdemeanor
Nancy WHEELER) True Bill Henry FULGHAM foreman

The State)
vs.) Ind^{t}. Pergury
W^{m}. TAYLOR) No Bill Henry FULGHAM foreman

Page 48

The State) Indictment for Misdemeanor &c.
vs.) Verdict of Guilty –
Archibald LASSITER) Ordered that the defendant Archibald LASSITER do pay a fine of one hundred dollars & be discharged upon payment of costs.

We the Grand Jurors at April term 1812 - Agreeable to the act of the Legislature we have examined into the county funds. We find in hands, in notes and bonds to the amount of six thousand and twenty seven dollars and sixty four cents. We find there has been paid out to the amount of $3748.36.

We further return our thanks to his Honor the Judge for his faithful and impartial attention. Henry FULGHAM foreman

Archibald LASITER
Michael HORN J^{r}.
Benjamin HARVEY
Jesse POWELL
Sutton TRUELUCK
Benjamin BROWN
John ROSIER
Abram VICKERS
Jacob SNELL
Joseph BARRON
Robert DEWETT
Hardy VICKERS

George DYKES	Lewis HOLLAND
John RAINEY	Daniel SNELL
John GRINSTEAD	Daniel COLE
Shadrick ATKINS	Daniel REGAN
William GOODSON	Sion DAVIS

The State)
vs.) Ind[t]. Assault &c.
James L. PERRY) James L. PERRY acknowledged himself bound to his Excellency the Governor in the sum of five hundred dollars and James T. THOMAS and John RAMSEY acknowledged themselves bound in the sum of two hundred & fifty dollars each conditioned to be void if the said James L. PERRY do appear at the next Superior Court in this county and not depart thence without the leave of said Court otherwise to remain in full force and virtue.

James L. PERRY {Seal}
James T. THOMAS {Seal}
Attest Rich[d]. H. THOMAS Clk. John RAMSEY {Seal}

Page 50

The State)
vs.) Ind[t]. Assault &c.
Colson ADAMS) Colson ADAMS acknowledged himself bound to his Excellency the Governor in the sum of five hundred dollars and William TAYLOR and William HALL acknowledged themselves bound in the sum of two hundred & fifty dollars each conditioned to be void if the said Colson ADAMS do appear at the next Superior Court in this county and not depart thence without the leave of said Court otherwise to remain in full force & virtue.

Colson ADAMS {Seal}
Attest W[m]. TAYLOR {Seal}
Rich[d]. H. THOMAS Clk. W[m]. HALL {Seal}

Page 51

The State)
vs.) Ind[t]. Larceny
Wm. PROCKTOR) William PROCKTOR acknowledged himself bound to his Excellency the Governor in the sum of five hundred dollars and John TEMPLES and Thomas TEMPLES acknowledged themselves bound in the sum of two hundred & fifty dollars each conditioned to be void if the said William PROCTOR do appear at the next Superior Court in this county and not depart thence without the leave of said Court otherwise to remain in full force & virtue.

W[m]. PROCTOR {Seal}
Attest John TEMPLES {Seal}
Rich[d]. H. THOMAS Clk. Thomas TEMPLES {Seal}

~~The State)~~
~~vs.) Indt. Misdemeanor~~
~~Archibald LASITER) Archibald LASITER acknowledged himself bound to his Excellency the Governor in the sum five two hundred dollars and William YARBROUGH acknowledged himself bound in~~

The State)
vs.) Ind^{t}. Misdemeanor
Archibald LASITER) We Archibald LASITER & William YARBROUGH acknowledge themselves bound to his Excellency the Governor or his successors in office in the sum of two hundred dollars, conditioned to be void if the above bound Archibald LASITER does well and truly pay unto the Sup^{r}. Court of the County of Pulaski \one hundred dollars/ on the first day of the \next/ term then to be void otherwise to remain in full fource & virtue.

Attest — Archibald LASSITER {Seal}
Rich^{d}. H. THOMAS Clk. — William YARBROUGH {Seal}

Page 53

Retison DAVIS Endee)
vs.) Case
Sampson BRASWELL)
& James BRASWELL) The defendants Sampson BRASWELL & James BRASWELL with Abraham VICKERS their security comes forward pays all costs and stays the execution sixty days.

his
Simpson x BRASWELL {Seal}
mark
Attest — Ja^{s}. BRASWELL {Seal}
his
Rich^{d}. H. THOMAS Clk. — Abraham x VICKERS {Seal}
mark

Ex^{d}. Peter EARLY

The Court then adjourned till court in course. Attest Rich^{d}. H. THOMAS Clk.

Page 54, May 1812

Jeremiah W. WILLIAMS)
vs.) Indebitatus Assum[p]set
Noah WHEELER) In this case the defendent being dissatisfied with the verdict of the jury comes \forward/ ~~into court~~ pays all costs and prays an appeal and enters William RAMSEY himself security in terms of the law.

2nd May 1812 — Noah WHEELER
Attest Rich^{d}. H. THOMAS Clk. — William RAMSEY

Page 55, October 1812

October Term 1812. The Superior Court for the County of Pulaski met agreeably to law. Present his Honor Judge EARLY.

The following persons appeared and were sworn on the Grand Jury at the present term:

1 Murdoch M^{c}LEOD foreman	11 Benjamin SMITH
2 William JOHNSON	12 Josiah EVERETT
3 Daniel SNELL	13 John SHERROD
4 John SNELLING	14 Joseph SESSIONS
5 Samuel KING	15 Oran D. WATSON
6 James T. THOMAS	16 Mark MASON
7 John STEGALL	17 George G. GAINES
8 W^{m}. S. LANCASTER	18 Thomas M^{c}GRIFF
9 William HALL	19 Needham STEPHENS
10 Joseph REEVES	20 Lester CRAWFORD

The following persons appeared and were sworn as Petitt Jurors:

N°. 1

1 Benjamin POSEY	7 Elisha GARBIT
2 Daniel CORNWELL	8 John LEE J^{r}.
3 Sherrod PHILIPS	9 Charles DANIEL
4 Phelix DYKES	10 Archibald ODAM
5 William ALLEN	11 Jordan DEES
6 Samuel HART	12 Reubin ROLLING

Page 56

N°. 2 Petitt Jury

1 Joel WALKER	7 William HAMMACK
2 William ROBERTS	8 Moses GIDDINGS
3 William PHILIPS S^{r}.	9 John BRYAN
4 Chesley DAVIS	10 John DIXON
5 William BRYAN	11 Nimrod PHILIPS
6 Benjamin HARRISON	12 Bailey HARRELL

The State)
vs.) Ind^{t}. Assault
John A. WILLIAMS) True Bill Murdoch M^{c}LEOD foreman

The State)
vs.) Ind^{t}. Assault
Nathl. HUNT) True Bill Murdoch M^{c}LEOD foreman

The State)
vs.) Ind^{t}. Assault
John A. WILLIAMS) John A. WILLIAMS acknowledged himself bound to his Excellency the Governor in the sum of two hundred dollars and Elijah WALLACE and Thomas A. HILL acknowledged themselves bound in the sum of one hundred dollars each conditioned to be void if the said John A. WILLIAMS do appear at the next Superior Court in this county & not depart thence without the leave of said Court otherwise to remain in full force & virtue. Jno. A. WILLIAMS {Seal}
Attest Elijah WALLACE {Seal}
Richard H. THOMAS Clk. Thos. A. HILL {Seal}

The Grand Jury returned the following bills into Court:

The State)
vs.) Ind^{t}. Assault
Joseph COOPER) True Bill Murdoch M^{c}LEOD foreman

The State)
vs.) Ind^{t}. Larceny
John PARRIS) No Bill Murdoch M^{c}LEOD foreman

Richard MOYA) Spc. Case
vs.) Jury N°. 1
Isham SHUFFIELD) We find for the plantiff the sum of sixty six dollars with cost of suit. A. ODOM foreman

The Court then adjourned till tomorrow nine Oclock.
Ex^{d}. Peter EARLY

Tuesday 27th October 1812. The Court met agreeable to adjournment.

Page 58

Levi BUSH ad mor)
de bonis non of)
W^{m}. BUSH Junr. dec^{d}.) Case
vs.) Jury N°. 2
Edmund HOGAN &)
John HOGAN) We find for the plantiff the sum of four hundred & eight dollars with interest and cost. John DICKSON foreman

The State)
vs.) Ind^{t}. for passing base coin
Vachel DAVIS) No Bill Murdoch McLEOD fore^{n}

The State)
vs.) Ind^{t}. for passing base coin
William SMITH) True Bill Murdoch McLEOD fore^{n}

The State)
vs.) Ind^{t}. for passing base coin
William SMITH) True Bill Murdoch McLEOD for^{n}

[*above entered twice in original*]

William TAYLOR) Trespass & false imprisonment
vs.) Jury N°. 2
Benjamin BROWN) We the Jury find for the defendant with cost of suit.
John DIXON for^{n}

Richard MOYA)
vs.) Spc. Case
Isham SHUFFIELD) In this case the defendant being dissatisfied with the verdict of the Jury comes forward pays all costs and prays an appeal and enters Asa PIPKIN with himself security in terms of the law.

27th October 1812. Isham SHUFFIELD
Richd. H. THOMAS Clk. Asa PIPKIN

John BROWN) Jury No. 1st
vs.)
Wheatten PINES)
Archibld. H. ODOM) Trespass vi et armis
James DENARD)
& Daniel PINES) We the Jurors find for the plantiff thirteen dollars with cost of suit.
A. ODOM foreman

Nicholas LONG)
administrator) Debt
vs.)
Elijah BARKER) I confess judgement to the plantiffs for the sum of thirty six dollars & fifty four cents with cost of suit.
27th October 1812. Elijah his x mark BARKER

Page 60

The State)
vs.) Assault
Joseph COOPER) Joseph COOPER acknowledges himself bound to his Excellency the Governor or his successors in office in the penal sum of two hundred dollars and Amos WHEELER & John JONES Senr. acknowledge themselves bound in the sum of one hundred dollars each conditioned to be void if the said Joseph COOPER do appear \from day to throughout this/ ~~at the next Superior~~ Court in this county & not to depart without leave of the Court otherwise to remain in full force & virtue.

Joseph COOPER {Seal}
Attest Richd. H. THOMAS Clk. Amos his x mark WHEELER {Seal}
John his x mark JONES {Seal}

William MERRITT)
& Richard ASBURY) Debt
vs.) In open court –
Elijah WALLACE)
& William JELKS) We confess judgement for eighty nine dollars with interest & cost.
E. WALLACE
William JELKS

The State)
vs.) Larceny
John PARRIS) No Bill Murdoch M^{c}LEOD for^{n}.

Page 61

Christopher SHEPARD)
for the use of Philip COOK)
vs.) Debt
Micajah H. POWEL &)
William JELKS) We confess judgement for the sum of sixty dollars with interest & cost October 27th 1812. W^{m}. CROCKER for defendant

Ambrose MURPHY)
for E. NUNN) Case
vs.) Jury N°. 2
John A. WILLIAMS) We find for the plantiff fifty dollars with ~~cost of suit~~ interest & cost. John DICKSON for^{n}.

Six months after date I promise to pay Elijah CLARK or bearor the sum of fifty dollars value received April 2^{d} 1810.

(Indorsment) I in dorce the within note to A[m]brose MURPHY to be responsible in the event of the maker of the note failing to pay the same.

April 3^{d} 1811 Elijah CLARK

Georgia)
Pulaski County) Appeared in open court Thomas W. HARRIS made oath that he held a note in his hands for collection of which the foregoing as near as he can recollect is a true copy with the indorsment that the same is lost or mislaid that he has made...

Page 62

diligant search for it & cannot find it Sworn to in open court October 27th 1812.
Attest Rich^{d}. H. THOMAS Clk. Thomas W. HARRIS

Nichols LONG)
administrator)
vs.) Case
James RAMSEY &) Jury N°. 2
Elijah WALLACE) We the Jury find for the plaintiff one hundred & eighty nine dollars with interest & cost of suit. John DICKSON for^{n}.

Ex^{d}. Peter EARLY

And the court then adjourned untill tomorrow morning nine Oclock.

Page 63

Wednesday 28th of October 1812 – The Court met agreeable to adjournment.

Seaborn JONES) Case
vs.) Jury No. 1
Admr. of R. THOMPSON) We find for the plaintiff thirty seven dollars & forty one cents with costs.
A. ODOM forn.

William HALL)
vs.) Fi fa
Lodawick LORD) On motion of counsel for deft. it is ordered that the Shff. do produce the above fi fa with his actings & doings thereon instanter.

Redmond SISSON) Debt
vs.) Jury No. 1
William GOODSON) We find for the plaintiff thirty three dollars interest & cost.
A. ODOM forn.

Thompson BIRD) Debt
vs.) Jury No. 1
Edmund HOGAN) We find for the plaintiff the sum of one hundred & fifty nine dollars twelve & one half cents with interest & cost.
A. ODOM forn.

Page 64

A. SLAUGHTER)
& C. SALEUZAN?) Case
vs.) Jury No. 1
Edm. HOGAN) We \the jury/ find for the plaintiffs the sum of two hundred dollars with interest & cost – October 28th 1812.
A. ODOM forn.

J. & A. STINSON)
vs.) Case
Murdoch McLEOD) I confess judgement to the plaintiff in the sum of one hundred & seventy five dollars with interest & costs.
Bedney FRANKLIN for deft.

Thomas DICKSON &)
John G. UNDERWOOD) Case
vs. Admrs.) Jury No. 1
Murdoch McLEOD) We find for the defendant the sum of two hundred ~~dollars~~ & thirty six dollars with interest & costs.
A. ODOM forn.

Warren HART Indee)
vs.)
Isaac TURNAGE) Debt
otherwise called Isaac)
BLOUNT Indorser) Dismissed.

John DOE ex. dem.)
Abner HOLLIDAY) Trespass in Ejectment
vs.)
Richard ROE Furney) Jury N°. 2
F. GATLIN tenant) We find for the defendant with costs.
John DICKSON for^{n}.

CROWELL & BUTLER)
endorsees for the use of)
John CROWELL) Case
vs.)
Jonathan TAYLOR) I confess judgement to the plaintiff in the sum of forty five dollars with interest & cost.
his
Jonathan x TAYLOR
mark

CROWELL & BUTLER)
for the use of)
John CROWELL) Debt
vs.)
William RAY) I confess judgement to the plaintiff for one hundred fifty nine dollars 62$\frac{1}{2}$ cents with interest & cost.
his
William x RAY
mark

The State)
vs.) Assault
Bartholomew GAINEY) True Bill Murdoch M^{c}LEOD for^{n}.

Thomas BUTLER)
for the use of)
John CROWELL) Debt
vs.) Jury N°. 2
John RAMSEY &)
W^{m}. RAMSEY) We find for the plaintiffs the sum of thirty two dollars & seventy five cents with interest & cost. John DICKSON for^{n}.

Page 66

Daniel WATKINS)
vs.) Debt
James L. PERRY) I confess judgement to the plaintiff for seventy six dollars & twenty five cents with interest & cost. James L. PERRY

Allen TOOKE &)
Arthur TOOKE) Debt
vs.)
W^{m}. GOODSON) I confess judgement to the plaintiffs in the sum of two hundred & twenty dollars & forty three & three-fourths cents with interest & cost.

his
W^{m}. x GOODSON
mark

Thomas BUTLER for the)
use of John CROWELL) Debt
vs.) Jury N°. 2
Jonathan VICKERS) We find for the plaintiff sixty one dollars sixty two & a half cents with interest & cost. John DICKSON for^{n}.

James SHACKELFORD)
for Henry SHACKELFORD) Debt
vs.)
John RAMSEY) In open court I confess judgement for fifty dollars with interest & cost reserving the right of appeal. 28th Octr. 1812.
Adam G. SAFFOLD def^{t}. atty.

Allen TOOKE & Co.)
vs.) Debt
Wm. GOODSON) I confess judgement to the plaintiff in the sum of fifty four dollars & sixty two cents with interest & cost.
his
W^{m}. x GOODSON
mark

Page 67

Simon SMITH for the)
use of Allen TOOKE) Debt
vs.) Jury N°. 2
Jesse FULGHAM &)
Henry FULGHAM) We find for the plaintiff seventy eight dollars with interest & cost. John DICKSON for^{n}.

Thomas BUTLER for the)
use of John CROWELL) Debt
vs.)
Thomas A. HILL) I confess judgement to the plaintiffs in the sum of thirty six dollars & eighty seven & a half cents with interest & cost.
FRANKLIN for def^{t}.

The State)
vs.) Ind^{t}. Forgery
Vachel DAVIS) True Bill Murdoch M^{c}LEOD for^{n}.

Page 68

Allen TOOKE & Co.) Debt
vs.) Jury N°. 1
Lewis LEE) We the jury find for the plaintiffs the sum of fifty nine dollars with interest & costs. A. ODOM for^{n}.

John M. VASS for the use)
of Archibald McMILLAN) Debt
vs.)
Christopher D. EDWARDS) In open court I confess judgement to the plaintiff for the sum of seventy dollars with interest & cost.

Christopher EDWARDS

Justices of the Inferior)
Court for the use of)
James L. PERRY) Debt
vs.)
Lewis LEE &)
Robert DESHAZO) I confess judgement to the plaintiff for seventy five dollars & fifty cents with interest & cost.

Wm. CROCKER
atty. for Ptffs.

Allen TOOKE)
& Company) Debt
vs.) Jury No. 1
Daniel W. SHINE) We the Jury find for the plaintiffs the sum of thirty six dollars twelve & a half cents with interest & cost.

A. ODOM forn.

Page 69

Allen TOOKE)
& Company) Debt
vs.)
John JONES Senr.) October Term 1812. I confess judgement to the plaintiffs in the sum of thirty one dollars six & a quarter cents with interest & cost of suit.

his
John x JONES Sr.
mark

Allen TOOKE)
& Company) Debt
vs.)
Henry HAGAN) In open court I confess judgement to the plaintiffs for the sum of sixty dollars twelve & a half cents with interest & cost.

Henry HAGAN

Allen TOOKE)
& Company) Debt
vs.) Jury No. 1
John DEES) We the Jury find for the plaintiff the sum of thirty three dollars eighty one & one fourth cents with interest & cost.

A. ODOM forn.

Allen TOOKE)
& Company) Debt
vs.)
James RAMSEY) October Term 1812. In open court I confess judgement to the plaintiffs in the sum of fifty seven dollars fifty six & a quarter cents with interest & cost. B. FRANKLIN for Def[t].

Page 70

Justices of the Inferior)
Court for the use of)
James L. PERRY) Debt
vs.)
Thos. JOHNSON &)
John B. PACKER) Settle at Pltffs. cost.

Allen TOOKE)
& Company)
vs.) Debt
John RAMSEY &)
W[m]. RAMSEY) October Term 1812. In open court I confess judgement to the plaintiff in the sum of fifty five dollars eighty two & a half cents with interest & cost. B. FRANKLIN for Def[t].

Allen TOOKE)
& Company) Debt
vs.) Jury N[o]. 1
Noah WHEELER) We find for the plaintiffs the sum of forty nine dollars & fifty cents with interest & cost. A. ODOM for[n].

Dudly DUNN assignee)
vs.) Case
W[m]. GARLINTON &) Jury N[o]. 1
Edwin GARLINTON) We find for the plaintiff the sum of thirty six dollars with interest & cost. A. ODOM for[n].

Page 71

Elisha HIGGS for the)
use of John CROWELL) Debt
vs.)
Clement LANIER) In open court I confess judgement to the plaintiff for fifty dollars with interest & cost. Clement LANIER

James WHEELER) Case
vs.) Jury N[o]. 2
Jonathan VICKERS) We find for the plaintiff sixty dollars & cost of suit.
John DICKSON for[n].

Elijah CLARK)
vs.) Debt
Allin TOOKE &)
Arthur TOOKE) We confess judgement ot the plantiff for the sum of seventy eight dollars eighty one & one fourth cents with interest & cost.

Allin TOOKE
Arthur TOOKE

The State) Assault
vs.) Jury N°. 2
Joseph COOPER) We the Jury find not guilty. John DICKSON for^{n}.

Ex^{d}. Peter EARLY

And the Court the adjourned untill tomorrow morning nine oclock.

Page 72

Thursday the 29th October 1812. The Court met agreeably to adjournment.

William HALL)
vs.) Fi fa
Ladowick LORD) The Sheriff having made a complete return and also the fi fa sought the rule ni si is therefore discharged.

The State) Indictment) John T. HOWARD
vs.) for passing base) Levi NELSON
William SMITH) coin) Joseph WOOD
) Ja^{s}. M. TAYLOR
witnesses sworn

Jury Sworn

1 Felix DYKES	7 John BRIANT
2 William ALLEN	8 Drury MAYO
3 Elisha GARBIT	9 Daniel COLE
4 Jordan DEES	10 Thomas PAXTON
5 William BRIANT	11 Jesse LIVELY
6 William HAMMOCK	12 James BRASWELL

We find the prisoner guilty. James BRASWELL for^{n}.

Ex^{d}. Peter EARLY

And the Court the adjourned untill tomorrow morning eight oclock.

Page 73

Friday the 30th October 1812. The Court met agreeably to adjournment.

The State)
vs.)
James LANIER)
Clement LANIER)
Wm. S. LANCASTER) James LANIER being called & not appearing and Clement LANIER and William S. LANCASTER having no cause to shew why judgement should not be entered against them for the amount of their recognizance whereupon it is considered by the Court that the plaintiff recover of the defendants Clement LANIER & William S. LANCASTER the sum of one thousand dollars and the sum of [*blank*] for his cost and the defendants in mercy &c.

B. FRANKLIN Sol.

The State)
vs.)
John A. WILLIAMS) The security Orandatus WATSON having surrendered the principal John A. WILLIAMS; Ordered that the said Orandatus WATSON be henceforth discharged from his recognizance.

The State)
vs.) Indt. for passing base coin
Vachel DAVIS) No bill Murdoch McLEOD forn.

Page 74

Pulaski Sup. Ct. October Term 1812.

The Grand Inquest for the Body of Pulaski on their oath present, Bailey ROBINSON and John SCARBROUGH the one for performing ordinary labor on the Sabbath and the other to viz) John SCARBROUGH for galloping his horse through the streets on the same day in time of divine worship – We present Gideon KELLAM for the highly immoral practice of retailing spirituous liquors on Sabbath days and as a future preventation recommend to the County and City Police a more strict observance of the law in such cases made & provided.

We cannot pass over in silence the truly distressed situation of our fellow citizens which has been produced by a depreciation of the staple commmodity of our country, and a universal restriction on trade, a national calamity that could not have been avoided; and production of much mischief by a sale of property which in many cases has not paid cost – these facts being known and the dreadful consiquences to accoust? every man in common life has induced a large majority of the inhabitants of said county to hold a meeting on the subject, the result of which is – that the operations of the law cease for a limited time in civil cases & in such a way as the Legislature of the State may deem most advisable and the members elected from this County are instructed to adopt measures to that effect.

If being the wish of the people – we return his Honor Judge EARLY our undivided thanks for his very prompt & decided opinions in all judicial matters that has come before him during the present term as well as the great patience manifested during a lengthy session – notwithstanding the fatigue experienced on a circuit too extensive for any one man to perform without manifest inconvenience to his health. We therefore recommend to the legislature to turn their attention to that fact, and if a division of the circuit do not meet their approbation they certainly in our humble opinion can have no objection to pay their officers in proportion to the labor rendered – We reuqest that these our presentments be published together with any remarks that his Honor may think proper to make.

1 Murdoch M^c^LEOD for^n^.	10 Joseph REEVES
2 Orandatus WATSON	11 John SNELLING
3 Mark MASON	12 Samuel KING
4 Thomas McGRIFF	13 Josiah EVERETT
5 Neidham STEPHENS	14 Lester CRAWFORD
6 Benjamin SMITH	15 David SNELL
7 James T. THOMAS	16 John SHERROD
8 William HALL	17 Joseph SESSIONS
9 John STEGALL	18 William JOHNSON

Page 76

The State) Indt.
vs.) Forgery & passing
Vachel DAVIS) base coin

Jury Sworn

1 Samuel HART	7 Frederic WOLF
2 Reubin ROLLING	8 William CARDIN
3 William PHILIPS Sr.	9 William WOOD
4 Edmund GIDDINS	10 John SHAW
5 John LEE	11 Jesse JONES
6 John YARBROUGH	12 Wm. T. RENEAU

Witnesses Sworn
) John McRAE
) Elizabeth McRAE
) Samuel REGAN
) James SHATTIEN
) Christopher EDWARDS
) John B. PACKIR
) James RAMSEY
) Samuel FOULE
) James M. TAYLOR
) Rachel SMITH
) Joseph WOOD
) John GRINSTEAD
) Benjamin MEWBORN
) John T. HOWARD
) James L. PERRY
) Frederic WOLF
) William WOOD

We find the prisoner not guilty. Wm. T. RENEAU forn.

Exd. Peter EARLY

And the Court then adjourned untill tomorrow morning nine pclock.

Saturday 31st October 1812. The Court met agreeably to adjournment.

The following persons were drawn to serve as Grand Jurors at the next term:

1 Archibald LASSETTER
2 Christopher RHODES
3 William H. GROSS
4 Lewis HOLLAND
5 Isaac BURKHALTER
6 Benjamin BRUTON
7 John STEWART
8 Docr. M. H. POWELL
9 Joab HORN
10 William DESHAZO
11 Daniel REGAN
12 Robirt MATHEWS
13 James McNORTON
14 Asa PIPKIN
15 William GOODSON
16 James BRACEWELL
17 Daniel COLE
18 John GILSTRAP
19 Benjamin BROWN
20 William JELKS
21 Reubin WARREN
22 William HAINEY
23 John LESTER
24 Archibald H. ODOM
25 William MAHAFEE
26 Jacob SNELL
27 William YARBROUGH
28 John HARVEY
29 James M. TAYLOR
30 William ISLER

Page 78

The following persons were drawn to serve as Petitt Jurors at the next term:

1 Adam BILLINGS
2 Solomon LAMB
3 James JONES
4 Solomon SUTTON
5 Elijah BARKER
6 Thomas TOMBLEY
7 Edmund RUNNELS
8 George KELLEY
9 Umfrey POSEY
10 Edmund HESTER
11 William SMITH
12 Maliki KELLEY
13 John LEE Younger
14 William WINN
15 Burwell PHILIPS
16 Thomas SHEPHERD
17 William RAY
18 Willis BRIAN
19 John DEES
20 Hugh TAYLOR
21 William LITTLE
22 Thomas CUNIGIN [*Cuningham?*]
23 James DYKES
24 John SYLVESTER
25 Daniel THOMPSON
26 William HAMILTON
27 Isaac HARRELL
28 Neil McCORMICK
29 Ezekiel PHILIPS
30 William HILLIARD
31 William LESTER
32 Samuel PERKINS
33 Noah WHEELER
34 Nimrod SMITH
35 Jacob SINGLETARY
36 William SMITH
37 Daniel DYKES
38 Isham SHUFFIELD
39 Moses SUTTON
40 Noah CALHOON
41 John COLEMAN
42 ~~Phili~~ Christopher McRAE
43 Henry MILLS
44 Jacob SPICKARD
45 Marmaduke KENT
46 Dennis ADAMS
47 James RATLIFF
48 Henry CENTERFEIT
49 Linnerl BROWN
50 Thomas PARRIMORE

The State) Indictment for passing base coin
vs.) & conviction
William SMITH) Sentence of the Court: You William SMITH are to be kept in close confinement untill Friday the Twentieth day of November next. You are then between the hours of eleven oclock in the forenoon & one oclock in the afternoon of that day to be taken to a gallows at or near the town of Hartford in this County & there between the hours aforesaid on the day aforesaid you are to be hung by the neck untill you are dead – and the Lord have mercy on your soul.

The State) Indict.
vs.) forgery &c.
Vachel DAVIS) The prisoner being found not guilty – on motion it is ordered that he be discharged on the payment of costs.

Page 80

Ex[d]. Peter EARLY
The Court then adjourned until court in course. Attest Rich[d]. H. THOMAS Clk.

John DOE ex dem.)
Abner HOLLIDAY)
vs.) Trespass in Ejectment
Richard ROE Furney)
F. GATLIN Tenant) The plaintiff being dissatisfied with the verdict in this case comes by his attorney Thomas FITCH & prays an appeal & pays up the cost & tenders Allen SCARBOROUGH for his security & an appeal is granted him this ~~31st~~ October 1812.
Thomas FITCH
Attorney for pltff. {Seal}
{Seal}

End of Book 1; Loose Page, November 1812

Abel PAULK)
vs.) Case
James RAMSEY &)
ElijahWALLACE) The defendants being dissatisfied with the verdict of the Jury comes forward pays all costs \& prays an appeal/ and enters William LYON security in terms of the law.
James RAMSEY {LS}
Attest
Elijah WALLACE {LS}
Rich[d]. H. THOMAS Clk.
William LYON {LS}

Elijah CLARK)
vs.) Debt
Allen TOOKE &)
Arthur TOOKE) The defendants Allen TOOKE & Arthur TOOKE with Turner EVERETT their security comes forward stays execution in terms of the law. 5th of November 1812.
Allen TOOKE {LS}
Attest
Arthur TOOKE {LS}
Rich[d]. H. THOMAS Clk.
Turner EVERETT {LS}

Simon SMITH for the)
use of Allen TOOKE)
vs.) Debt
Jesse FULGHAM &)
Henry FULGHAM) The defendants Jesse FULGHAM & Henry FULGHAM with Turner EVERETT their security comes forward stays execution in terms of the law. 5th November 1812.

his
Jesse x FULGHAM {LS}
mark
H. FULGHAM {LS}
Turner EVERETT {LS}

Attest
Richd. H. THOMAS

Back of loose page, November 1812

Christopher B. SHEPARD)
for the use of Philip COOK)
vs.) Debt
Micajah H. POWEL)
& William JELKS) The defendants Micajah H. POWEL & William JELKS with Turner EVERETT their security comes forward and stays execution in terms of the law. 5th of November 1814.

Micajah H. POWELL {LS}
William JELKS {LS}
Turner EVERETT {LS}

Attest
Richd. H. THOMAS Clk.

Allen TOOKE)
vs.) Debt
James RAMSEY) The defendant James RAMSEY with Elijah WALLACE his security comes forward & stays execution in terms of the law.

James RAMSEY {LS}
Elijah WALLACE {LS}

Attest
Richd. H. THOMAS

William MERITT &)
Richard ASBURY) Debt
vs.)
Elijah WALLACE) The defendants Elijah WALLACE & William JELKS with James RAMSEY their security comes forward & stays execution in terms of the law.

Elijah WALLACE {LS}
William JELKS {LS}
James R[AMSEY {LS}]

Attest
Richd. H. THOMAS Clk.

[*End*]

SUPERIOR COURT
MINUTES, BOOK 2
1813-1816

In the original the pages are not numbered and the 17th through 28th pages are out of order. The misplaced pages are presented here in correct order; their placement in the original is indicated by the number in parentheses.

April 20th 1813. The Superior Court for the County of Pulaski met agreeably to law. Present his Honor – Judge EARLY.

The Solicitor General of this circuit failing to attend at the present term, It is ordered that Moses FORT Esqr. be & he is hereby is appointed Solicitor General pro tempore, with power to do & perform all & singular the duties appertaining to that office.

The following persons appeared & were sworn on the grand jury at the present term:

1 James M. TAYLOR forn.
2 Archibald LASSETTER
3 Christopher RHODE
4 William H. GROSS
5 Lewis HOLLAND
6 Isaac BURKHALTER
7 Micajah H. POWELL
8 Joab HORN
9 William DESHAZO
10 Daniel REGAN
11 Benjamin BROWN
12 William JELKS
13 Archibald H. ODOM
14 Jacob SNELL
15 William YARBROUGH
16 William ISLER
17 William HAINEY
18 James BRACEWELL
19 Daniel COLE
20 John GILSTRAP
21 Reuben WARREN

The following persons appeared & were sworn as Petitt Jurors:

Page 2

Petitt Jury No. 1

1 Adam BILLINGS
2 Solomon LAM
3 Thomas TOMBLY
4 George KELLEY
5 Umfrey POSEY
6 Edmund HESTER
7 William W. SMITH
8 Maliki KELLEY
9 John LEE
10 John DEES
11 William LITTLE
12 Thomas CUNIGIN

Petitt Jury No. 2

1 James DYKES
2 William HAMBLETON
3 Ezekiah PHILLIPS
4 William HILLIARD
5 William LESTER
6 Nimrod SMITH
7 Henry MILLS
8 Daniel DYKES
9 Moses SUTTON
10 ~~Noah CALHOUN~~
Dennis ADAMS
11 John COLEMAN
12 Christopher McRAE

Noah CALHOUN having been summoned & sworn as a Pettit Juryman at this term & having afterwards absented himself without leave, it is ordered that he pay a fine of five dollars.

Page 3

Josiah STEWART) Case
vs. Indorsee)
Conrad AUGLY) Dismissed by the plaintiff.

James L. PERRY)
vs.) Trespass vi et armis
W$^{m.}$ T. RENEAU) Settled at defendants cost.

~~Blakley EDINS)~~
~~vs.) Slander Jury No. 2~~
~~James BEATEY)~~

Thomas SHEPHERD appeard & was sworn on the Pettit Jury N°. 1 in place of John LEE. Dennis ADAMS appeared & was sworn on the Pettit Jury N°. 2 in place of Noah CALHOUN.

Lodowick LARD)
vs.) Spc. action
Allen TOOKE) It being stated that \W^{m}./ WILLIAMS Esqr. late a magistrate of Tattnal County now resides in this County & that he still holds the books lately kept by him as magistrate & that the same books are material in this case; On motion of plffs. atto. it is ordered that the clerk issue subpoena duces tecum directed to the said William WILLIAMS.

The Grand Jury came into Court and returned the following bills:

The State)
vs.) Indictment Misdemeanor
Samuel REGAN, Martha REGAN) True Bill against Martha REGAN.
David APLIN & Catherine APLIN) Ja^{s}. M. TAYLOR fore^{n}.

Page 4

The State)
vs.) Indc^{t}. assault
Samuel REGAN, Martha REGAN) True Bill vs. Martha REGAN.
David APLIN & Catherine APLIN) Ja^{s}. M. TAYLOR fore^{n}.

The State)
vs.) Indc^{t}. assault
Polly LAWSON) True Bill. Ja^{s}. M. TAYLOR fore^{n}.

The State)
vs.) Ind^{t}. assault
Elizabeth ROBERTSON) True Bill Ja^{s}. M. TAYLOR fore^{n}.

John DOE ex. dem.)
John FIELDER) Jury N°. 1
vs.) Trespass in ejectment
Richard ROE)
John LEE tenant) We find for the plaintiff the premises in dispute with cost of suit.
Thomas SHEPHERD for^{n}.

John DOE ex. dem.)
John FIELDER)
vs.) Trespass in ejectment
John ~~DOE~~ ROE)
John LEE tenant) In this case the defendant being dissatisfied with the verdict of the jury comes into Court pays all cost & prays an appeal and Abraham YEARTA enters himself security in terms of the law.

Attest Rich[d]. H. THOMAS Clk.

his
John x LEE {LS}
mark
Abraham YERTA {LS}

The State)
vs.)
Benjamin HARVEY) Benjamin HARVEY acknowledges himself bound to his Excellency the Governor in the sum of one thousand dollars and William DESHAZO and Thomas HARVEY acknowledge themselves bound in the sum of five hundred dollars each conditioned to be void if the said Benjamin HARVEY do appear in \the Superior/ Court by nine oclock tomorrow morning in this County & not to depart thence without leave of said Court otherwise to remain in full force & virtue.

Rich[d]. H. THOMAS Clk.

Benja. HARVEY {LS}
W[m]. DESHAZO {LS}
Thomas HARVY {LS}

Page 6

The State)
vs.)
William HORN) William HORN acknowledges himself bound to his Excellency the Governor in the sum of one thousand dollars and Thomas PHILIPS and Thomas BUTLER acknowedge themselves bound in the sum of five hundred dollars each conditioned to be void if the said William HORN do appear in the Superior Court by nine oclock tomorrow morning in this County and not to depart thence without leave of said Court, otherwise to remain in force & virtue.

Attest
Rich[d]. H. THOMAS Clk.

W[m]. HORNE {LS}
Tom PHILIPS {LS}
Tho[s]. BUTLER {LS}

Blakley EDINS) Jury N[o]. 2
vs.) Case for words
James BEATY) We the jurors find for the plaintiff seventy five dollars with cost of suit.

Christopher M[c]RAE for[n].

Ex[d]. Peter EARLY

And the Court then adjourned untill tomorrow morning nine oclock.

Page 7

Tuesday 27th day of April 1813. The Court then met agreeably to adjournment.

Ordered that the fine yesterday imposed on Noah CALHOUN a defaulting juror be remitted. Marmaduke KENT appeared in court and was sworn on the Pettit Jury N[o]. 1 in place of Thomas CUNIGIN discharged.

Farish CARTER for the use)
of Richardson O. SEURRY) Case
vs.)
James M. TAYLOR) I confess judgement to plaintiff for eight hundred & seventy dollars with interest & cost. 27th April 1813.
Ja^{s}. M. TAYLOR

Commissioners of the Town of Hartford)
for the use of Philip COOK) Debt
vs.)
Richard W. ELLIS & Thomas A. HILL) I confess judgement to plaintiffs for the use aforesaid for forty four dollars with interest & cost. 27th April 1813.
Thomas A. HILL

Patrick M^{c}GRIFF)
vs.) Debt
James W. SHINE) I confess judgement to the plaintiff for forty one dollars 81 1/4 cents with interest from the time it became due & cost of suit reserving the right of appeal on the usual terms. Thos. FITCH defts. atto.

Page 8

Allen TOOKE & Company)
vs.) Debt
James W. SHINE) I confess judgement to the plaintiff for the sum of thirty three dollars & forty cents with interest & cost reserving the right of appeal on the usual terms. T. FITCH defts. atto.

Robert MATHEWS) Case
vs. Indorsee) Jury N°. 2
John MOSES Indorser) We find for the plaintiff fifty three dollars with interest & cost. Christopher M^{c}RAE for^{n}.

Farish CARTER) Debt
vs.) Jury N°. 1
Barna HART) We find for the plaintiff thirty six dollars with interest & cost.
Thomas SHEPHERD for^{n}.

Lester CRAWFORD)
vs. Indorsee) Case
Benjamin POSEY) I confess judgement to the plaintiff for the sum of fifty nine dollars & twenty five cents with interest & cost.
his
Benjamin P Posey
mark

Page 9

Thompson BIRD for the)
use of Benjn. MEWBORN) Debt
vs.)
William RAY) We find for the plaintiff forty two dollars & seventy five cents with interest & cost. Christopher M^{c}RAE for^{n}.

Jno. BUTLER for the use)
of Leed HARRIS & Co.) Debt
vs.)
Arch^{d}. H. ODOM) I confess judgement to the plaintiff for one hundred & twenty five dollars interest & cost. A. H. ODOM

Leed HARRIS & Co.)
vs.) Debt
Arch^{d}. H. ODOM) I confess judgement to the plaintiff for fifty eight dollars & seventy five cents interest & cost. A. H. ODOM

Com^{rs}. &c for the use)
of Benjn. MEWBORN)
vs.) Debt
Rich^{d}. W. ELLIS &)
Thomas A. HILL) I confess judgement to the plaintiff for sixty five dollars & seventy two cents with interest & cost. Thomas A. HILL

Page 10

Lodowick LAIRD)
vs.) Mal practice
Allen TOOKE) John SNELLING being in possession of an original deed made by the defendant as Sheriff of Pulaski County to a lot of land sold as the property of the plaintiff which is material which is material for the defendants defence in the above case on motion of Robert RUTHERFORD atto. pro deft. It is ordered that a subpoena duces tecum issue to the said SNELLING commanding him to appear at the next Superior Court for said County & then & there procure the said deed to be used by said defendant in said case.

S. JONES)
vs.) Case
R. HODGES) I confess judgement to the plaintiff for the sum of thirty five dollars with interest & cost 27th April 1813. Robert HODGES

Blakley EDINS)
vs.) Mal pros
Aaron SCARBOROUGH) Henry FULGHAM Esquire being in possession of the original affidavit & warrant against the plff. and which ~~is material for the prosecution of~~ \is the ground of the above action and/ which is material for the prosecution of the plffs. demand on motion of Thomas W. HARRIS atto. pro plff. It is ordered that a subpoena duces tecum issue to the said Henry FULGHAM Esquire commanding him to appear at the next Superior Court for said County & then & there produce the said affidavit & warrant to be used by said plff in said case.

Page 11

The Grand Jury came in the Court and returned the following bills:

The State)
vs.) Ind^{t}. Misdemeanor
Saml. REGAN) True Bill Ja^{s}. M. TAYLOR for^{n}.

The State)
vs.) Ind^{t}. Assault
James DEES) No Bill Ja^{s}. M. TAYLOR for^{n}.

The State)
vs.) Ind^{t}. Assault
Joseph WOOD) True Bill Ja^{s}. M. TAYLOR for^{n}.

The State)
vs.) Ind^{t}. Assault
David APLING) True Bill Arch^{d}. LASSETER for^{n}. pro tem

The State)
vs.) Ind^{t}. Perjury
Elizabeth B. ROBERSON) True Bill Ja^{s}. M. TAYLOR for^{n}.

The State)
vs.) Ind^{t}. Stabbing
William HORN) True Bill Ja^{s}. M. TAYLOR for^{n}.

Benjamin HARVEY having been recognized to appear in Court at nine oclock this morning & sufficient cause having been shewn, Ordered that he be discharged forthwith from said recognizance.

Page 12

The State)
vs.) Ind^{t}. Assault
David APLING) David APLING acknowledges himself bound to his Excellency the Governor in the sum of two hundred dollars and Elijah WALLACE & Isaac GOOLSBY acknowledge themselves bound in the sum of one hundred dollars each conditioned to be void if the said David APLING do appear at the next Superior Court in this County and not depart thence without leave of said Court otherwise to remain in full force & virtue. David APPLING {LS}
Rich^{d}. H. THOMAS Clk. Elijah WALLACE {LS}
Isaac GOOLSBY {LS}

Micajah H. POWELL) Case
vs.) Jury N°. 1
William JELKS) We find for the plaintiff sixty dollars with cost of suit.
Thomas SHEPHERD for^{n}.

Ex^{d}. Peter EARLY
The Court then adjourned till tomorrow morning nine oclock.

Wednesday 28th April 1813. The Court then met agreeably to adjournment. ~~Wednesday 28th April 1813.~~

The following persons were drawn to serve as Grand Jurors at the next term-

1 Colson ADAMS
2 Drury MAYO
3 Archd. ODOM
4 James TOMBERLIN
5 Charles CARDIN
6 Robert THOMPSON
7 Bartlett McDANIEL
8 Benjamin SMITH
9 Zion DAVIS
10 John SNELLING
11 Daniel SNELL
12 Charles MAYO
13 Sutton TRUELUCK
14 John WILCOX
15 John GRINSTEAD
16 Shadrach ATKINSON
17 James CLARK
18 Jefrey MORNFORD
19 Sands STANDLY
20 Thomas JOHNSON
21 Robert DANIEL
22 Thomas McDANIEL
23 John SWEARINGEN
24 Orandatus WATSON
25 David GARTMAN
26 Hardy VICKERS
27 John GRACE
28 Elijah WALLACE
29 Michael HORN
30 Thomas A. HILL

Page 14

The following persons were drawn to serve as Pettit Jurors at the next term-

1 Samuel SMITH
2 Samuel MILLER
3 Joseph REGAN
4 Edward BOTT?
5 James W. SHINE
6 Etheldred HARREL
7 Alexander SMITH
8 Jacob TAYLOR
9 William McCORMICK
10 William CARDIN
11 Barna HART
12 John TEMPLES
13 Henry COOPER
14 James RAINEY
15 Biggars SINGLETON
16 Thomas HOWELL
17 Martin HORN
18 James TEMPLES
19 Levi HARRELL
20 William BOLLING
21 Moses KIRKLAND
22 Henry BEATY
23 Isaac BLOUNT
24 James BARROW
25 Isham CARR
26 John HAGAN
27 Thomas WESLEY
28 Nathan MADDOX
29 William MOORE
30 Joshua HARRIS
31 Thomas ROGERS
32 James MILLER
33 Lewis THOMAS
34 John KELLEY
35 Asa HARRELL
36 John BARROW
37 William SMITH
38 John BENNET
39 Stephen HAGAN
40 Benjmain WEEKS
41 Jordan LEOPARD
42 John HARREL
43 Moses HARREL
44 John BRYAN
45 Josiah TAYLOR
46 Jeremiah GILSTRAP
47 Charles CREECH
48 Joel WALKER
49 Washington LANCASTER
50 Abraham YEARTA

CROWELL & BUTLER)
vs.) Fi fa
John J. FORD) In this case it being stated & made appear to the Court that lot N^{o}. three hundred & four in the twenty first district of Wilkinson now Pulaski county was sold under the above fi fa by the Shff. of said County in the first Tuesday in September eighteen hundred & twelve & was purchased by Henry TATE & the Shff. having refused to put said TATE in possession On motion It is ordered that the Shff. of Pulaski County do proceed to put in possession of said land Henry TATE or any person by him legally authorised.

The State)
vs.) Ind^{t}. Stabbing
William HORN) William HORN acknowledges himself bound to his Excellency the Governor in the sum of one thousand dollars and Thomas BUTLER acknowledges himself bound in the sum of one thousand dollars conditioned to be void if the said William HORN do appear at the next Superior Court to be held in & for the County of Pulaski and not to depart thence without leave of said Court otherwise to remain in full force & virtue. W^{m}. HORNE {LS}
Rich^{d}. H. THOMAS Clk. Thos. BUTLER {LS}

Page 16

The State)
vs.) Ind^{t}. Misdemeanor
Samuel REGAN) Jury N°. 2

		Witnesses Sworn
1 James DYKES	7 Henry MILLS	) Elizabeth ROBERSON
2 William HAMBLETON	8 Daniel DYKES	) Polly LAWSON
3 Ezekiah PHILLIPS	9 Mosses SUTTON	) James LAWSON
4 William HILLIARD	10 Noah CALHOUN	) David BROOM
5 William LESTER	11 John COLEMAN	) John A. WILLIAMS
6 Nimrod SMITH	12 Christopher M^{c}RAE	) Benjamin MEWBORN
		) Joel DAWSON
		) Noah WHEELER

We the jurors find the traversors not guilty. Christopher M^{c}RAE for^{n}.

The ~~State~~ Grand \Jury/ returned the following bill into Court:

The State)
vs.) Ind^{t}. Perjury
Samuel FOWL) No Bill. Ja^{s}. M. TAYLOR fm.

The State)
vs.) Ind^{t}. Misdemeanor
Samuel REGAN,)
Martha RIGGEN)
David APLIN &)
Catharine APLIN) Jury N°. 1

[*Pages 17-28 are out of order. See note on page 85*]

1 Adam BILLINGS	7 William W. SMITH	) Witnesses Sworn
2 Solomon LAMB	8 Maliki KELLEY	) Jas. M. TAYLOR
3 Thomas TOMBLY	9 Thomas SHEPHERD	) Elizabeth B. ROBERSON
4 George KELLEY	10 John DEES	) Polley LAWSON
5 Dennis ADAMS	11 William LITTLE	) Rebeckah ROBERSON
6 Edmund HESTER	12 Marmaduke KENT	) Sally RAY
		) Eliza ROSIER
		) Micajah H. POWELL
		) Benjamin MEWBORN
		) Joel DAWSON

We find the traverser not guilty.
Thomas SHEPHERD forn.

Georgia)
Pulaski County) We the Grand Jury for the body of the County aforesaid at April term eighteen hundred & thirteen present on our oaths as a grievance - that on examining the minutes of the Inferior Court we find that commissioners are generally appointed on the roads agreeable to law throughout said County. We also find through the neglect of the Clerk of said Court not notifying the commissioners agreeable to law the necessary repairs have been neglected.

We also present William BRACKEN for having obstructed the passage of the road near Gum Swamp leading from Hartford to Batys Ferry on the Oconee River April 11th 1813. William YARBROUGH, James FRIERSON, James M. TAYLOR, Witness.

We also present Robert THOMPSON for obstructing the passage of said road about five miles from Hartford on the 15th day of April 1813. Witness...

Page 18 (22)

Elijah WALLACE & John MILLER. We also present Asa PIPKIN for obstructing the passage of said road near the County line near his plantation on the 12th day of April 1813. William YARBROUGH, William ISLER & James M. TAYLOR. We also present Charles STEWART for retailing spirituous liquors without a licence on the 6th day of April 1813. Witness Archibald H. ODOM, William YARBROUGH, William JELKS. We also present Ebbenezer ELLIS for retailing spirituous liquors without a licence on the 11th of April 1813. Witness James FRIERSON, James M. TAYLOR. We also present Isome CARR for misdemeanor on the day of Devine Service in the Town of Hartford on the seventh day of March 1813 Witness Joseph WOOD, John SNELLING.

We highly apresiate his Honor Judge EARLY and thank him for his due attendance at this term.

James M. TAYLOR foreman	John GILSTRAP
Archibald LASSETER	Benjamin BROWN
Christopher RHODE	William JELKS
William H. GROSS	Archibald H. ODOM
Lewis HOLLAND	Jacob SNELL
Isaac BUCKHALTER	William YARBROUGH
Joab HORN	William ISLER
William DESHAZO	William HANEY

Daniel RIGGIN
James BRACEWELL
Daniel COLE
Reubin WARREN
Micajah H. POWELL

Page 19 (17)

The State)
vs.) Ind^{t}. Assault
Joseph WOOD) Joseph WOOD aknowledges himself bound to his Excellency the Governor in the sum of one hundred dollars and *[blank]* acknowledges himself bound likewise in the sum of one hundred dollars, conditioned to be void if the said Joseph WOOD do appear at the next Superior Court in this County and not to depart thence without leave of said Court otherwise to remain in full force & virtue.

Joseph WOOD {LS}
Rich^{d}. H. THOMAS Clk. {LS}

The State)
vs.) Ind^{t}. Assault
Polley LAWSON) Polly LAWSON aknowledges herself bound to his Excellency the Governor in the sum of one hundred dollars and Elizabeth B. ROBERTSON & Shadrack ROZAR acknowledges themselves bound likewise in the sum of fifty dollars each conditioned to be void if the said Polley LAWSON do appear at the next Superior Court in this County and not to depart thence without leave of said Court otherwise to remain in full force & virtue.

Polly LAWSON {LS}
Rich^{d}. H. THOMAS Clk. Elizabeth B. ROBESON {LS}
Shadrack ROZAR {LS}

Page 20 (18)

The State)
vs.) Ind^{t}. Assault
Martha RIGGEN) Indictment & conviction for an assault - Ordered that the defendant pay a fine of twenty dollars & be discharged on payment of costs.

The State)
vs.) Ind^{t}. Perjury
Elizabeth B. ROBERTSON) Elizabeth B. ROBERTSON aknowledges herself bound to his Excellency the Governor in the sum of one thousand dollars and Shadrach ROSIER & James LAWSON acknowledge themselves bound likewise in the sum five hundred dollars each conditioned to be void if the said Elizabeth B. ROBERTSON do appear at the next Superior Court in this County, and not to depart thence without leave of said Court otherwise to remain in full force & virtue.

Elizabeth B. ROBESON {LS}
Rich^{d}. H. THOMAS Clk. Shadrack ROZAR {LS}
James LAWSON {LS}

Micajah H. POWELL)
vs.) Case
William JELKS) In this case the defendant being dissatisfied with the verdict of the Jury comes into Court pays all cost & prays an appeal and James S. IVEY enters himself security in terms of the law. W. JELKS
R. H. THOMAS Clk. James S. IVEY
Exd. Peter EARLY
The Court then adjourned till Court in courçe. Richd. H. THOMAS Clk.

Page 22 (20)

Blakly EDDINS)
vs.) Case for words
James BEATY) In this case the defendant being dissattisfied with the verdict of the Jury comes into Court pays all cost and prays an appeal and Henry BEATY enters himself security in terms of the law. James BEATY
his
Richard H. THOMAS Clk. Henry x BEATY
mark

September 1813

I Archibald LASITER do solemly sw<u>are</u> that I will faithfully execute all writs, warrents, precepts, and processes directed to me as Sheriff of the County of Pulaski, and true returns make and in all things well and truly and without malice or partiality perform the duties of the office of Sheriff of Pulaski County, during my continuance in office and take only my lawful fees, so help me God sworn to before us this 18th September 1813.
James T. THOMAS J.I.C. Archd. LASSETER
Stephen GATLIN J.I.C. Richd. H. THOMAS Clk.

Page 23 (25)

I do solemly swear that I will execute all writs, warrants, precepts & processes directed to me as Sheriff of the County of Pulaski and true returns make and in all things well and truly, and without mal<u>a</u>ce or partiality perform the duties of the office of Sheriff of said County during my continuance in office, and take only my lawful fees so help me God.
Josiah EVERETT J.I.C.) Elijah WALLACE
James BRACEWELL J.I.C.)
N. STEVENS J.I.C.) Turner EVERETT Clk.

I Elijah WALLACE do solemnly swear that I will bear true faith and allegiance to the state of Georgia and to the utmost of my power and ability observe, conform to, support & defend the Constitution thereof, without \any/ reservation or equivocation whatsoever and the Constitution of the United States So help me God.
Josiah EVERETT J.I.C.)
N. STEVENS J.I.C.) E. WALLACE
James BRACEWELL J.I.C.)

April 25th 1814. The honorable the Superior Court for the County of Pulaski met agreeably to law. Present his Honor Judge HARRIS.

The following persons appeared & were sworn on the Grand Jury at the present term:

1 Murdoch M^{c}LEOD foreman
2 James TOMLINSON
3 Charles CARDIN
4 Robert THOMPSON
5 Zion DAVIS
6 Sutton TRULUCK
7 Shadrach ATKINSON
8 James CLARK
9 Thomas JOHNSON
10 Thomas M^{c}DANIEL
11 Robert DANIEL
12 John WILCOX
13 Charles MAYO
14 John SWEARINGEN
15 Orandatus WATSON
16 David GARTMAN
17 Michael HORN
18 Jefrey MONTFORD
19 John GRINSTEAD
20 Drury MAY
21 Archibald ODOM
22 Hardy VICKERS
23 Daniel SNELL

The following persons appeared and were sworn on the Petit Jury N°. 1

1 Joseph REGAN
2 James W. SHINE
3 Alex^{r}. SMITH
4 Thos. ROGERS
5 Barna HART
6 John TEMPLES
7 Henry COOPER
8 Biggars SINGLETON
9 Thomas HARREL
10 Levi HARREL
11 Isam CARR
12 Thomas WESLEY

Page 25 (27)

And on the Jury N°. 2

1 James MILLER
2 Lewis THOMAS
3 Asa HARRELL
4 John BARNETT [*Bennett?*]
5 Stephen HAGAN
6 John HARRELL
7 John BRYAN
8 Washington LANCASTER
9 Abram YEARTY
10 Haywood JONES
11 ~~John BIRD~~ Daniel DYKES
12 David APLIN

The Grand Jury came into Court and returned the following bills-

The State)
vs.) Ind^{t}. assault
Aaron SCARBOROUGH) True Bill Murdoch M^{c}LEOD for^{n}.

The State)
vs.)
John A. WILLIAMS, James CLARK)
Benjn. MEWBORN, W^{m}. SMITH) Ind^{t}. assault & battery
W^{m}. GOODSON, Benjamin BROWN Senr.)
William YARBROUGH Jn^{r}.) True Bill
James GOODSON & Robert DEWETT) Murdoch M^{c}LEOD for^{n}.

J. W. WILLIAMS)
vs.) Indebitatus assumpset
Noah WHEELER) I confess judgement to the plaintiff for the sum of eighteen dollars and one cent with cost of suit. Moses FORT defts. atty.

Benjamin CHAIRES)
vs.) Case
Hardy VICKERS) I confess judgement to plaintiff for six hundred & twenty dollars and eighty six cents with interest & cost.
James S. FRIERSON attory. for defendant

John DOE ex dem.)
Richard STEWART) Petit Jury No. 1
vs.)
Richard ROE) Trespass in ejectment
Leonard STRINGER)
Joseph STRINGER)
& William WYNN)
tenants in possession) We find for the plaintiff the premises in dispute.
Alexr. SMITH forman

Page 27 (23)

~~The State)~~
~~vs.) Indt. Assault & battery~~
~~John A. WILLIAMS) John A. WILLIAMS acknowledges himself bound to his Excellency the Governor in the sum of one thousand dollars, and William GOODSON & James GOODSON William SMITH acknowledge themselves bound likewise in the sum of five hundred dollars each conditioned to be void on his appearing at this Court from day to day untill discharged, otherwise to remain in in full force & virtue this 25th April 1814.~~
~~Attest~~
~~Turner EVERETT Clk.~~
~~Jno. A. WILLIAMS {LS}~~
~~his~~
~~William w GOODMAN {LS}~~
~~mark~~
~~Wm. SMITH {LS}~~

The State)
vs.) Indt. assault & battery
Elizabeth PIPKIN) No Bill Murdock McLEOD forn.

The State)
vs.)
John A. WILLIAMS, James CLARK) Indt. Stabing
Benjamin MEWBORN, William SMITH)
William GOODSON, Benjamin BROWN)
William YARBROUGH, James) True Bill
GOODSON & Robert DEWETT) Murdoch McLEOD forn.

Solomon A. HOPKINS) Debt
vs.) Petitt Jury N°. 2
Thomas HATTON) We find for the plaintiff forty two dollars sixty eight
& three forth cents with interest & cost. Washington LANCASTER for^{n}.

Solomon A. HOPKINS) Debt
vs.) Petitt Jury N°. 2
John M. VASS) We find for the plaintiff ninety nine dollars thirty four
& one fourth cents with interest & cost. Washington LANCASTER for^{n}.

Solomon A. HOPKINS) Debt
vs.) Petitt Jury N°. 2
Clement LANIER) We find for the plaintiff thirty seven dollars sixty two
& one half cents with interest & cost. Washington LANCASTER for^{n}.

Solomon A. HOPKINS) Debt
vs.) Petitt Jury N°. 2
Arch^{d}. LASSITER) We find for the plaintiff forty seven dollars thirty one
& one fourth cents with interest & cost. Washington LANCASTER for^{n}.

Page 29

Solomon A. HOPKINS) Debt
vs.) Petit Jury N°. 2.
William WARD) We find for the plaintiff thirty dollars fifty six & one
fourth cents with interest & cost. Washington LANCASTER for^{n}.

Solomon A. HOPKINS) Debt
vs.) Petit Jury N°. 2.
Abram HOLLIDAY) We find for plaintiff forty eight dollars & fifty cents
with interest & cost. Washington LANCASTER for^{n}.

Nimrod HENDRICK)
vs.) Case
Ephraim PHILIPS) Petitt Jury N°. 1.
Sharod PHILIPS)
Gabriel PHILIPS) We the jury find for the plaintiff the sum of four
hundred & forty nine dollars & thirteen cents with interest & cost.
Alex^{r}. SMITH forman

Solomon A. HOPKINS) Debt
vs.) Petitt Jury N°. 2.
Jonathan VICKERS) We find for the plaintiff the sum of two hundred &
four dollars eighty nine & three forth cents with interest & cost.
Washington LANCASTER for^{n}.

The State)
vs.) Ind^{t}. assault & battery
John A. WILLIAMS) John A. WILLIAMS acknowledges himself bound to his Excellency the Governor in the sum of one thousand dollars and Spire MILLS & John M^{c}CRAE acknowledge themselves bound \likewise/ in the sum of five hundred dollars each, conditioned to be void on his appearing at this Court from day to day untill discharged otherwise to remain in full force & virtue this 25th April 1814.

John A. WILLIAMS {LS}
Turner EVERITT Clk. John M^{c}CRAE {LS}
his
Spire x MILLS {LS}
mark

The Grand Jury came into court and returned the following bills-

The State)
vs.) Assault with intent to kill
John M^{c}REA) No Bill Murdoch M^{c}LEOD for^{n}.

The State)
vs.) Fornication
Joseph COOPER)
& Polly YOUNG) No Bill Murdoch M^{c}LEOD for^{n}.

Page 31

The State)
vs.) Sta<u>b</u>ing
Mary ROBINSON)
Patsey DORMAN) True bill vs. Mary ROBINSON, Patsey DORMAN,
Elizabeth SCOTT) Elizabeth SCOTT; No Bill against Sally RAY.
Sally RAY) Murdoch M^{c}LEOD for^{n}.

The State)
vs.) Ind^{t}. assault & battery
William GOODSON) William GOODSON acknowledges himself bound to his Excellency the Governor in the sum of one thousand dollars and Hardy VICKERS & Robert DANIEL acknowledge themselves bound \likewise/ in the sum five hundred dollars each, conditioned to be void on his appearing at this Court from day to day untill discharged otherwise to remain in full force & virtue this 25 April 1814.

his
Turner EVERITT Clk. William x GOODSON {LS}
mark
Hardy VICKERS {LS}
Robirt DANIEL {LS}

The State)
vs.) Assault & battery
William SMITH) William SMITH acknowledges himself bound to his Excellency the Governor in the sum of one thousand dollars and William LYON & Samuel JONES acknowledge themselves bound likewise in the sum of five hundred dollars each, (conditioned)...

conditioned to be void on his appearing at this Court from day to day untill discharged otherwise to remain in full force & virtue this 25th April 1814.

Wm. SMITH {LS}
Turner EVERITT Clk. William LYON {LS}
Sam. JONES {LS}

The State)
vs.) Indt. assault & battery
James GOODSON) James GOODSON acknowledges himself bound to his Excellency the Governor in the sum of one thousand dollars and Robert DANIEL & William LYON acknowledge themselves bound likewise in the sum of five hundred dollars each, conditioned to be void on his appearing at this Court from day to day untill discharged otherwise to remain in full force & virtue this 25th April 1814.

his
James x GOODSON {LS}
mark
Turner EVERITT Clk. Robirt DANIEL {LS}
William LYON {LS}

The State)
vs.) Indt. assault & battery
Robert DEWETT) Robert DEWETT acknowledges himself bound to his Excellency the Governor in the sum of one thousand dollars and Moses SUTTON & William YARBOROUGH acknowledge themselves bound likewise in the sum of five hundred dollars each conditioned to be void on his appearing at this Court from day to day untill discharged...

Page 33

otherwise to remain in full force & virtue this 25th April 1814.

Robert DEWET {LS}
Turner EVERITT Clk. William YARBROUGH {LS}
Moses SUTTON {LS}

The State)
vs.) Indt. assault & battery
Benjamin MEWBORN) Benjamin MEWBORN acknowledges himself bound to his Excellency the Governor in the sum of one thousand dollars and Shadrach ATKINSON & Saml. REGAN acknowledge themselves bound likewise in the sum of five hundred dollars each conditioned to be void on his appearing at this Court from day to day until discharged otherwise to remain in full force power & virtue this 25th April 1814.

Benja. MEWBORN {Seal}
Turner EVERITT Clk. Shadrach ATLINSON {Seal}
Samuel REGAN {Seal}

The State)
vs.) Indict. assault & baty.
William YARBOROUGH) William YARBOROUGH acknowledges himself bound to his Excellency the Governor in the sum of one thousand dollars and Archibald LASSITER & ALLEN SCARBOROUGH...

acknowledge themselves likewise bound in the sum of five hundred dollars each, conditioned to be void on his appearing at this Court from day to day during the present term or until discharged otherwise to be & remain in full force & virtue.

24 April 1814. William YARBROUGH {Seal}
Turner EVERITT Clk. Allen SCARBOROUGH {Seal}
Arch^d^. LASSETER {Seal}

The State)
vs.) Indic^t^. assault & battery
James CLARK) James CLARK acknowledges himself bound to his Excellency the Governor in the sum of one thousand dollars and James M. TAYLOR & Allen TOOKE in the same manner in the sum of five hundred dollars each conditioned to be void if the said James CLARK do appear at this Court from day to day during this term of this Court...

Page 35

and do not depart without leave of said Court else to remain in full force April 25th 1814.

Ja^s^. CLARK {Seal}
Turner EVERITT Clk. Ja^s^. M. TAYLOR {Seal}
Allen TOOKE {Seal}

The State)
vs.) Ind^t^. assault & baty.
Benjn. BROWN) Benjamin BROWN acknowledges himself bound to his Excellency the Governor in the sum of one thousand dollars and [*blank*] in like manner in the sum of five hundred dollars each conditioned to be void if the said Benjamin do appear from day to day during the present term of this Court and shall not depart without leave else to remain in full force power and...

ENTERED THROUGH MISTAKE

Page 36

virtue April 25th 1814. {Seal}
{Seal}
{Seal}

Ex^d^. S. W. HARRIS

The Court then adjourned untill tomorrow morning eight oclock.

Tuesday 26th April. The Court then met agreeably to adjournment. The following persons were drawn to serve as Grand Jurors at the next term of this Court:

1 Hincy WARREN
2 Clement LANEAR
3 William JOHNSTON
4 Abraham VICKERS
5 David SNELL
6 Archibald THOMPSON
7 Lester CRAWFORD
8 William BERNAM
9 George G. GAINS
10 William MAYO
11 Allen TOOK
12 Henry FULGUM
13 Robert DEWIT
14 John ROZIER

15 Samuel JONES
16 Edward BRYAN
17 John CRAWFORD
18 James DEES
19 Neil McALPIN
20 Jesse POWELL
21 Philip JONES
22 Joel DAWSON
23 William LYON
24 John RAINEY
25 John MOSES
26 George WALKER
27 James L. PERRY
28 Gideon MAYO
29 Drury DEES
30 Dickson JELKS

The following persons were drawn to serve as petit jurors at the next term:

1 Ephraim PHILIPS
2 Needham BRYAN
3 Robt. DESHAZO
4 Wm. YARBORO Jr.
5 Jesse LIVELY
6 Theo. SUTTON
7 Tho. HESTER
8 Fort ALFORD
9 Tho. ADAMS
10 Richd. TAYLOR
11 Jas. BASSON?
12 Levi BROWN
13 Sol. BREWER
14 Aaron SCARBORO
15 Nathan SOWELL
16 Richd. WYNNE
17 Mark WHEELER
18 Jas. ODAM
19 Jno. BRADSHAW
20 Moses GIDINS
21 Henry EVANS
22 Shad. LEE
23 Joshua LEE
24 Jno. CARDIN
25 Stephen PIPKIN
26 Jno. YON
27 Elijah HANKS
28 Moses KIRKLAND
29 ~~Tho~~ Edwd. GIDINS
30 Pat. McGRIFF
31 Wm. SMITH
32 Tho. ROGERS

Page 38

33 Jesse HARREL
34 Saml. STEWART
35 Ben. POSEY
36 Henry HAGAN
37 Fred. SWEARING
38 Sherod PHILIPS
39 Wm. KELLY
40 Jesse LEE
41 Jno. BIRD
42 Danl. SPARROW
43 Robert MUNFORD
44 Jno. PARIS
45 Fred. WOLF
46 Jno. A. WILLIAMS
47 Larey JOINER
48 Jacob JOINER
49 Tho. FRANKLIN
50 Saml. HUDSON
51 Jesse PENNINGTON
52 Jno. SMEDLEY

On motion of counsel for the State, Ordered that Allen TOOKE late Sheriff of Pulaski County return into Court all the executions in favor of the State of Georgia tax collectors placed in his hands with his actings and doings thereon instanter or shew cause to the contrary.

~~It appearing to the Court that a levy & sale was made by Allen TOOKE late Sheriff of Pulaski County of one half of a tract of land known in the general plan by lot number 269 in the 21st District of Wilkinson now Pulaski County as the~~

~~property of Benjamin MEWBORN to satisfy Noah WHEELER's execution, and that John COLE decd. became the purchaser at said sale for the sum of seventy seven dollars which sum has been paid to said TOOKE who has failed to make titles to the same - on motion of counsel ordered that the present Sheriff.~~

Page 39

The State)
vs.) Assault & battery
Aaron SCARBOROUGH) Aaron SCARBOROUGH acknowledges himself bound to his Excellency the Governor in the sum of two hundred dollars and Joseph BARRON acknowledges himself bound likewise in the sum of two hundred dollars conditioned to be void if the said Aaron SCARBOROUGH do appear at the next Superior Court of Pulaski and not depart thence without leave of said Court otherwise to remain in full force & virtue 26th April 1813 [*1814?*].

Aaron SCARBROUGH {Seal}
Turner EVERETT Joseph BA[RRON] {Seal}

The Grand Jury came into Court & returned the following bills:

The State)
vs.) Indt. Misdemeanor
John STEWART) True bill Murdoch McLEOD forn.

The State)
vs.) Assault & battery
Nancy STEWART)
Nancy WOOD) True bill vs. Nancy STEWART & Nancy WOOD
Elizabeth STEWART) No bill vs. Elizabeth STEWART.
Murdoch McLEOD forn.

Page 40

~~The State)~~
~~vs.) Misdemeanor~~
~~John STEWART) John STEWART acknowledges himself bound to his Excellency the Governor in the sum of five hundred dollars and [*blank*] acknowledge themselves bound likewise in the sum of~~

The State)
vs.) Misdemeanor
John STEWART) [*blank*] acknowledge themselves held and bound to his Excellency the Governor in the sum of five hundred dollars each Conditioned to be void if the said John STEWART do appear at the next Superior Court of said County and not depart thence without leave of said Court otherwise to remain in full force and virtue 26th April 1814.
{Seal}
{Seal}

It appearing to the Court that a levy & sale was made by Allen TOOKE late Sheriff of Pulaski County of one half of a tract of land known in the general plan by lot number 269 in the 21st district of Wilkinson now Pulaski County as the property of Benjamin MEWBORN to satisfy Noah WHEELERs execution and that John COLE dec^{d}. became the purchaser at said sale for the sum of seventy seven dollars which has been paid to said TOOKE who has...

Page 41

failed to make titles to the same. On motion of counsel Ordered that the present Sheriff Elijah WALLACE to proceed to perfect said sale by making titles to Prusia COLE widow & relict, William COLE & John K. MONTFORD who hath intermarried with Ann COLE heirs of the said John COLE dec^{d}.

The State)
vs.) Ind^{t}. assault & baty.
James CLARK) True bill Murdoch M^{c}LEOD foreman

The State)
vs.) Assault & baty.
Abraham HOLIDAY) True bill Murdoch M^{c}LEOD foreman

The State)
vs.) Ass^{t}. &c.
Turner EVERITT) No bill Murdoch M^{c}LEOD foreman

The State)
vs.) Assault & baty.
Green ROBERTSON alias)
Nat^{l}. Green ROBERTSON) True Bill Murdoch M^{c}LEOD foreman

The State)
vs.) Ass^{t}. & baty.
Jno. A. WILLIAMS, Ja^{s}. CLARK)
Ben. MEWBORN, W^{m}. SMITH) True bill against BROWN
W^{m}. GOODSON, Ben. BROWN S^{r}.) and no bill against the others
W^{m}. YARBORO, Ja^{s}. GOODSON)
& Robt. DEWET) Murdoch M^{c}LEOD foreman

Page 42

The State)
vs.) Ind^{t}. assault & battery
James CLARK) James CLARK acknowledges himself bound to his Excellency the Governor in the sum of two hundred dollars, and Richard H. THOMAS acknowledges himself bound likewise in the sum of two hundred dollars conditioned to be void if the said James CLARK do appear at the next Superior Court in said County, and not depart thence without leave of said Court, otherwise to remain in full force & virtue - 26th April 1814.

Turner EVERITT Clk. James CLARK {Seal}
R. H. THOMAS {Seal}

The State)
vs.) Indt. Stabing
John A. WILLIAMS)
and others) John A. WILLIAMS acknowledges himself to his Excellency the Governor in the sum of twelve hundred dollars and Isaac KIRKSEY & Spire MILLS acknowledge themselves bound likewise in the sum of six hundred dollars each conditioned to be void if the said Jno. A. WILLIAMS do appear at the next Superior Court of Pulaski County and not depart thence without leave of said Court, otherwise to remain in full force & virtue - 25th April 1814.

Jno. A. WILLIAMS {Seal}
Turner EVERITT Clk. Isaac KIRKSEY {Seal}
his
Spire x MILLS {Seal}
mark

Page 43

The State)
vs.) Indt. Stabing
Benjamin MEWBORN) Benjamin MEWBORN acknowledges himself bound to his Excellency the Governor in the sum of twelve hundred dollars and Daniel COLE & Shadrach ATKINSON acknowledge themselves bound likewise in the sum of six hundred dollars each conditioned to be void if the said Benjn. MEWBORN do appear at the next Superior Court in Pulaski and not depart thence without leave of said Court, otherwise to remain in full force & virtue 26th April 1814.

Benjamin MEWBORN {Seal}
Shadrach ATKINSON {Seal}
Daniel COLE {Seal}

The State)
vs.) Indt. Stabing
William GOODSON) William GOODSON acknowledges himself bound to his Excellency the Governor in the sum of twelve hundred dollars and William HALL & Benjamin SMITH acknowledge themselves bound likewise in the sum of six hundred dollars each, conditioned to be void if said Wm. GOODSON do appear at the next Superior Court in said County and not depart thence without leave of said Court, otherwise to remain in full force & virtue 26th April 1814.

his
William x GOOSON {Seal}
mark
Turner EVERITT Clk. Wm. HALL {Seal}
his
Benjamin x SMITH {Seal}
mark

The State)
vs.) Ind^t^. Stabing
James GOODSON) James GOODSON acknowledges himself bound to his Excellency the Governor in the sum of twelve hundred dollars and William JELKS and John SMITH acknowledge themselves bound likewise in the sum of six hundred dollars each, conditioned to be void if said Ja[s]. GOODSON do appear at the next Superior Court in said County and not to depart thence without leave of said Court, otherwise to remain in full force & virtue 26th April 1814.

Turner EVERITT Clk.

James x GOOSON {Seal} (his mark)
W. JELKS {Seal}
John SMITH {Seal}

The State)
vs.) Ind[t]. Stabing
William SMITH) William SMITH acknowledges himself bound to his Excellency the Governor in the sum of twelve hundred dollars and Charles CARDIN & Washington LANCASTER acknowledge themselves bound likewise in the sum of six hundred dollars each, conditioned to be void if said W[m]. SMITH do appear at the next Superior Court in Pulaski County and not depart thence without leave of said Court, 26th April 1814.

Turner EVERITT Clk.

William SMITH {Seal}
Charles CARDIN {Seal}
Washington LANCASTER {Seal}

Page 45

The State)
vs.) Ind[t]. Stabing
Robert DEWETT) Robert DEWETT acknowledges himself bound to his Excellency the Governor in the sum of twelve hundred dollars and Soloman SUTTON & Henry DEWETT acknowledge themselves bound likewise in the sum of six hundred dollars each, conditioned to be void if the said Robert DEWETT do appear at the next Superior Court in Pulaski County and not depart thence without leave of said Court, otherwise to remain in full force & virtue.
26th April 1814.

Turner EVERITT Clk.

Robert DEWET {Seal}
Solomon x SUTTON {Seal} (his mark)
Henry DEWETT {Seal}

The State)
vs.) Ind[t]. Stabing
James CLARK) James CLARK acknowledges himself bound to his Excellency the Governor in the sum of twelve hundred dollars and Sanders COLESON & Edward BLACKSHEAR acknowledge themselves bound likewise in the sum of six hundred dollars each, conditioned to be void if said James CLARK do appear at the next Superior Court in said County and not to depart thence without leave of said Court, otherwise to remain in full force & virtue.

26th April 1814. James CLARK {Seal}
Turner EVERITT Clk. Sanders COLSON {Seal}
Edward BLACKSHEAR {Seal}

Page 46

The State)
vs.) Indt. Stabing
Wm. YARBOROUGH) William YARBOROUGH acknowledges himself bound to his Excellency the Governor in the sum of twelve hundred dollars and Furney F. GATLIN and Moses SUTTON acknowledge themselves bound likewise in the sum of six hundred dollars each, conditioned to be void if said Wiliam YARBORO do appear at the next Superior Court and not depart thence without leave of said Court, otherwise to remain in full force & virtue 26th April 1814.

William YARBROUGH {Seal}
Turner EVERITT Clk. Furney F. GATLIN {Seal}
Moses SUTTON {Seal}

Lasseter CRAWFORD)
vs.) Case & bail
Benjamin POSEY &) April Term 1813
Benjamin BROWN) Benjamin BROWN security for the appearance of Benjamin POSEY defendant in the above case having brought into Court the body of the said POSEY & is now ready to deliver him over to the Sheriff on motion of counsel it is ordered that making such delivery an exoneration be entered on the bail bond taken in the above & the said BROWN be discharged from his liability.

The State) Misdemeanor
vs.) True bill
John STEWART) On motion ordered that the said John STEWART stand committed until he gives security for his appearance at the next Court & pays the cost also conditioned to keep the peace towards the good citizens of this State particularly towards Robert HART.

Exd. S. W. HARRIS
The Court then adjourned untill court in course. Turner EVERETT Clk.

Page 47

The State)
vs.) Indt. Misdemeanor
John STEWART) James M. TAYLOR, Henry COOPER, John J. FORD, William LYON, Daniel McNEAR, Thomas PHILIPS, William JELKS, Federick WOLF, Baily ROBINSON, William PIPKIN, William CALK & William LITTLE & Charles STEWART acknowledge themselves bound to his Excellency the Governor in the sum of five hundred dollars each, conditioned to be void if the said John STEWART do appear at the next Superior Court in Pulaski County and not to depart thence without leave of said Court, conditioned also that the said John STEWART do keep the peace towards the good citizens of this State, and

particularly towards Robert HART, otherwise to remain in full force & virtue 26th April 1814. Turner EVERETT Clk.

Jas. M. TAYLOR {LS}
Henry COOPER {LS}
Tom PHILIPS {LS}
William JELKS {LS}
William LYON {LS}
John J. FORD {LS}
his
William x CAUK {LS}
mark
B. ROBINSON {LS}

Daniel McNAIR {LS}
Wm. LITTLE {LS}
his
Fedrick x WOOLF {LS}
mark
his
William x PIPKIN {LS}
mark
his
Charles x STEWART {LS}
mark

Page 48, October 1814

Monday the 24th Octr. 1814. The Superior Court for the County of Pulaski met agreeably to law - present his honor Judge HARRIS.

The following persons ~~were~~ \appeared & were/ sworn on the Grand Jury at the present term:

1 Henry FULGHAM for.
2 William JOHNSON
3 David SNELL
4 William BERNAM
5 Allen TOOKE
6 Robert DEWIT
7 Edward BRYANT
8 Neil McALPIN
9 Jesse POWELL
10 William LYON
11 Drury DEES
12 George WALKER
13 James L. PERRY
14 Dixon JELKS
15 Archibald THOMPSON
16 John ROZIER
17 Abram VICKERS
18 Hinche WARREN
19 Wm. YARBROUGH Sr.
20 Samuel JONES
21 Joel DAWSON
22 James DEES
23 William MAYO

The following persons appeared and were sworn on the Petit Jury No. 1

1 ~~Aaron SCARBOROUGH~~
Zelah PULLING
2 John YAWN
3 John BRADSHAW
4 Henry EVENS
5 ~~Mark WHEELER~~
Mitchell DORMAN
6 William YARBOROUGH
7 James ODOM
8 Fort ALFORD
9 Nathan SOWELL
10 Solomon BREWER
11 Thomas HESTER
12 Jesse LIVELY

Page 49

Petit Jury No. 2

1 John BIRD
2 Moses KIRKLIN
3 Stephen PIPKIN
4 Patrick McGRIFF
5 ~~Samuel STEWART~~
Lewis HOLLAND
6 Jesse PENNINGTON
7 Theophilus SUTTON
8 Henry HAGAN
9 Daniel SPARROW
10 Thomas FRANKLIN
11 John CARDIN
12 John L. SMITH

Benjn. HARVEY)
vs.) Trespass vi et armis
Allen SCARBOROUGH) We the jurors do find for the plaintiff thirty two dollars with costs.
Henry HAGAN foreman

Blakely EDINS) Case Jury N°. 1
vs.) Verdict
Aaron SCARBOROUGH) We find for the defendant with costs.
John BRADSHAW foreman

The Grand Jury returned into Court & returned the following bills:

The State)
vs.) Stabing
Daniel MAGEE) True Bill Henry FULGHAM foreman

Page 50

The State)
vs.) Assault & battery
John J. FORD) True bill foreman

The State)
vs.) Assault & battery
Thos. COLE) True bill Henry FULGHAM foreman

Soloman SUTTON)
vs.) Trespass vi et armis
Amos WHEELER &)
Nancy WHEELER) We the Jury find for the plaintiff ~~the plaintiff~~ the sum of thirty five dollars with cost.
John BRADSHAW foreman

John STEWART by)
his next friend & father) Trespass on the case
Charles STEWART) for words &c Jury N°. 1
vs.)
Robert HART) We the Jury find for the plaintiff two hundred dollars with cost.
John BRADSHAW foreman

Page 51

The State)
vs.) Ind^{t}. Misdemeanor
John STEWART) John STEWART acknowledges himself bound to his Excellency the Governor in the sum of five hundred dollars and Daniel COLE his security likewise in the sum of five hundred dollars, conditioned to be void if the said John STEWART do appear in Court tomorrow morning eight oclock and not to depart thence without leave of said Court 24th Oct. 1814.
Turner EVERITT Clk. Daniel COLE {LS}

The Court the adjourned untill tomorrow morning half past eight oclock.
T. EVERETT Clk.

Ex[d]. S. W. HARRIS
Tuesday 25th Oct[r]. 1814. The Court met pursuant to adjournment present his Honor Judge HARRIS.

Bailey ROBINSON)
vs.) Trespass vi et armis
John M[c]CRAE) We the jurors do find for the plaintiff twenty five dollars with cost.
Henry HAGIN foreman

Solomon SUTTON)
vs.) Trespass vi et armis
Amos WHEELER &)
Nancy WHEELER) On motion of counsel for def[t]. ordered that plaintiffs counsel shew cause instanter why the verdict in the above case should not be set aside and a nonsuit awarded on the following For that there is no time laid in the declaration. This case laid over for advisement till next term with...

Page 52

liberty to the defendant then to enter an appeal.

The Grand Jury came into court & returned the following bills:

The State)
vs.) Assault & battery
Isaac KIRKSEY) No bill. Henry FULGHAM for[n].

The State)
vs.) Ind[t]. cattle stealing
James TEMPLES) True bill. Henry FULGHAM for[n].

The State)
vs.) Larceny
John TEMPLES) True bill against John VARNER, No bill against John
John VARNER) TEMPLES. Henry FULGHAM for[n].

Page 53

The State)
vs.) Indict. assault
Elizabeth ROBERTSON now)
Elizabeth B. CRUTCHFIELD)

Same)
vs.) Indictment perjury
Same) In these cases the recognizance of the said Elizabeth for her appearance at the Court being forfeited by the Sol. Gen[l]. & she having at this term on motion ordered that scire facias do not issue.

Theod^{k}. MONTFORD)
& Company) Case
vs.) Jury N°. 1
Benjamin MEWBORN) We find for the plaintiffs three hundred and two dollars sixty six and three fourth cents with costs. John BRADSHAW for^{n}.

Benjamin HARVEY)
vs.) Trespass armis verdict
Allen SCARBORO) In this case the defendant being dissatisfied with the verdict of the jury comes into Court & pays all cost and prays an appeal in terms of the law & gives Charles CARDEN security. Allen SCARBOROUGH {LS}
Charles CARDIN {LS}

The State)
vs.) Cattle stealing
W^{m}. PROCTOR) True bill Henry FULGHAM foreman

Page 54

The State)
vs.) Larceny True Bill
Henry MILLS &)
Alex^{r}. M^{c}DANIEL) Henry FULGHAM foreman

The State)
vs.) Larceny
John TEMPLES) True bill against John VARNER no bill against
John VARNER) John TEMPLES. Henry FULGHAM foreman

The State)
vs.) Ind^{t}. larceny
John VARNER) John VARNER acknowledges himself bound to his Excellency the Governor in the sum of five hundred dollars and John TEMPLES and Thomas TEMPLES securitys each in the sum of two hundred and fifty dollars conditioned to be void if the said John VARNER do appear at the next Superior Court to be held in & for the County aforesaid on the fourth Monday in April next and not depart thence without leave of said Court 25th October 1814.

John VARNER {LS}
Turner EVERETT Clk. John TEMPLES {LS}
his
Thomas x TEMPLES {LS}
mark

Page 55

The State) Assault & battery True bill
vs.) Henry FULGHAM foreman
Polly LAWSON) Polly LAWSON acknowledges herself bound to his Excellency the Governor in the sum of two hundred dollars and James LAWSON and William GOODSON each in the sum of two hundred dollars conditioned to be void if the said Polly LAWSON tomorrow at nine oclock appear in Court and continue

untill duly discharged by due course of law. {LS}
25th October 1814. James LAWSON {LS}
his
Turner EVERITT Clk. William x GOODSON {LS}
mark

The State)
vs.) Hog stealing
Henry MILLS) Henry MILLS acknowledges himself bound to his Excellency the Governor in the sum of two hundred dollars and Samuel REGAN his security in the sum of two hundred dollars likewise, conditioned to be void if the said Henry MILLS do appear in Court tomorrow morning by nine oclock and not to depart thence without leave of said court this 25th October 1814.

his
Turner EVERETT Clk. Henry **H** MILLS {LS}
mark
Samuel REGAN {LS}

Page 56

The State)
vs.) Hog stealing
Alexander DANIEL) Alexander DANIEL acknowledges himself bound to his Excellency the Governor in the sum of two hundred dollars and Joseph GRAHAM his security also in the sum of two hundred dollars, conditioned to be void if the said Alexander DANIEL do appear in Court tomorrow morning nine oclock and not depart thence without leave of said Court 25th October 1814.

Alexander DANIEL {LS}
Turner EVERETT Clk. Joseph GRAHAM {LS}

Exd. S. W. HARRIS

The Court then ~~met agreeably to~~ adjourn~~ment~~ed 'till half past eight oclock tomorrow morning. Turner EVERETT Clk.

~~Blakely EDINS~~
~~vs.~~
~~James~~

Court met pursuant to adjournment this Wednesday 26 Octr. 1814.

Page 57

Blakely EDINS)
vs.) Case for words
James BEATY) Special jury sworn

1 Henry FULGHAM	7 James L. PERRY
2 William JOHNSON	8 Dixon JELKS
3 David SNELL	9 Archd. THOMPSON
4 Wm. BROWN	10 Hinche WARREN
5 Neil McALPIN	11 Saml. JONES
6 Wm. LYON	12 Wm. MAYO

We find for the plaintiff three hundred dollars with costs of suit.

Henry FULGHAM foreman

The following persons were drawn to serve on the Grand Jury at the next term:

1 Jas. AVERIT
2 Simon BARDIN
3 Saunders COLSON
4 Murdock McLEOD
5 Jas. RAMSAY
6 Blakley EDINS
7 James ROUNTREE
8 Benjn. HARVEY
9 Joseph BARRON
10 Natl. MERCER
11 Richd. H. THOMAS
12 Saml. RAGAIN
13 Stephen MITCHELL
14 Chesley DAVIS
15 Jno. SHARRARD
16 Mark MASON
17 Jas. BRACEWELL
18 Wm. HALL
19 Wm. MEHAFFEE
20 Danl. COLE
21 Danl. RAGAIN
22 Jno. LEE Jr.
23 Wm. H. GROSS
24 Tho. McGRIFF
25 Wm. DESHAZO
26 Wm. GOODSON
27 Wm. IZLER
28 Archd. H. ODOM
29 Jno. STUART
30 Benjn. BRUTON

Page 58

The following persons were drawn to serve at the next term as Petit Jurors:

1 Theos. ROGERS
2 Joel REEVES
3 Ben. HARRISON
4 Aaron JOHNSON
5 Peter HAGIN
6 Ben. JOHNSON
7 Isaac PHILLIPS
8 Arthur SHUFFIELD
9 Hugh INGRAM
10 Isham HAGIN
11 Tho. PHILLIPS
12 Jas. BEDDINGFIELD
13 Jno. NELSON
14 Edwd. LASSITER
15 Jno. JONES
16 Isaac FOREMAN
17 Philip WHICHERT
18 Abram NIPPER
19 Jno. J. FORD
20 Danl. CORNWELL
21 ~~Bailey HARRIL~~ Henry DEWIT
22 Ben. MEWBORN
23 Grantham HORN
24 Jno. LEE Sr.
25 Thos. EVERIT
26 Arthur TOOKE
27 Philemon BRYAN
28 Levi HARRELL
29 Josiah WINBURN
30 Laban KENT
31 William LONG
32 Jno. MANNING
33 Tho. TAYLOR
34 Chs. STUART
35 Willson BASS
36 Jerh. BEALL
37 Jesse WILLIAMS
38 Reuben ROUNTREE
39 Felix DYKES
40 West SHUFFIELD
41 Spire MILLS
42 Ben. STEGALL
43 Lewis BAGGET
44 Lawrence FULSOM
45 Wm. TAYLOR
46 Jno. MILLER
47 Bartley C. WILLIAMS
48 Jas. CARDIN
49 Jno. JONES [#2]
50 Wm. HAMMOCK
51 Nicholas BAGGET
52 Holden DUNN

William HILLARD was sworn on the Petit Jury No. 1 in place of Jesse LIVELY.

The State)
vs.) Indictment stabbing
Daniel MAGEE) Jury Sworn No. 1

1 Zelah PULLEN	7 James ODOM
2 John YAWN	8 Fort ALFORD
3 John BRADSHAW	9 Nathan SOWELL
4 Henry EVANS	10 Solomon BREWER
5 Mitchell DORMON	11 Thomas HESTER
6 William YARBOROUGH	12 William HILLYARD

We the jurors find the defendant guilty. John BRADSHAW for.

Blakley EDINS) Case for malicious prosecution
vs.) Verdict for defendant
Aaron SCARBORO) In this case the plaintiff being dissatisfied with the verdict of the Jury comes forward pays all cost gives Allen TOOKE as his security in terms of the law for the eventual condemnation money and prays an appeal which is granted Oct. 26 1814. Blakly EDINS {Seal}
Turner EVERITT Clk. Allen TOOKE {Seal}

Page 60

Samuel STEWART took the place of Lewis HOLLAND on the Petit Jury No. 2.

The State) Same) Assault
vs.) Perjury vs.) &
Elizabeth B. CRUTCHFIELD) Same) Battery

We acknowledge ourselves to wit Joab CRUTCHFIELD & James L. PERRY indebted to the Governor his successors in office in the sum of six hundred dollars each to be void on the condition that the above Elizabeth do appear at the next Superior Court of this County on the first day thereof and do not depart without leave of said Court. Joab CRUTCHFIELD {Seal}
Turner EVERETT Clk. James L. PERRY {Seal}

The State)
vs.) Indictment Cattle Stealing
Thomas TEMPLES) True Bill Henry FULGHAM foreman

The State)
vs.) Larceny
Henry MILLS &) Jury No. 2 sworn
Alexander McDANIEL)

1 John BIRD	7 Theophilus SUTTON
2 Moses KIRKLIN	8 Henry HAGAN
3 Stephen PIPKIN	9 Daniel SPARROW
4 Patrick McGRIFF	10 Thomas FRANKLIN
5 Samuel STUART	11 John CARDEN
6 Jesse PENINGTON	12 John L. SMITH

We the Jurors do find the defendant guilty. Henry HAGIN foreman

The State)
vs.) Ind^{t}. assault
Theodrick MONTFORT) True Bill Henry FULGHAM foreman
Arraigned and plead guilty ~~& my fee paid~~
Fined $5.00 October term 1814. Bedney FRANKLIN Sol. Genl.

Georgia) Superior Cort October Term 1814.
Pulaski County) We the Grand Inquest for the County aforesaid have agreed on the following presentments - We the present Wilson BASS for retailing spiritous liquors wihtout licence also for keeping a riotous house on the sabbath day. We present as a grievance John K. MONTFORT for pulling down the cover built over the public well in the town of Hartford and the wall around the same. We also present as a grievance Thos. M^{c}DANIEL, Thomas MILLS, Daniel MAGEE, John K. MONTFORT and William GARLINGTON commissioners of the Town of Hartford for not keeping the public square and streets of said town in better order.

We also present the bad situaion of the Uchee Road so far as respects Gum Swamp or Little Oakmulgy and reccommend the commissioners thereof immediately to repair the same.

Page 62

We have with pleasure witnessed the strict and impartial attendance of his Honor Judge Harris of the discharge of his official duty during the present Session.

Henry FULGHAM foreman	James L. PERRY
William JOHNSON	Dixon JELKS
David SNELL	Archibald THOMPSON
William BERMAN [*Bernam*]	John ROZIER
Allen TOOKE	Abraham VICKERS
Robert DEWIT	Kinchey WARREN
Edward BRYAN	William YARBOROUGH
Neil M^{c}COLPIN	Samuel JONES
Jesse POWELL	Drury DEES
William LYON	James DEES
George WALKER	Joel DAWSON
	William MAYO

The State)
vs.) Ind^{t}. assault
Polly DAWSON) Jury N°. 1 sworn

1 Zelah PULLING	7 James ODOM
2 John YAWN	8 Fort ALFORD
3 John BRADSHAW	9 Nathan SOWELL
4 Henry EVANS	10 Solomon BREWER
5 Mitchell DORMAN	11 Thomas HESTER
6 William YARBOROUGH	12 William HILLIARD

We the Jury find the defendant guilty. John BRADSHAW foreman

The State)
vs.) Cattle stealing
Thomas TEMPLES) Daniel DYKES Esqr. acknowledges himself bound to his Excellency the Governor in the sum of fifty dollars, conditioned to be void if the said DYKES do appear at the next Superior \Court/ in & for the County of Pulaski as a witness in said case on the part of the State.
this 25th Octr. 1814. Daniel DYCKES {LS}
Turner EVERETT Clk.

Blakely EDINS resp^{t}.) Case
vs.) for words
James BATY app^{t}.) Verdict for three hundred dollars.

On motion of counsel for defendant it is ordered that plaintiffs counsel shew cause on the first day of next term why the verdict should not be set asside and a new trial awarded on the following grounds: 1st For that the plaintiff did not prove the words as laid in the declaration; 2nd For that the Court refused to admit testimony to prove that the defendant had reasonable grounds of suspicion under the plea of not guilty in mitigation of damages; 3rd For that the damages & the verdict contrary to law equity and the Justice of the case.

The testimony offered and regected was a copy of an...

Page 64

indictment from Twiggs Superior Court found against Blakely EDINS for a misdemeanour for false swearing and also testimony to prove that EDINS swore to a lie before the Justice of the Peace at the time the defendants father was bound over to appear at Twiggs Court for burning CARVERs? barn and relative to the same transaction for which the indictment was found a true bill by the Grand Jury.

The State)
vs.) Stabbing
W^{m}. HORNE) The witnesses not being present on the part of the State & the State therefore not being ready to proceed, On motion it is ordered that the defendant William HORNE be discharged.

The State)
vs.) Indictment Larceny
Henry MILLS) In this case it appearing that the testimony that the traverser had been expressly employed by the prosecuter Doctor GARBETT & who is the prosecutor and who claimed the hog which is the subject of the prosecution to take care of this hog with others and that he would pay him for his trouble that the hog had been raised by the defendant & sold by him to one HOLLAND and by him to one GARBETT and that the hog had returned to MILLS house where he...

was employed by GARBETT about two days before this MILLS had acknowledged it to be GARBETTs hog that in this situation the traverser on the twenty fourth of December last killed the hog at his neighbour DANIELs - that he never denied killing the hog and that he proved that he had a fair character from infancy that the hog was in his mark and he never denied killing him - On motion of traversers counsel it is ordered that a new trial be granted in this case unless cause be shewn to the contrary at the next term on the following grounds: 1st That the verdict is contrary to law & evidence; 2nd The the traverser was legally and in fact in possession of the property killed & the facts do not shew that there was a felonious conversion of property.

The Court then adjourned till court in course Turner EVERETT Clk. Exd. S. W. HARRIS

The State)
vs.) Larceny
Henry MILLS) Henry MILLS acknowledges himself bound to his Excellency the Governor in the sum of five hundred dollars. Samuel REGAN his security likewise in the sum of five hundred dollars - conditioned to be void if the said MILLS do appear at the next Superior Court to be held in & for the County of Pulaski on the fourth Monday in April next and not depart without leave of said Court this 26th Octr. 1814.

Turner EVERETT Clk.

his
Henry **H** MILLS {LS}
mark
Samuel REGAN {LS}

Page 66

The State)
vs.) Indt. Stabing
Daniel MAGEE) Daniel MAGEE acknowledges himself bound in the sum of one thousand dollars to his Excellency the Governor or his successor in office & Stephen GATLIN and James RAMSEY his securities acknowledge themselves bound likewise in the sum of five hundred dollars each, conditioned to be void if the said Daniel MAGEE does appear at the next Superior Court to be held in & for the County of Pulaski County on the fourth Monday in April next, and not depart thence without the leave of said Court this 27th day of October 1814.

Daniel MAGEE {LS}
Attest
Turner EVERETT Clk.

Stephen GATLIN {LS}
James RAMSEY {LS}

The State)
vs.) Indictment Larceny
Alexander McDANIEL) Alexander McDANIEL acknowledges himself bound in the sum of five hundred dollars to his Excellency the Governor or his successors in office and George VARNER his security acknowledges himself bound also in the sum of five hundred dollars conditioned to be void if the said...

Alexander McDANIEL does appear at the next Superior Court to be held in and for the County aforesaid on the fourth Monday in April next, and not depart thence without the leave of said Court this 27th day of October 1814.

Alexander DANIEL [!] {Seal}
his
Attest Turner EVERETT Clk. George x VARNER {Seal}
mark

January 1815

Farish CARTER for the use)
of Richardson O. SEURRY?) Case
vs.)
James M. TAYLOR) I Stephen GATLIN acknowledge myself bound as security to the defendant for the principal interest & cost in the above case in terms of the alleviating law. this 4th day of January 1815.
Attest Turner EVERETT Clk. Stephen GATLIN

Page 68

Nimrod HENDRICK)
vs.) Case
Ephraim PHILIPS)
Sherrard PHILIPS &)
Gabriel PHILIPS) I Burwell PHILIPS acknowledge myself bound as security to the defendants for the principal interest & cost in the above case in terms of the alleviating law. this 4th January 1815.
his
Attest Turner EVERETT Clk. Burwell x PHILIPS
mark

Ambrose MURPHY)
for E. NUNN) Case
vs.) Jury No. 2
John A. WILLIAMS) We find for the plaintiff fifty dollars with interest and cost. October term 1812. John DICKSON forn.

I William JELKS acknowledge myself bound as security to the defendant for the principal interest & cost in the above case in terms of the alleviating law this 4th January 1815.
Attest Turner EVERETT Clk. W. JELKS

Page 69

Benjamin CHAIRS)
vs.) Case
Hardy VICKERS) I William LESTER acknowledge myself bound as security to the defendant for the principal interest and cost in the above case in term of the alleviating law. this 4th January 1815.
Attest Turner EVERETT Clk. William LESTER

J. & A. STINSON)
vs.) Judgement for Pltf.
Murdock McLEOD) I Archibald H. ODOM acknowledge myself bound as security to the defendant for the principal interest and costs in the above case in terms of the law in such cases made and provided this 4th Jany. 181[5].

A. H. ODOM

Page 70, April 1815

Monday the 24th April 1815. The Superior Court for the County of Pulaski met agreeable to law Present his honor Judge HARRIS.

The following persons appeared & were sworn on the Grand Jury at the present term:

1 Murdock McLEOD forman
2 Sanders COLSON
3 James EVERETT
4 Blakley EDINS
5 John SHARRARD
6 Mark MASON
7 James BRACEWELL
8 William MEHAFFEE
9 Daniel COLE
10 William H. GROSS
11 Thomas McGRIFF
12 William GOODSON
13 Simon BARDIN
14 Samuel REGAN
15 James ROUNTREE
16 William DESHAZO
17 Benjamin HARVY
18 John LEE
19 William HALL
20 John STEWEART
21 Benjamin BRUTON
22 Nathaniel MERCER

The State)
vs.) Indt. Stabing & conviction
Danl. MAGEE) A pardon having been produced in the above case It is ordered that the defendant Daniel MAGEE be discharged so far as the State is concerned.

Page 71

The following persons appeared & were sworn on the Petit Jury at the present term.

Jury No. 1

1 Spire MILLS
2 Benjamin STEGALL
3 Lewis BAGGET
4 William TAYLOR
5 Nicholas BAGGET
6 Lawrence FOLSOM
7 William WILLIAMS
8 John JONES
9 Isaac FOREMAN
10 James GOODSON
11 Felix DYKES
12 Benjamin HARRISON

Jury No. 2

1 William HAMMACK
2 Philemon BRYANT
3 Benjamin MEWBORN
4 Aaron JOHNSON
5 Arthur TOOKE
6 Henry DEWIT
7 Daniel CORNWALL
8 Josiah WINBORN
9 Philip WHITCHARD
10 William LONG
11 Hugh INGRAM
12 Joel REEVES

John EASLEY for the)
use of Dudly JONES) Debt
vs.) Jury No. 2
James RAMSEY) We find for the plaintiff forty one dollars with interest & cost.
Daniel CORNWALL forn.

Page 72

Robert HART)
vs.) Trespass on the case for words &c
Nancy STEWART &)
Charles STEWART) Non suit.

William HALL) Jury No. 1
vs.) Debt
William COOPER) We find for the plaintiff five hundred dollars with interest & cost of suit.
W. WILLIAMS forn.

Joseph SESSIONS) Asst. & battery
vs.) Jury No. 1
John J. FORD) We find for the plaintiff one hundred dollars with cost of suit.
Wm. WILLIAMS forn.

Robert MATHEWS)
vs. Indorsee) Case
John MOSES Indorser) On motion it is ordered that the Clerk deliver the note declared on to Robert RUTHERFORD that proceedings may be had against the maker for the benefit of the indorser.

Page 73

Joseph SESSIONS) Case for slander
vs.) Jury No. 2
John J. FORD) We find for the plaintiff one hundred & seventy dollars with cost of suit.
Daniel CORNWALL forn.

The Court then adjourned untill tomorrow morning half after seven oclock. Exd. Stephen W. HARRIS

Joseph WOOD) Petition
vs.) Jury No. 2
William McDANIEL) We find for the plaintiff twenty dollars with interest & cost.
Daniel CORNWALL forn.

The Grand Jury returned the following bill:

The State)
vs.) Indt. Perjury
Blakley EDINS) No bill. M. McLEOD forn.

The State)
vs.) Ind^{t}. Cattle Stealing
James TEMPLES) James TEMPLES acknowledges himself bound to his Excellency the Governor in the sum of five hundred dollars, and Charles CARDIN and John VARNER his securities also in the sum of two hundred & fifty dollars each, conditioned to be void if the said James TEMPLES do appear at the next Superior Court to be held in & for the County of Pulaski on the fourth Monday in October next, and not depart thence without leave of said Court, this 25th April 1815.

his
Test. Turner EVERETT Clk. James x TEMPLES {LS}
mark
Charles CARDIN {LS}
John VARNER {LS}

The State)
vs.) Ind^{t}. Cattle Stealing
Thomas TEMPLES) Thomas TEMPLES acknowledges himself bound to his Excellency the Governor in the sum of five hundred dollars, and Charles CARDIN and John VARNER his securities also in the sum of two hundred & fifty dollars each, conditioned to be void if the said Thomas TEMPLES do appear at the next Superior Court to be held in & for the County of Pulaski on the fourth Monday in October next, and not depart thence without leave of...

Page 75

said Court, this 25th April 1815.
his
Thomas x TEMPLES {LS}
mark
Test. Turner EVERETT Clk. Charles CARDIN {LS}
John VARNER {LS}

Solomon SUTTON)
vs.) Trespass vi et armis
Nancy WHEELER &)
Amos WHEELER) Amos WHEELER being dissatisfied with the verdict of the Jury rendered in the above case came forward pays all cost enters John BRADSHAW security in terms of the law & craves an appeal which is granted him.

his
Turner EVERITT Clk. Amos x WHEELER {Seal}
mark
John BRADSHAW {Seal}

Blakley EDINS)
vs.) Rule nisi for new trial
James BEATY) The above rule having been obtained at the last Court \and the case being settled between the parties/ ~~& sufficient cause having been shewn~~ on motion it is ordered that said rule nisi be discharged.

Joseph WOOD)
vs.) Debt on attachment
William McDANIEL) In this case Thomas McDANIEL having been security in a replevy bond given to the Sheriff and his successors in office & it being stated that the defendant will require his testimony in the above case & he offers William WILLIAMS as security in his place & said WILLIAMS consenting to become his security for the eventual money it is ordered that the said Thomas McDANIEL be discharged from his said bond & the said WILLIAMS be received in his place he consenting to this rule by signing ~~his~~ the same 25th April 1815.

Wm. WILLIAMS

Page 77

The State)
vs.) Indt. Asslt. & Battery
Colson ADAMS) Colson ADAMS acknowledges himself bound to his Excellency the Governor in the sum of two hundred dollars also William TAYLOR his security in the sum of two hundred dollars Conditioned to be void if the said Colson ADAMS do appear at the next Superior Court to be held in & for the County of Pulaski on the fourth Monday in October next and not depart thence without leave of said Court. Colson ADAMS {LS}
Test Turner EVERETT Clk. William TAYLOR {LS}

Abel PAULK respt.)
vs.)
James RAMSAY &)
Elijah WALLACE)
appelants) Special Jury

1 William MEHAFFEE	7 William DESHAZO
2 Daniel COLE	8 Benjamin HARVEY
3 Thomas McGRIFF	9 John LEE
4 William GOODSON	10 William HALL
5 Simon BARDIN	11 John STEWART
6 Samuel REGAN	12 Nathaniel MERCER

We the Jurors find for the plaintiff one hundred & sixty two dollars, with interest & cost of suit. Nathaniel MERCER forn.

Page 78

John DOE ex dem.)
John FIELDER)
vs. Respondant) Ejectment
Richard ROE John LEE) Same special sworn
Tenant in possession appt.) We find for the plaintiff the premises in dispute with cost of suit.
Natl. MERCER forn.

The State)
vs.) Larceny
Henry MILLS) Verdict guilty

Rule nisi for a new trial obtained at the last Court cause having been shewn why a new trial should not be granted ordered that the rule nisi be discharged.

John A. WILLIAMS)
vs.) Divorce
Hester WILLIAMS) Special Jury Sworn

1 Mark MASON
2 W^{m}. MEHAFFEE
3 Daniel COLE
4 W^{m}. H. GROSS
5 Simon BARDIN
6 Saml. RAGAN
7 James ROUNTREE
8 William DESHAZO
9 Benjamin HARVEY
10 John LEE
11 William HALL
12 Benjn. BRUTON

Dismissed

Page 79

The following persons were drawn to serve as Grand Jurors at the ensuing term:

1 Thos. JOHNSTON
2 Abram VICKERS
3 Christopher RHODES
4 Isaac BUCKHALTER
5 Thos. M. DANIEL [*McDaniel*]
6 John GILSTRAP
7 Sands STANLEY
8 Orandatis WATSON
9 Drury MAYO
10 Charles CARDIN
11 Sutton TRUELUCK
12 George WALKER
13 John LESTER
14 Michael HORN
15 Jno. SWARENGAME
16 Joel DAWSON
17 David SNELL
18 Hincy WARREN
19 Archibald THOMPSON
20 W^{m}. JOHNSON
21 James CLARKE
22 John ROZIER
23 Robert DANIELL
24 William LYON
25 William BURNAM
26 Chas. MAYO
27 John WILCOX
28 Benjn. SMITH
29 Robt. HODGES
30 W^{m}. MAYO
31 Zion DAVIS
32 Allen TOOKE

The following persons were drawn to serve as Petit Jurors at the ensuing term.

1 Reuben IRWIN
2 W^{m}. GRINSTEAD
3 Nimrod PHILLIPS
4 John BAGGET
5 Daniel SHINE
6 W^{m}. BRYAN
7 Thos. TEMPLES
8 W^{m}. TAYLOR S^{r}.
9 Jonathan TAYLOR
10 Jason BRINSON
11 W^{m}. HARRELL
12 Elisha BRANUM
13 Elias PHILLIPS
14 Elisha EVANS
15 Little J. SMITH
16 Jesse PIPKIN
17 Haywood JONES
18 Daniel MYERS
19 John RADCLIFF
20 Ezekiel JONAKIN
21 Jacob YEARTA
22 Jno. DANILL
23 W^{m}. TAYLOR
24 John CLARKE

25 Jacob TAYLOR
26 John HARROLD
27 Stephen HAGAN
28 Henry COOPER
29 Jordan LEPART
30 Washington LANCASTER
31 Thos. HESTER
32 Wm. YARBOROUGH
33 Josiah TAYLOR
34 Wm. BARRON
35 Richd. TAYLOR
36 James BUSS [*Bush?*]
37 Fort ALFORD
38 Jesse LIVELY
39 Joel WALKER
40 John BRADSHAW
41 Henry EVANS
42 Aaron SCARBORO
43 Ephraim PHILLIPS
44 Malachia KELLY
45 Thos. ROGERS
46 Nathan SAWEL
47 Thos. ADAMS
48 Asa HARROLD
49 Elijah HANKS
50 Richard WYNN
51 Needham BRYAN
52 Benjn. POSEY

The Grand Jury came into Court and returned the following bill:

The State	)		
vs.	)	Assault & b.	
Theoderick MONTFORT	)	True bill	Murdoch McLEOD forn.

The Court then adjourned till tomorrow morning six oclock.

Page 81

Pulaski Sup. Court April Term 1815. It is with more than ordinary pleasure that the grand inquest for the body of Pulaski meets his Honor Judge HARRIS in an oficial capacity; and equally pleasing to this body in returing without finding any criminal matter worthy of presentment.

This body hopes that proper & effectual measures be taken to exempt William NIPPER a blind man from the payment of poll tax. This body cannot conclude without expressing the high sense and respect in which they hold the official conduct and stability of his Honor and further say they find no ground even to suspect the smallest dereliction of principle, and would be happy in his long presidency. They request the publication of this presentment in one of the public papers of the circuit.

Simon BARDIN
James A. EVERETT
Wm. HALL
Benj. BRUTON
Danl. COLE
Wm. GOODSON
Sam REGAN
John LEE
M. McLEOD forn.
Wm. MAHAFFEE
Blakley EDINS
Wm. DESHAZO
James ROUNDTREE
John STEWART
Wm. H. GROSS
Tho. McGRIFF
Natl. MERCER
Mark MASON
James BRASEWELL
Sanders COLSON
Benj. HARVEY

Exd. S. W. HARRIS

Court met pursuant to adjournment. The Court then adjourned untill Court in course. Test Turner EVERITT Clk. Exd. S.W. HARRIS

October 1815

Monday 23rd October 1815. The Superior Court for the County of Pulaski met agreeable to law. Present his Honor Judge HARRIS.

The State)
vs.) Fi fa
Archd. LASSETER &)
Wm. S. LANCASTER) The above execution having been discharged & payed off by the admr. of LANCASTER who was the security of LASSITER to the State, On motion of Thomas W. HARRIS It is ordered that the said execution be delivered to Washington LANCASTER the admr. of the security for this benefit & he to have full control thereof.

Page 83

The State)
vs.) Fi fa
Archd. LASSETER &)
Wm. S. LANCASTER) The Shff. having raised the sum of two hundred & forty nine dollars out of the property of Archibald LASSETER & the Admr. of Wm. S. LANCASTER the original security having paid off the above execution, on motion of Thomas W. HARRIS it is ordered that the Shff. do shew cause so soon as counsel can be heard why he does not pay the aforesaid sum of two hundred & forty nine dollars to the atto. of said Washington LANCASTER in satisfaction of said execution.

MERRRETT & ASBERRY)
vs.) Rule nisi
E. WALLACE Shff.) Fi fa
& James RAMSEY) Wm. YARBOROUGH Coroner having produced the said fi fa and having failed to raise the money thereon on motion it is ordered that he pay the amount thereof by nine oclock tomorrow or shew cause to the contrary.

John EASLY for the)
use of Dudly JONES) Fi fa
vs.)
James RAMSEY) Ordered that the Shff. do return the above execution instanter into Court with his actings & doings thereon.

Page 84

The following persons appeared and were sworn to serve as Grand Jurors, who made choice of Allen TOOKE for the foreman.

1 Allen TOOKE foreman
2 Cristopher RHODES
3 Thomas McDANIEL
4 Sutton TRULUCK
5 George WALKER
6 Michael HORN
7 Joel DAWSON
8 David SNELL
9 Hinchey WARREN
10 William JOHNSTON
11 Robert DANIEL
12 William LYON
13 Wm. BURNAM
14 Charles MAYO
15 Robert HODGES
16 William MAYO
17 Zion DAVIS
18 John SWEARINGAME
19 Archibld. THOMPSON
20 James CLARK
21 Benjamin SMITH
22
23 [*no names*]

The following persons were called and sworn to serve as Petit Jurors during the present term.

Jury No. 1

1 Nimrod PHILLIPS
2 Daniel SHINES?
3 William BRYAN
4 ~~Thom. TEMPLES~~
Daniel MAGEE
5 Jonathan TAYLOR
6 Jason BRINSON
7 William HARRELL
8 Elias PHILIPS
9 Elisha EVANS
10 Little J. SMITH
11 Haywood JONES
12 John DANIEL

Page 85

Jury No. 2

1 William TAYLOR
2 Jacob TAYLOR
3 John HARRELL
4 Washington LANCASTER
5 William YARBOROUGH
6 Fort ALFORD
7 Jesse LIVELY
8 John BRADSHAW
9 Mallicaie KELLY
10 Thos. ROGERS
11 Nathan SOWELL
12 Asa HARRELL

Burrell PHILIPS)
vs.) Trover &c
•Ephraim PHILLIPS) Sherrod PHILIPS having been duly & legally subpoenaed in the above case on the part of the plaintiff & having failed to attend Court, on motion it is ordered that an attachment issue to enforce the attendance of said Sherrod PHILIPS.

The State)
vs.) Indictment Cattle Stealing
Thos. TEMPLES) The bail of the said Thomas TEMPLES in the above case having surrendered him into Court, ordered the said bail be exonerated.

Georgia, Pulaski Superior Court Octr. term 1815. It appearing to the Court that at October term eighteen hundred & fourteen a true bill was found by the Grand Jury of this County against William PROCTOR for cattle stealing - that a bench warrant issued thereon & that the said William by virtue thereof has been apprehended and committed to the common jail of Wilkinson County where he is now confined, Ordered that Elijah WALLACE Sheriff of this County by himself or his proper Deputy proceed forthwith to the said common jail of the County of Wilkinson to receive into his custody the body of the said William & that he have him under safe ~~& secure~~ guard before this Court as soon as may be to answer to the aforesaid accusation and the jailor of Wilkinson County is hereby ordered & requested on the production of a copy of this order by the said Sheriff or his Deputy without delay to deliver unto his custody the body of the said William PROCTOR.

Page 87

The State)
vs.) Ind^{t}. Cattle Stealing
Thomas TEMPLES) Thomas TEMPLES acknowledges himself bound to his Excellency the Governor in the sum of five hundred dollars and James TEMPLES his security also in the sum of\five hundred/ dollars, conditioned to be void if the said Thomas TEMPLES do appear in this Court from day to day and not depart from said Court without leave of said Court ths 23rd day of October 1815.

Turner EVERETT Clk.

his
Thomas x TEMPLES {LS}
mark
his
James x TEMPLES {LS}
mark

William LYON bear.) Case
vs.) Jury N°. 2
John B. PACKER) We find for the plaintiff sixty six dollars eighteen & three fourth cents interest & cost.
Washington LANCASTER for^{n}.

Shadrach ATKINSON)
for the use &c) Debt
vs.) Jury N°. 2
William BURNAM) We find for the plaintiff ninety one dollars with interest & cost.
Washington LANCASTER for^{n}.

Page 88

Ann TARPLEY)
vs.) Debt
W^{m}. LYON) We find for the plaintiff eighty six dollars interest & cost.
Washington LANCASTER for^{n}.

Shadrach ATKINSON for the)
use of James M. TAYLOR) Debt
vs.)
Thomas JONES &) Jury N°. 2
William BURNAM) We find for the plaintiff two hundred & twenty three dollars with interest & cost. Washington LANCASTER for^{n}.

Warren HART for use &c)
vs.) Debt
Benjamin STEGALL &)
Thos. THOMLING) I confess judgement for fifty three dollars & fifty cents interest & cost. Benj. STEGALL

Ex^{rs}. S. A. HOPKINS)
vs.) Debt
Elijah WALLACE) I confess judgement for one hundred & fifty five dollars eighty five cents & one half interest & cost. Elijah WALLACE

Page 89

Ex^{rs}. Sol. A. HOPKINS) Debt
vs.) Jury N°. 2
Elijah WALLACE) We find for the plaintiff thirty five dollars eighty severn cents & one half interest & cost. Washington LANCASTER for^{n}.

Ladowick LAIRD) Special Action
vs.) Jury N°. 1
Allen TOOKE) We find for the plaintiff the sum of four hundred and eighty nine dollars with cost of suit. Jason BRINSON for^{n}.

Ex^{d}. Stephen W. HARRIS

Court then adjourned untill 9 oclock tomorrow morning.

October 24th 1815. Court met pursuant to adjournment present his Honor Judge HARRIS.

Page 90

Bailey ROBERSON)
vs.) Judgement
Joseph WOOD) Magistrates Court Pulaski County the plaintiff having recovered a final judgement before David BROOM and Bartly M^{c}DANIEL and they having went out of office before they issued execution & John A. WILLIAMS & William WILLIAMS having succeeded them in said District and having refused to issue a fifa on motion, it is ordered that the said John A. & William shew cause tomorrow at nine oclock why they do not issue said fi fa and that a copy of this rule be served on them.

John EASLY for the)
use of Dudly JONES) Fi fa
vs.)
James RAMSEY) The Sheriff having raised the sum of forty seven dollars & twenty cents on the above fi fa ordered that he do pay that amount to Thomas W. HARRIS the plffs. atto.

Page 91

The Grand Jury came into Court & returned the following bills-

The State)
vs.) Ind^{t}. Assault
William RAY) True bill Allen TOOKE forman

The State)
vs.) Assault & battery
Rebecca ROBERTSON) No bill Allen TOOKE forman

The State)
vs.) Ind^{t}. Assault
Sol. FRANKLIN) True bill Allen TOOKE forman

The State)
vs.) Ind^{t}. Assault
William RAY) True bill Allen TOOKE forman

The State)
vs.) Assault & battery
Patrick ROBERTSON) No bill Allen TOOKE forman

Page 92

The State)
vs.) Fi fa
Arch^{d}. LASSETER) A rule nisi having been obtained on the Shff. for him to shew cause why he should not pay over to the atto. of Washington LANCASTER the sum of two hundred & forty nine dollars it being the amount left in his hand (after payment of cost) raised out of the property of Arch^{d}. LASSETER & no sufficient cause having been shewn It is ordered that he do pay over to Thomas W. HARRIS the atto. of Washington LANCASTER the above amount.

William MELTON) Debt
vs.) Jury N°. 2
Leonard STRINGER) We find for the plaintiff the sum of fifty six dollars with interest & cost. Washington LANCASTER for^{n}.

Patrick ROBERTSON)
vs.) Case
Prussia COLE adm^{x}.) Jury N°. 1
of John COLE dec^{d}.) We find in favor of the plaintiff one hundred dollars
with cost of suit. Jason BRINSON for^{n}.

Page 93

George BUCKHANAN) Debt
vs.) Jury N°. 2
Daniel M^{c}LENAN) We find for the plaintiff thirty two dollars & seventy
five cents with interest & cost. Washington LANCASTER for^{n}.

Jeremiah BAKER)
vs. Indorsee) Case
Daniel W. SHINE &) Jury N°. 1
James W. SHINE) We find for the plaintiff one hundred & seventy five
dollars with interest & cost. Jason BRINSON for^{n}.

Allen TOOKE & Co. for)
the use of Allen TOOKE) Debt
vs.) Jury N°. 1
Arch^{d}. LASSETER) We find for the plaintiff fifty one dollars eighty one
& a quarter cents with interest & cost. Jason BRINSON for^{n}.

Allen MARTIN) Case
vs.) Jury N°. 1
Bailey ROBINSON) We find for the plaintiff fifty five dollars with interest &
cost. Jason BRINSON for^{n}.

Page 94

Thomas WOOLDREDGE)
vs. Indorsee) Case
Henry FULGHAM) I confess judgement to plaintiff for forty four
dollars & seventy one cents with interest & cost. Tho. W. HARRIS def^{ts}. atto.

Ex^{rs}. Sol. A. HOPKINS) Debt
vs.) Jury N°. 2
Daniel W. SHINE) We find for the plaintiff fifty nine dollars forty three
cents & three quarters interest & cost. Washington LANCASTER for^{n}.

Arthur & Allen TOOKE)
for the use of John ISLER)
vs.) Case
The Ex^{rs}. & Ex^{tx}. of) Jury N°. 2
Solomon A. HOPKINS dec^{d}.) We find for the plaintiff the sum of two hundred
& sixty six dollars with interest & cost. Washington LANCASTER for^{n}.

Ex^rs. S. A. HOPKINS) Debt
vs.) Jury N°. 1
David APLING) We find for the plaintiff fifty dollars and twenty five cents interest & cost. Jason BRINSON for^n.

Ex^rs. S. A. HOPKINS) Debt
vs.)
James L. PERRY) I confess judgement for one hundred & seventy two dollars eighty seven & a half cents with interest & cost reserving the right of appeal. Robt. RUTHERFORD deft. atty.

Page 95

Ex^rs. Sol. A. HOPKINS) Debt
vs.) Jury N°. 2
Thomas M^cDANIEL et al) We find for the plaintiff one thousand & forty dollars & seventy five cents interest & cost. Washington LANCASTER for^n.

Ex^rs. Sol. A. HOPKINS) Debt
vs.) Jury N°. 2
Jno. A. WILLIAMS &)
James L. PERRY) We find for the plaintiff seventy two dollars & fifty cents interest & cost. Washington LANCASTER for^n.

Ex^rs. Sol. A. HOPKINS) Debt
vs.) Jury N°. 2
Thomas M^cDANIEL) We find for the plaintiff eighty nine dollars fifty one cents & one half interest & cost. Washington LANCASTER for^n.

Cullen WOOTON) Case
vs.) Jury N°. 2
James L. PERRY) I confess judgement to the plantiff in the sum of seventy dollars with interest & cost reserving the right of appeal. James L. PERRY

Nich^s. L. PRISTER)
vs.) Case
Daniel MAGEE) I confess judgement to the plaintiff in the sum of three hundred and seventy five dollars with interest & cost. Daniel MAGEE

Page 96

John A. WILLIAMS)) Pulaski Superior Court
vs.) Divorce) October Term 1815
Hester WILLIAMS))

It appearing to the Court from the Sheriffs return that the defendant is not to be found in said County. It is ordered that service be forfeited? by the next term of this Court the publication of this rule in one of the public gazetts of this circuit at least once a month for three months.

Joel ELLIS)
vs.) Case
Henry SMITH &) Jury N°. 1
Thomas SMITH) We find for the plaintiff the sum of eighty five dollars with
interest & cost. Jason BRINSON for^{n}.

James BUSH)
for the use of) Debt
Thomas BUTLER) Jury N°. 1
vs.)
James RAMSEY) We find for the plaintiff the sum of eighty nine dollars &
sixty two & a half cents with interest & cost. Jason BRINSON for^{n}.

Kinchen DAWSON) Case
vs. bearer) Jury N°. 2
William RAMSEY) We find for the plaintiff thirty five dollars with interest &
cost. W. LANCASTER for^{n}.

Page 97

Jacob SNELL adm^{r}.) Debt
vs.) Jury N°. 2
William RAMSEY)
& James RAMSEY) We find for the plaintiff one hundred & fifty two dollars
with interest & cost. Washington LANCASTER for^{n}.

Thomas BUTLER) Debt
vs.) Jury N°. 1
Archibald LASSETER) We find for the plaintiff forty five dollars & fifty cents
with interest & cost. Jason BRINSON foreman

The Grand Jury came into Court & returned the following bills-

The State)
vs.) Indictment cattle stealing
John TEMPLES) True bill Allen TOOKE for^{n}.

The State)
vs.) Ind^{t}. cattle stealing
John BOLING) True bill Allen TOOKE for^{n}.

The State)
vs.) Indictment cattle stealing
John J. FORD) True bill Allen TOOKE for^{n}.

Lodowick LAIRD)
vs.) Special action on the case
Allen TOOKE) In this case the defendant being dissatisfied with the verdict of the jury comes into court & pays all cost and prays an appeal in terms of the law and gives Arthur TOOKE security.
Test. Turner EVERETT Clk.

Allen TOOKE {LS}
Arthur TOOKE {LS}
E. WALLACE {LS}

Thomas BUTLER)
for the use of)
Joel CRAWFORD) Debt
& Robt. CUMMINS)
vs.)
Shadrach ATKINSON) I confess judgement to the plaintiff for the sum of two hundred & eighty dollars and seventy five cents with interest and cost Octr. 24th 1815.

Shadrach ATKINSON

David WILLIAMS)
vs. indorsee) Case
Shadrack ATKINSON) I confess judgement to the plantiff for the sum of one hundred and seventy one dollars with interest & cost of suit.

Shadrack ATKINSON

Samuel JONES)
vs.) Debt
Shadrack ATKINSON) I confess judgement to the plantiff for the sum of one hundred & eighty four dollars with interest & cost of suit.

Shadrack ATKINSON

Page 99

~~The Court then adjourned untill tomorrow morning 9 oclock.~~

The Ad^{r}. of Micajah H. POWELL)
vs.) Case
William JELKS) Special Jury sworn

1 Allen TOOKE
2 Christopher RHODES
3 Sutton TRULUCK
4 Thomas M^{c}DANIEL
5 George WALKER
6 Michael HORN
7 Joel DAWSON
8 David SNELL
9 Hinchey WARREN
10 William JOHNSTON
11 Robert DANIEL
12 William BUR[N]AM

We find for the defendant with cost of suit. Allen TOOKE foreman

Ex^{d}. Stephen W. HARRIS

The Court then adjourned untill tomorrow morning nine oclock.

Wednesday 25th October 1815. The Court then met agreeable to adjourment.

Georgia) Samuel RATLIFF for the) Rule nisi
Pulaski County) use of Jeffrey MONTFORT) for the
) vs) foreclosure
) John IZLER) of mortgage

Upon the petition of Samuel RATLIFF for the use of Jeffrey MONTFORT praying the foreclosure of the equity of redemption in & to a certain lot or square of land in the twenty fourth district of Wilkinson County when surveyed but now Pulaski known by the number three hundred and thirty one containing two hundred two & one half acres which was mortgaged by John ISLER the better to secure the payment of two notes of hand one of which was for six hundred & fifty dollars due the first of March eighteen hundred & twelve three hundred & forty dollars of which besides interest is yet due & unpaid. On motion of Thomas W. HARRIS attorney for the petitioner it is ordered that unless the principal interest & cost due on said mortgage be paid into Court within twelve months therefrom that the equity of redemption which the mortgager has in & to the mortgaged premises shall be henceforward forever barred & foreclosed and such other proceedings be had thereon as are agreeable to law, and that a copy of this rule be served on the...

Page 101

mortgagor or his special agent at least six months before the money is directed to be paid or publish once a month in one of the public gazetts for twelve months.

Blakley EDINS) Case for mal pros
vs.) Jury N°. 1
Aaron SCARBOROUGH) We find for the plaintiff five hundred dollars with cost of suit.
Jason BRINSON for^{n}.

Thomas BUTLER) Debt
vs.) Jury N°. 2
William LYON) We find for the plaintiff the sum of three hundred & twenty seven dollars fifty four & a half cents with interest & cost.
Washington LANCASTER for^{n}.

Robert DESHAZO) Debt
vs.) Jury N°. 1
James L. PERRY)
& David BROOM) We find for the plaintiff sixty dollars & cents with interest & cost.
Jason BRINSON for^{n}.

Thomas BUTLER) Debt
vs.) Jury N°. 2
John MOSES) We find for the plaintiff the sum of ~~one hundred~~ \sixty two/ dollars & fifty ~~cents three~~ cents with interest & cost.
Washington LANCASTER for^{n}.

Allen TOOKE & Co. for)
the use of Allen TOOKE) Debt
vs.) Jury No. 1
William McCORMICK) We find for the plaintiff forty dollars sixty two & one half cents with interest & cost. Jason BRINSON forn.

Thomas BUTLER) Debt
vs.) Jury No. 2
Wm. McCORMICK) We the jury find for the plaintiffs fifty one dollars six & a quarter cents with interest & cost. Washington LANCASTER forn.

Thomas McDANIEL) Debt
vs.) Jury No. 2
Spire MILLS) We find for the plaintiff fifty three dollars ninety three & three quarter cents with interest & cost. Jason BRINSON forn.

James M. TAYLOR)
vs.) Debt
Benja. MEWBORN) In open Court I confess judgement for twenty eight dollars with interest & cost. T. W. HARRIS pro deft.

Page 103

John A. WILLIAMS for)
the use of Josiah EVERETT)
vs.) Debt
Danl. MAGEE) I confess judgement to the plaintiff for the sum of twenty nine dollars and seventy five cents with interest & cost.
Daniel MAGEE

George BUCKHANAN)
vs.) Debt
Daniel McLEANAN) The defendant Daniel McLENAN with John McLEAN his security comes forward & stays execution in terms of the law.
Daniel McLENNAN {LS}
Test. Turner EVERETT Clk. John McLENNAN {LS}

Thomas WOOLDREDGE)
vs. indorsee) Case
Henry FULGHAM) The defendant Henry FULGHAM with Blakley EDINS his security comes forward & stays execution in terms of the law.
H. FULGHAM {LS}
Test. Turner EVERETT Clk. Blakly EDINS {LS}

Page 104

The Grand Jury came into court and returned the following bills-

The State)
vs.) Ind^{t}. Murder
Archibald LASSETER) True bill against Archibald LASSETER
& James CLARK) No bill against James CLARK
Allen TOOKE foreman

The State)
vs.) Ind^{t}. Petit Larceny
Frederick WOLF) No bill Allen TOOKE for^{n}.

The State)
vs.) Ind^{t}. Cattle Stealing
Thomas TEMPLES) True bill Allen TOOKE for^{n}.

The State)
vs.) Ind^{t}. Cattle Stealing
John BROWN) True bill Allen TOOKE for^{n}.

The State)
vs.) Ind^{t}. assault with intent to ravish
Bartlett BROWN) No bill Allen TOOKE for^{n}.

Page 105

Ex^{rs}. S. A. HOPKINS) Debt
vs.) Jury N°. 1
John PARRIS) We find for the plaintiff twenty six dollars thirty seven and a half cents with interest & cost. Jason BRINSON for^{n}.

Ex^{rs}. Sol. A. HOPKINS)
vs.) Debt
Benj. MEWBORN) In open Court I confess judgement for forty three dollars fifteen & a half cents with interest & cost.
Tho. W. HARRIS Def^{ts}. Atto.

The State)
vs.) Ind^{t}. Cattle Stealing
Thomas TEMPLES) Jury N°. 2

1 William TAYLOR	7 Jesse LIVELY
2 Jacob TAYLOR	8 John BRADSHAW
3 John HARRELL	9 Malikia KELLY
4 Washington LANCASTER	10 Thomas ROGERS
5 William YARBOROUGH	11 Nathan SOWELL
6 Fort ALFORD	12 Asa HARRELL

We the jury find the defendant guilty. Washington LANCASTER foreman

The State) Indt. Mony Stealing
vs.)
William PROCTOR) In this case Christopher EDWARDS & Mary EDWARDS being material witnesses in this case they & each of them do acknowledge themselves bound in the sum of two hundred and fifty dollars and Daniel McLEANAN & John McLENAN their securities in the sum of two hundred & fifty dollars each, conditioned to be void if the said Christopher EDWARDS & Mary EDWARDS do appear at the Superior Court of Pulaski as a witness against said PROCTOR and not to depart without leave of said Court this 25th Octr. 1815.

Christopher EDWARDS {LS}
her
Marey x EDWARDS {LS}
mark
D. McLENNAN {LS}
John McLENNAN {LS}

Test.
Turner EVERETT Clk.

Exd. Stephen W. HARRIS
The Court then adjounrned till nine oclock tomorrow morning.

Page 107

Thursday 26th October 1815. The Court met pursuant to adjourment. Present the honorable Stephen W. HARRIS.

MERRET and ASBURY)
vs.) Fi fa
E. WALLACE Shff. &)
J. RAMSEY) A rule nisi having been obtained for the coroner Wm. YARBOROUGH to shew cause why he should not pay over the money due the said fi fa and <u>know</u> cause having been shewn on motion it is ordered that the said Coroner do pay over the principle and interest of said fi fa instanter to R. RUTHERFORD plaintiffs atto.

The Grand Jury came into Court & returned the following bills-

The State) Indt. Assault
vs.)
Blakly EDINS) No bill Allen TOOKE foreman

The State) Indt. adultery & fornication
vs.)
James L. PERRY &)
Viny HOLLIMAN) True bill Allen TOOKE foreman

Page 108

A rule absolute having been obtained for Wm. YARBOROUGH to pay over instanter the amount of a fi fa against E. WALLACE Sheriff and W. JELKS & J. RAMSEY and he having failed to do so & having absented himself from this

Court on motion it is ordered that he be arrested by the Sheriff of this County for the contempt and be confined in the jail of this County until he pays over in this office or the plfs. atto. the principal & interest of said fi fa.

Abel POLK)
vs.) Fi fa
Elijah WALLACE) On motion it is ordered that the Coroner do return the above fi fa into Court with his actings & doings thereon instanter.

The State) Indictment for cattle stealing &
vs.) verdict of guilty
Thomas TEMPLES) Thomas TEMPLES you will on Saturday next the twenty eighth day of October instant be set in the pillery for two hours between the hours of twelve & three oclock on that day & you will also be publickly whipped on your bare back between the hours of twelve & three oclock on...

Page 109

~~that day~~ Thursday, Friday, & Saturday, the twenty sixth, twenty seventh & twenty eighth day of October instant receiving ~~on each day~~ thirty nine lashes, on each day. You will also be branded on the shoulder with the letter R on Saturday the twenty eighth of October instant between the hours of twelve and one oclock and be imprisoned for four days and then you will be discharged upon payment of costs.

The Grand Jury came into Court & returned the following bills-

The State)
vs.) Indt. passing a counterfeit bank bill
William NEIL) True bill Allen TOOKE forn.

The State)
vs.) Indt. assault
William MUSGROVE) No bill Allen TOOKE forn.

The State)
vs.) Indt. assault
Kinchen DAWSON) No bill Allen TOOKE forn.

Page 110

J. BROWN for the use)
of E. WALLACE) Judgement on a
vs.) promissory note
Theodrick MONTFORT)
& Co. Indorsor) No cause having been shewn why Wm. W. WILLIAMS the presiding Justice in the above case would not deliver said note to the defendant on motion of council it is ordered that said note be delivered upon the defendant giving said Justice a receipt for said note.

Blakly EDINS)
vs.) Mal pros
Aaron SCARBOROUGH) In this case the defendant Aaron SCARBOROUGH being dissatisfied with the verdict of the Jury comes into Court & pays all cost and prays an appeal in terms of the law and gives James DEES security.

Aaron SCARBROUGH {LS}
Test. Turner EVERETT Clk. James DEES {LS}

Page 111

The State)
vs.) Ind^{t}. fornication
Joseph COOPER) The defendant Joseph COOPER acknowledges himself bound to his Excellency the Governor in the sum of two hundred dollars and Colson ADAMS his security in the sum of two hundred dollars also - conditioned to be void if the said Joseph COOPER do appear at the next Superior Court to be held in & for the County of Pulaski on the fourth Monday in April next, and not to depart thence without leave of said Court. Joseph COOPER {LS}
Test. Turner EVERETT Clk. Colson ADAMS {LS}

The State)
vs.) Ind^{t}. Cattle stealing
John J. FORD) The defendant John J. FORD acknowledges himself bound to his Excellency the Governor in the sum of five hundred dollars and Joseph GRAYHAM & Green? GRAYHAM his securities in the sum of two hundred & fifty dollars each, conditioned to be void if the said John J. FORD do appear at the next Superior Court to be held in & for the County of Pulaski on the fourth Monday in April next and not to depart thence without leave of said Court.

John J. FORD {LS}
Test Turner EVERETT Clk. Joseph GRAHAM {LS}
G. G. GRAHAM {LS}

Page 112

Joel SIMANTON?)
plaintiff in execution) Trial of Right of Property
vs.) Jury N°. 1
William LYON) We find the property in dispute subject to the executions.

Jason BRINSON for^{n}.

The State) Assault & battery
vs.) Jury N°. 1
John J. FORD) We find the defendant guilty.
Fined ten dollars. Jason BRINSON for^{n}.

The State)
vs.) Ind[t]. Assault
William RAY) William RAY acknowledges himself bound to his Excellency the Governor in the sum of four hundred and his security John WILCOX acknowledges himself bound also in the sum of four hundred dollars, conditioned to be void if the said William RAY do appear at the next Superior Court to be held in and for the County of Pulaski on the fourth Monday in April next, and not to depart therefrom without leave of said Court.

his
William x RAY {LS}
mark

Test. Turner EVERETT Clk. John WILLCOX {LS}

Ex[d]. Stephen W. HARRIS

Page 113

The Court then adjourned untill tomorrow morning seven oclock.

Friday 27th October 1815. The Court then met pursuant to adjournment. The following persons were drawn to serve as Grand Jurors at the next term of this Court.

1 Stephen MITCHELL S[r].
2 Charnick THARP
3 Daniel COLE
4 Daniel MAGEE
5 William JELKS
6 George G. GAINS
7 Charles CARDIN S[r].
8 Thomas PHILIPS
9 Mark MASON
10 Daniel DYKES
11 Sands STANLY
12 Christopher M[c]RAE
13 James BALTHROP
14 Jason BRINSON
15 Jacob SNELL
16 William HORNE
17 John GILSTRAP
18 David GIRTMAN
19 Robert THOMPSON
20 Thomas SMITH
21 Joab HORNE
22 William HILLIARD
23 Daniel W. SHINE
24 Gideon MAYO
25 John RHODES
26 Stephen GATLIN
27 Bolling SWEARINGAME
28 Needham STEPHENS
29 Blakly EDINS
30 Washington LANCASTER
31 Benjamin HARVY
32 John DONALSON

Page 114

The following persons were drawn to serve on the Petitt Jury at the next term of this Court:

1 Thomas ADKINSON
2 Richard STORY
3 John JONES
4 William PATE
5 Isaac HARRELL
6 James SALTER
7 Jesse FENN
8 Arthur SHUFFIELD
9 Moses SUTTON
10 Barnet G. THOMAS

11 Marmaduke KENT
12 John BRUTON
13 Patrick McGRIFF
14 Isham SHUFFIELD
15 Benjamin JOHNSTON
16 John ROGERS
17 John BIRD
18 David BADSON?
19 Robert MATTHEWS
20 Jacob PARKERSON
21 Thomas BAGGETT
22 Matthew SMITH
23 Moses HARRIS
24 Harvey HARRISON
25 William JOHNS
26 Bryant SHUFIELD
27 Lewis BAGGET
28 Thomas EVERETT
29 Jesse JUMP
30 George FOLSOM
31 Charles MAYO
32 John OPREY?
33 Benjamin MEWBORN
34 John COLEMAN
35 Reubin WARREN
36 James GALAMORE
37 Moses KIRKLAND
38 John B. BROWN
39 Samuel PERKINS
40 Thomas ROGERS
41 Charles CREECH
42 Daniel HENDERSON
43 John DANIEL
44 Samuel HART
45 Isaac SMITH
46 Etheldred HARRELL
47 Thomas SMITH Jr.
48 Randall RICHARDSON
49 William LITTLE
50 Zacheriah DAVIS
51 Nathan MATTOX
52 Allen PERKINS

Page 115

Exd. Stephen W. HARRIS
The Court then adjourned untill Court in course. Turner EVERETT Clk.

Exr. Solomon A. HOPKINS)
vs.) Debt
Thomas McDANIEL) ~~The defendant Thomas McDANIEL~~ In this case the defendant Thomas McDANIEL being dissatisfied with the verdict of the jury comes forward and pays all cost and prays an appeal in terms of the law and gives Neil McALPIN security this 27th October 1815.

Thomas McDANIEL
his
Test. Turner EVERETT Clk. Neil x McAPLIN
mark

Page 116

The State)
vs.) Indictment Cattle Stealing
Thomas TEMPLES) The defendant Thomas TEMPLES acknowledges himself bound to his Excellency the Governor in the sum of five hundred dollars and James TEMPLES his security acknowledges himself bound likewise in the sum of five hundred dollars also conditioned to be void if the said Thomas TEMPLES do appear at the next Superior Court to be held in & for the County of Pulaski on the fourth

Monday in April next, and not to depart thence without leave of said Court, this 30th October 1815.

his
Thomas x TEMPLES {LS}
mark
his
Test. Turner EVERETT Clk. James x TEMPLES {LS}
mark

Patrick ROBERTSON)
vs.) Case
Prutia COLE admx.)
John COLE decd.) In this case the defendant Prutia COLE being dissatisfied with the verdict of the Jury comes forward & pays all cost and prays an appeal in terms of the law and gives Theodrick MONTFORT security this 31st October 1815.

Prussia COLE
Theodk. MONTFORT

Page 117, April 1816

~~October~~ April 22 1816. ~~The court met pursuant to adjournment present his Honor Judge HARRIS.~~ Monday 22nd of April 1816 the Superior Court for the County of Pulaski met agreeable to law. Present his Honor Judge HARRIS.

The following persons appeared and were sworn to serve as Grand Jurors who made choice of Stephen GATLIN for their foreman.

1 Stephen GATLIN for.
2 Stephen MITCHELL
3 Daniel MAGEE
4 William JELKS
5 Thomas PHILLIPS
6 Daniel DYKES
7 Christopher McRAE
8 James BALTRIP
9 Jason BRINSON
10 John GILLSTRAP
11 David GIRTMAN
12 Thomas SMITH
13 William HILLIARD
14 William HORNE
15 Daniel W. SHINE
16 Needham STEPHENS
17 Washington LANCASTER
18 John DONALSON
19 Sands STANLEY
20 Daniel COLE
21 Robt. THOMPSON

Page 118

The following persons were called and sworn to serve as Pettit Jurors during the present term. Pettit Jury No. 1

1 Thomas ADKINSON
2 John JONES
3 William PATE
4 James SALTER
5 Jessee FENN
6 ~~Arthur SHUFFIELD~~
Ruben WARREN
7 Moses SUTTON
8 Isham SHUFFIELD
9 John ROGERS
10 Thomas BAGGOT
11 Jessee JUMP
12 George FOLSOM

Pettit Jury N°. 2

1 ~~Ruben WARREN~~
Samuel HART
2 James GALLIMORE
3 Moses KIRKLAND
4 Etheldred HOWEL
5 Randol RICHARDSON
6 William LITTLE
7 Zachariah DAVIS
8 Nathaniel MATTOX
9 Charles MAYO
10 William JOHNSON
11 Lewis BAGGOT
12 John DANIEL

Thomas BUTLER for the)
use of Joel CRAWFORD)
& Robert CUMMINS)
vs.)
Shadrack ADKINSON) In this case it appearing to the Court that there was a mistake made at the last term of this Court in entering up judgement it is ordered that the same be corrected up nunc pro tunck.

Page 119

Ex^{rs}. of Sollomon A. HOPKINS) Debt
vs.) Jury N°. 1
Danl. CORNWAL) We find for the plaintiff ninety five dollars six cents & a quarter interest & cost. Ruben WARREN forem.

Thomas M^{c}DANIEL) Case
vs.) Jury N°. 1
Samuel FOWL) We \the Jury/ find for the plaintiff fifty six dollars & cost of suit. Reubin WARREN foreman

The Grand Jury returned into Court & returned the following bill

The State)
vs.) Ind^{t}. Cattle stealing
Benjn. JOHNSON) No bill Stephen GATLIN foreman

The Grand Jury came into Court & returned the following bill

The State)
vs.) Ind^{t}. Larceny
Joseph COFUSE?) No bill Stephen GATLIN foreman

Page 120

The Grand Jury returned into Court & returned the following bills

The State) Retailing Spirituous liquors
vs.) without a licence
Isaac KIRKSEY) True bill Stephen GATLIN foreman

On Jury N°. 1, Thomas ROGERS sworn in the place of John ROGERS & Reuben ROLAND in the place of George FOLSOM.

Daniel MAGEE b^{r}.)
vs.) Case
JONES & EVERRETT) We the Jury find for the plaintiff seventy two dollars with interest & cost of suit. Reubin WARREN foreman
Nine? dollars cost paid in this case to Clk.

Page 121-22 torn out; Page 123

Burrel PHILLIPS)
vs.) Trover & conversion
Ephraim PHILLIPS) We the Jury find for the plaintiff five hundred dollars which may be discharged by the delivery of the negroe Buck in ten days & cost of suit &c. Charles MAYO foreman

Hamlin COOK)
vs.) Ind^{t}. Ass^{t}.
Turner EVERETT) Dismissed.

Ex^{d}. Stephen W. HARRIS
Court then adjourned untill tomorrow morning 8 oclock.

Page 124

Tuesday April 23rd 1816. The Court met pursuant to adjournment. Rule nisi. Upon the petition of the Commissioners of the Court House & Jail of said County – successors in office, to the Town of Hartford by Richard JONES their attorney, praying the forclosure of the equity of redemption in & to a certain lot of land in the town of Hartford in said County known & distinguished in the plan of said town by number four in square letter E containing one half acre, which was mortgaged by Robert GRAHAM to said commissioners or their successors in office for the securing the payment of the sum of fifty one dollars; On motion, it is ordered that the said Robert GRAHAM do pay the amount of principal interest & costs due on said mortgage into the Clerks office of this Court within twelve months from this date or the equity of redemption in & to said mortgaged premises shall be hereforth barred & forever forclosed, according to the statute in such cases made & provided, & it is further ordered that a copy of this rule be published once a month for 12 months, or served upon the mortgagor or his special agent at least six months previous to the expiration of the time in which the money is required to be paid.

Page 125

G e o r g i a) Superior Court April term 1816
Pulaski County) Rule nisi

Upon the petition of the Commissioners of the Court House & Jail of said County by Richard JONES their attorney, praying the foreclosure of the equity of redemption in and to a certain lot of land in the town of Hartford in said County known & distinguished in the plan of said town by number forty one in square letter W on Lancaster Street containing one half acre which was mortgaged by William GARLINGTON to said commissioners for the better securing the payment of ninety dollars; On motion it is ordered that the said William GARLINGTON or his representatives do pay the principal interest & cost into the Clerks office of this ~~Superior~~ Court within twelve months from this date or otherwise the equity of redemption in and to said premises shall be henceforth and forever foreclosed according to the statute in such cases made & provided and it is further ordered that this rule be published in one of the gazettes of this State once a month for twelve months or served upon the mortgager or his agent at least six months previous to the expiration of the time in which the money is directed to be paid &c.

Page 126

Jury No. 1. Abram YERTA appeared and was sworn in place of Isham SHUFFIELD & ~~Daniel McCLENNAN~~ in the place of James SALTER.

Georgia) By the Honorable Stephen W. HARRIS Judge
Pulaski County) of the Superior Court of the Ocmulgee Cirquit

To Jason BRINSON Justice of the Peace for Captain LESTERs company district in the County aforesaid - Greeting. It having been made to appear to the satisfaction of the Court that a judgement was obtained in the Justices Court in said company district before said Jason BRINSON Esqr. against Zachariah BUSBY in favor of Elias WOODRUFF for the use of Richard JONES and that said BRINSON has hitherto refused & still refuses to issue execution alledgeing as a reason for such refusal the aleviating acts of this State, It is therefore ordered that a Writ of Mandamas do issue by the Clerk requiring the said Jason BRINSON Esqr. to issue execution forthwith.

Page 127

Wm. H. GROSS for the)
use of James EVERETT) Case
vs.)
Shadrack ATKINSON) I confess judgement to the plaintiff for the sum of one hundred & twenty dollars principal & seventeen dollars interest & cost of suit.

Joel CRAWFORD defts. atto.

Wm. PHELPS) Jury No. 2
vs.) Assumpsit
Chappel BOND) We find for the defendant cost of suit.

Charles MAYO foreman

Thomas BUTLER)
vs.) Debt
Nathan SEWALL) We find for the plaintiff forty six dollars sixty eight cents & $^{1}/_{4}$ of a cent with interest & cost. Rubin WARREN foreman

Page 128

Burrell PHILLIPS)
vs.) Trover & convertion
Epharim PHILLIPS) In this case the defendant being dissatisfied with the verdict of the Jury comes forward & pays all costs and prays an appeal in terms of the law Nathaniel MERCER security who comes forward and subscribes himself as such.
Ephraim PHILIPS
Edward SMITH Clk.
Nathl. MERCER

Robert HILL)
vs.) Debt
John M^{c}RAE) We find for the plaintiff thirty dollars & thirty three cents with int. & cost. Rubin WARREN foreman

The Grand Jury came into Court & returned the following bills:

The State)
vs.) Asst. & battery
Joseph WOOD) True bill Stephen GATLIN foreman

The State)
vs.)
~~John~~ Thomas LIVELY) Ind^{t}. Asst. & battery
James PITMAN)
Kire? RODGERS)
& John SHATEEN?) True bill Stephen GATLIN foreman

Page 129

Mary HIGGS br.)
vs.) Case
Jordan DEES) I confess judgement to the plaintiff for the sum of sixty four dollars & eighty nine cents with interest & cost.
Rich^{d}. JONES def^{ts}. atto.

Adm^{rs}. of Joshua HARRIS) Jury N°. 1
vs.) Debt Ex^{m}.
John PARRIS) We find for the plaintiff thirty two dollars with interest & cost. Ruben WARREN foreman

Admrs. of Joshua HARRIS) " No. 1
vs.) Case Exm.
John PARRIS) We find for the plaintiff thirty three dollars thirty seven & a half cents with interest & cost. Ruben WARREN foreman

James BARROW)
vs.) Debt
William HORNE) I confess judgement to the plaintiff for the sum of one hundred & twelve dollars & |6| cents with interest & cost.
Stays execution altenal? sixty days. Seabourn JONES defts. atty.

Page 130

MONTFORT & EVERETT for)
the use of Theodk. MONTFORT) Jury No. 1
vs.) Debt
Benjamin MEUBORN) We the jurors find for the plaintiff two hundred and fifty eight \dols./ eighty seven & a half cents with interest and cost.
Reuben WARREN foreman

Joseph COOPER) Jury No. 2
vs.) Trespass vi et armis
Christopher EDWARDS) We the Jurors find for the plaintiff twenty five dollars & cost of suit. Charles MAYO foreman

Edward LASSITER) Jury No. 1
vs.) Case
James L. PERRY) We find for the plaintiff one hundred and seventy six dollars with interest & cost. Ruben WARREN foreman

Page 131

Edward LASSITER)
vs.) Verdict for the plaintiff
James L. PERRY) The plaintiff will take notice that on the first day of the next term or so soon thereafter as council can be heard he will be required to shew why the verdict shall not be set aside and a verdict ~~to wit~~ rendered in favor of defendt. ~~to wit~~ on the following grounds to wit 1st for that the contract laid is one not made between the parties and the Court permitted one proved which was made between Archibald LASSITER of agent of plaintiff & defendant.

Charles Y. CALDWELL)
vs. bearer) Case
Richd. McGRIFF) Settled & cost paid.

Henry BRITT bearer) Case
vs.) Jury No.
John McRAE) We find for the plaintiff one hundred dollars with interest & cost. Reubin WARREN foreman

In open Court I confess judgement to the plaintiff for the sum of thirty four dollars & forty three & three fourths cents with interest & cost.

Seabourn JONES Def[ds]. atty.

Henry TOLK bearer)
vs.) Case
William HORNE) In open Court I confess judgement to the plaintiff for the sum of thirty four dollars & forty three & three fourth cents with interest & cost.

Seabourn JONES Def[s]. atty.

Mary RABSOM)
vs.) Debt
William GARBETT) I confess judgement to the plaintiff in the sum of two hundred & sixty six dollars and thirty one cents with interest and cost with liberty of an appeal. W[m]. GARBETT

Jacob SNELL surviving admini-)
strator of W[m]. A. HARPER dec[d].) N[o]. 2
for the use of Daniel RHODES) Case
vs.)
W[m]. RAMSEY surv[g]. promisor) We find for the plaintiff ninety dollars & with interest & cost. Charles MAYO foreman

Page 133-34 torn out; Page 135

The Grand Jury came returned into Court and returned the following bill:

The State)
vs.) Assault & battery
Christopher EDWARDS) True bill Stephen GATLIN foreman

Theodrick MONTFORT)
vs.) Case
William WILLIAMS)
& Jacob SPICKARD) We find for the plaintiff twenty five dollars with interest and cost of suit. Reuben WARREN foreman

Appeared in Court Mr. John ROGERS and took his seat on Jury N[o]. 2.

James M. TAYLOR)
adm[r]. of the estate of)
Micajah H. POWEL) Case
vs.)
John M[c]LENAN) We find for the plaintiff forty three dollars & fifty cents with interest and cost. Reuben WARREN foreman

John M^c^RAE)
vs.) Case
James L. PERRY) Nonsuit

John M^c^CORMIC)
vs.) Case
Edward SMITH) We the jury find for the plaintiff fifty dollars with cost of suit.
Charles MAYO foreman

Robert THOMPSON)
vs.) Debt
William WINN) We find for the plaintiff thirty two dollars and sixty cents with interest & cost.
Charles MAYO foreman

Robert DESHAZO)
vs. Indorsee) Case
Murdock M^c^LEOD) We find for the plaintiff seventy five dollars with interest & cost.
Charles MAYO foreman

Exrs. of Solomon A. HOPKINS)
vs.) Case
William RAY) I confess judgement to the plaintiff for the sum of one hundred and ninety one dollars and ninety one & three fourth cents with interest & cost.
his
William x RAY
mark

Page 137

Henry F. SIMMONS)
vs. br.) Case
John WILLCOX) I confess judgement to the plaintiff for the sum of one hundred and forty five dollars with interest & cost.
Thomas W. HARRIS defts. atty.

Robert CUMMINS)
vs. Indorsee) Case
James A. EVERET) We find for the plaintiff one hundred and thirty one dollars with interest & cost.
Charles MAYO foreman

John & Thomas LAWSON)
vs.) Debt
James L. PERRY &)
William PERRY) We find for the plaintiff Thomson LAWSON survivor the sum of one hundred eighty \eight/ dollars with interest & cost.
Charles MAYO foreman

The State)
vs.) Murder
John DONOLSON) True Bill Stephen GATLIN foreman

Georgia) Superior Court April Term 1816
Pulaski County) Rule nisi

Upon the petition of the commissioners of the Town of Hartford |aka| of the Court house & jail of said County by their attorney Richard JONES praying the foreclosure of the equity of redemtion in and to all that lott of land situated in the Town of Hartford known in plan of said Town by No. one in square letter I on Broad Street containing one half acre which was mortgaged by Hugh ALSTON the said commissioners for the better securing the payment of the sum of one hundred & forty one dollars - on motion it is ordered that the said Hugh ALSTON do pay the amount of principal interest & cost into the Clerks office of this Court within twelve months from this date otherwise the equity of redemption in and to said mortgaged premises will be thenceforth bared & forever foreclosed according to the statute in such cases made & provided and it is further ordered that a copy of this rule be published in one of the gazettes of this State once a month for ~~at~~ twelve months from this date or served on the mortgager or his agent for at least six months previous to the ~~time~~ expiration of the time in which the money is ordered to be paid.

Page 139

Georgia) The Superior Court April Term 1816
Pulaski County) Rule nisi

Upon the petition of the commissioners of the Court house & jail of said County successors of the commissions of the Town of Hartford by Richard JONES their attorney praying the foreclosure of the equity of redemption on and to a certain lott of land situated in the Town of Hartford in said County known in plan of said Town by by number three in square letter A containing one half acre which was mortgaged by George W. DANIEL to said commissioners for the better securing the payment of the sum of fifty six dollars - on motion it is ordered that the said George W. DANIEL do pay the amount of principal interest & cost into the Clerks office of this Court within the term of twelve months from this date or otherwise the equity of redemption in and to said mortgaged premises will be henceforth barred and forever foreclosed according to the statute in such case made & provided & it is further ordered that a copy of said rule be published in one of the gazettes of this State once a month for twelve months or served on the mortgager or his agent at least six months previous to the expiration of the time in which the money is ordered to be paid.

Page 140

Georgia) Superior Court April Term 1816
Pulaski County) Rule nisi

Upon the commissioners of the Court house and jail of said County praying the foreclosure of the equity of redemption in and to two certain lots of land in the Town of Hartford in said County one of which is known in the plan of said Town by number three in square letter C, containing one half acre the other by number six in same square containing the same which was mortgaged by Martin HARDIN to the said commissioners for the securing the payment of four hundred and ninety six dollars - on motion of Richard JONES attorney for the petitioners it is ordered that the said Martin HARDIN pay the amount of principal interest & cost due on said mortgage into the Clerks office of this ~~Superior~~ Court within twelve months from this date or otherwise the equity of redemption in and to said mortgaged premises will be thenceforth barred and forever foreclosed according to the statute in such case made & provided and it is further ordered that a copy of this rule be published in one of the publick gazettes of this State once a month for twelve months or served on the mortgager or his special agent at least six months previous to the the time within which the money is ordered to be paid.

Page 141

Georgia) April Term 1816
Pulaski County) Rule nisi

Upon the petition of the Town of Hartford, alias of the Court house & jail of said County by Richard JONES their attorney praying the foreclosure of the equity of redemption in and to a certain lot of land in the Town of Hartford in said County known in plan of said Town by number two in square letter B, containing one half acre which was mortgaged by James A. EVERETT & John MONTFORT to said commissioners for the better securing the payment of the sum of three hundred & eleven dollars - on motion it is ordered that said James A. EVERETT and John MONTFORT do pay the amount of principal interest & cost into the Clerks office of this Court within the term of twelve months from this date or otherwise the equity of redemption in and to said mortgaged premises will be henceforth barred and forever foreclosed according to the statute in such case made & provided and it is further ordered that a copy of this rule be published in one of the publick gazettes of this State once a month for twelve months or served on the mortgager or their agents at least six months previous to the expiration of the time in which the money is ordered to be paid.

Page 142

Georgia) Superior Court April Term 1816
Pulaski County) Rule nisi

Upon the petition of the commissioners Court house & jail of said County successors in office of the commirs. of the Town of Hartford by Richard JONES their atty. praying the foreclosure of the equity of redemption in and to a certain lott of land in this Town of Hartford in said County known and distinguished in the plan of said Town by number three in square letter B, containing one half acre which was mortgaged by James GRAHAM to said commissioners & their successors in office for the better securing the payment of the sum of one hundred & two dollars - on motion it is ordered that unless the said James GRAHAM do pay the amount of principal interest & cost due on said mortgaged premises into the Clerks office of this Court within twelve months from this date the equity of redemption in and to said mortgaged premises be thenceforth & forever barred and foreclosed and it is further ordered that a copy of this rule be published in one of the gazettes of this State once a month for twelve months or served on the mortgager or his special agent at least six months previous to the expiration of the time in which the money is ordered to be paid.

It appearing to the Court that there is money in the hands of the Sherriff being an overplus? from the sale of a house & lott sold to satisfy executions against Thomas A. HILL and subject to satisfy the executions against William LYON - On motion it is ordered that the said Sherriff do pay over the balance in his hands to the said executions against William LYON now in his hands.

William RAY)
vs.) Attachment
Neal McALPIN) Neal McALPIN being sworn as garnisher in the above case & having filed his affidavit in the Clerks office of this Court & a verdict having been obtained in the above case On motion it is ordered that judgement be signed against both the defendant & said Neal McALPIN garnisher according to his affidavit or the amount admitted to be admitted to be due by said affidavit.

~~Robert HILL)~~
~~vs.)~~
~~John McRAE)~~ Exd. S. W. HARRIS

Page 144

William CURETON)
vs.) Case
Sands STANLEY) Dismissed

William RAY)
vs.) Attachment
Edmond HOGAN) We find for the plaintiff fifty dollars with interest & cost.
Rubin WARREN foreman

Exr. Micajah H. POWELL)
vs. respt.) Case
William JELKS appt.) It appearing to the Court that the appellants counsel omitted at the last term to sign judgement for costs against the respondent, it is on motion ordered that said counsel do sign judgement at this term in said case, nunc pro tunc.

Appeared and was sworn and took his seat on Jury No. 1 in place of William PATE.

John A. WILLIAMS)
vs.) Divorce
Hester WILLIAMS) In this case it appearing to the Court that the original bill has been lost out of the office of the Clerk of this Court ordered that plaintiffs council be permited to substitute a copy in lue of the original.

The State)
vs.) For passing counterfeit bank bills
William NEIL) William NEAL acknowledges himself bound to his Excellency the Governor and his successors in office in the sum of one thousand dollars and his security Charles MAYO and Lewis HOLLAND in the sum of five hundred each, conditioned to be void if the said William NEAL do appear at the next Superior Court to be held in and for the County of Pulaski on the fourth Monday in October next and not depart therefrom without the leave of the Court then & there to answer to a bill of indictment to be preferd. against him by the Solisitor Genl. for passing a counterfeit bank bill, this 23rd day of April 1816.

W^{m}. NEIL { }
Edward SMITH Clk. Charles MAYO { }
Lewis HOLLAND { }

William GARBETT adm^{r}.)
of Brockenberry ANDREWS) Trover and convertion
vs.)
Samuel HART) We find for the defendant with cost.
Rubin WARREN foreman

Page 146

John A. WILLIAMS)
vs.) Divorce
Hester WILLIAMS) It appearing to the Court that from the return of the Sherriff that the defendant in the above case is not to be found in this County Ordered that service be perfected by publishing this rule once a month for three months in one of the gazetes within this cirquit.

Ex^{rs}. of Sol. A. HOPKINS)
vs.) Verdict
James L. PERRY) It appearing to the Court that in signing judgement in the above case an error has been made by which the plaintiffs demand was dimished upwards of one hundred dollars and that an execution has issued pursuant to said eroneous judgement it is on motion of plaintiffs council ordered that said execution be returned to the Clerks office and the said erroneous judgement be corrected and an alias fi[e]ri facias issue for the balance of said debt now truly & justly due.

The State)
vs.) Stabing
Archibald DANIEL) No bill Stephen GATLIN foreman

Page 147

The State) Assault & battery
vs.) Plea of guilty
Christopher EDWARDS) Ordered that said Christopher EDWARDS pay a fine of twenty five dollars & be discharged on payment of cost.

The State) Assault & battery
vs.) Plea of guilty
Joseph WOOD) Whereupon it is ordered that said Joseph WOOD pay a fine of ~~twenty~~ five dollars & be discharged on payment of cost.

The State)
vs.)
Thomas STANTON) Ind^{t}. Assault & battery
Hezekiah WOOD &)
John CHASTAIN) Thomas STANTON, Hezekiah WOOD & John CHASTAIN acknowledge themselves bound to his Excellency the Governor & his successors in office in the sum of three hundred dollars and James CHASTAIN & Jesse LIVELY their securities in the sum of two hundred and fifty dollars each, conditioned that if the said Thomas STANTON, Hezekiah WOOD & John CHASTAIN do appear at the next Superior Court to be held in and for the County of Pulaski on the fourth Monday in October next & not depart therefrom without the liberty of the Court this obligation \then/ to be void.

Thomas STANTON { }
his
Hezekiah x WOOD { }
mark
James M. CHASTAIN { }
his
Jessee x LIVELY { }
mark

Attest
Edward SMITH Clk.

Page 148

The following persons were drawn to serve as Grand Jurors at the next term:

1 John A. WILLIAMS
2 Elijah WALLACE
3 Edward BLACKSHEAR
4 William M^{c}CORMACK
5 Joel DAWSON
6 Micahel HORN Junr.
7 James CLARK
8 ~~William B~~
Thomas JOHNSON Senr.
9 James S. IVEY
10 Isaac BUCKHALTER
11 Daniel P. SNELL
12 George WALKER
13 Joseph B. BRYAN
14 John DEES
15 Henry FULGHAM
16 Hinchey WARREN
17 John B. PACKER
18 Simon BARDIN
19 William YARBROUGH Senr.
20 Orandatus WATSON
21 Daniel RIGGIN
22 Thomas MILLS (laddler)
23 Thomas HOWELL
24 John GRINSTEAD
25 Furney F. GATLIN
26 Richard H. THOMAS
27 Gideon KELLAM
28 Thomas M^{c}GRIFF
29 Abraham YERTA
30 William ISLER
31 Joseph SESSIONS
32 Turner EVERETT

The following persons were drawn to serve as Petit Jurors at the next term

1 John ROSIER
2 John McCORMAC
3 James WILLIAMS
4 Haywood JONES
5 Ezekial JERNIGAN
6 Umphrey POSEY
7 Nathan SOWELL
8 Thomas WORSLEY
9 Josiah CASON
10 James CRABB
11 Joel WALKER
12 Edward BRYAN
13 Arthur TOOKE
14 John NELSON
15 Wm. YARBROUGH Junr.
16 William WHIGGAM
17 Joseph RIGGIN
18 Nicholas BAGGETT
19 John PIERCE
20 John McCORMAC [#2]
21 Wiley WILLIAMS
22 John LEE
23 Thomas CARDIN
24 Zion DAVIS
25 John MOSES
26 Levi HARRELL
27 Dixon JELKS
28 Philip WHICHARD
29 Kinchen DAWSON
30 Elijah BARKER
31 Jessee HARRELL
32 Asa HARRELL
33 Nimrod PHILIPS
34 Moses GIDDINS
35 Amos WHEELER
36 John TAYLOR
37 John JONES Junr.
38 Lawrence FOLSOM
39 William PHILIPS
40 Zela PULLIN
41 Alexander VARNER
42 Frederick WOOLF
43 John BRADSHAW
44 Henry MORRIS
45 John BARTHAM
46 John HAGAN
47 William HARRELL
48 John STEGALL
49 Noah CALHOON
50 Robert DEWETT
51 Jacob HARRELL
52 John HARRELL

Page 150

The State) Indt. Assault & battery
vs.) A plea of guilty
William RAY) Ordered that William RAY pay a fine of ten dollars & be discharged on payment of costs.

The State) Indt. Assault & battery
vs.) & a plea of guilty
William RAY) Ordered that the said William RAY pay a fine of five dollars & be discharged on payment of costs.

Mason KIMMY for)
the use of Allen CARR) Case
vs.) or Debt
Henry SHEPPARD) Elisha FARNEL the bail of defendant appears in open Court and surrenders his principal Henry SHEPPARD and prays an exoneration whereupon it is ordered that he be discharged from his said securityship.

Chloa PATE)
vs.) Fi fa
Asa PIPKIN) The Sherriff having raised the sum of nineteen dollars & twenty cents in this case under executions of a younger date, Ordered that he do pay over to plaintiff in the above case or her order the sum so raised.

Page 151

Mason KIMMEY for)
the use of Allen CARR) Debt
vs.)
Henry SHEPPARD)

Daniel MAGEE bearer)
vs.) Case
JONES & EVERRITT) In this case the defendants come forward pays cost & prays a stay of execution sixty days which is granted & James CLARK enters himself as security.

his
Haywood x JONES
mark
Jas. M. TAYLOR

Robert DESHAZO) Case &
vs. Indorsee) bail
Sands STANLEY) In this case the Sherriff having omited to take any bail ordered that he be considered & deemed as bail in the said case.

Mary HIGGS bearer)
vs.) Case
Jordan DEES) I confess judgement to the plaintiff for the sum of sixty four dollars & eighty nine cents with interest & cost.

Rich[d]. JONES Plffs.[!] Atty.

Page 152

The State) Ind[t]. retailing spirituous liquors
vs.) without licence
Isaac KIRKSEY) Isaac KIRKSEY acknowledges himself indebted to his Excellency the Governor & his successors in office in the sum of four hundred dollars & James CHASTAIN his security in the sum of two hundred dollars conditioned that if the said Isaac KIRKSEY be and appear at the next Superior Court to be held in and for the County of Pulaski on the fourth Monday in October next & not depart therefrom without the leave of said Court then and in that case this obligation to be void.

Isaac KIRKSEY
James M. CHASTAIN

Attest Edward SMITH Clk.

Benjamin HARVEY)
vs.) Trespass vi et armis
Allen SCARBOROUGH) We find for plaintiff by consent of parties twenty five dollars with cost of suit.

Tom PHILLIPS foreman

The State)
vs.) Murder
John DONOLDSON) We find the traverser not guilty.
Saml. FOWL foreman

Page 153

Rule nisi. Upon the petition of Benjn. HAYS stateing that the original deed for lott number one hundred and forty one in the twenty second district of Wilkinson now Pulaski County from Stephen LAWRENCE to Joseph DENSON dated the twenty eighth of December eighteen hundred and ten is lost or so mislaid that it cannot now be found and he haveing prayed the Court for the establishment of the said copy in lieu of the lost original; On motion it is ordered that the said copy be established in lieu of the lost original deed on or before the first day of the next term unless cause be shewn to the contrary and that a copy of this rule be published in one of the publick gazettes ~~of~~ once a month for six months.

Georgia) Rule nisi
Pulaski County) Upon the petition of William S. BATTLE for the use of John W. BATTLE stateing that Drew DEES on the twelfth day of October eighteen hundred and fifteen made and executed his certain deed of ~~conveyance~~ mortgage for a certain tract of land number one hundred & thirty three in...

Page 154

in the twenty first district Wilkinson County now Pulaski in favor of the said William the better to secure the payment of two notes of hand given by said ~~William~~ Drew to said William on the thirteenth day of Novem^{r}. eighteen hundred and ten and bearing interest from said date for four hundred dollars each \one/ made payable one year after date and the other two years after date and praying the foreclosure of the equity of redemption which the said Drew has in and to said morgaged premises and it appearing to the Court that said notes are entirely unpaid, On motion of Thomas W. HARRIS attorney for the petitioner it is ordered that the principal interest and cost due on said mortgaged be paid into the Clerks office ~~of~~ within twelve months herefrom or that the equity of redemption in and to said mortgaged premises be henceforward for ever \barrd &/ foreclosed and the other usual proceedings be had according to law and that a copy of this rule be published in one of the gazettes of this State twelve months or be served on the mortgager or his special agent...

Page 155

or attorney at least six months before the money is directed to be paid into Court.

Examined Stephen W. HARRIS
The Court then adjourned untill Court in course.

Theodrick MONTFORT)
vs.) Case
William WILLIAMS &)
Jacob SPICKARD) In this case the defendants being dissatisfied with the verdict of the jury comes forward and pays all costs and prays an appeal in terms of the law and gives Peter HARVEY as their security who comes forward and subscribes himself as such 25th of April 1816. Wm. WILLIAMS { }
Attest his
Edward SMITH Clk. Jacob x SPICKARD { }
mark
Peter J. HARVEY { }

Page 156

Thomas McDANIEL)
vs.)
Samuel FOWL) In this case the plaintiff ~~being~~ being dissatisfyed with the verdict of the jury comes forward and pays all costs and prays an appeal in terms of the law & gives William JELKS as security who comes forward and subscribes himself as such the 26th of April 1816. Thomas McDANIEL
Edward SMITH Clk. W. JELKS

James M. TAYLOR)
administrator of the estate)
of Micajah H. POWEL) Case
vs.)
John McLENAN) In this case the defendant comes forward & prays a stay of execution sixty days which is granted & gives Daniel McLENAN as his security 27th of April 1816. John McLEENNAN
Attest Edward SMITH Clk. Dan. McLENNAN

Page 157

Mary RABSOM)
vs.) Debt
William GARBETT) In this case the defendant being dissatisfied with the verdict of the jury comes forward & pays all costs & prays an an appeal in terms of the law & gives [*blank*] as his security who comes forward & subscribes himself as such 27th of April 1816. [*no signatures*]

October 1816

Monday October 27th 1816. The Superior Court for the County of Pulaski met agreeable to law. Present his honor Judge HARRIS.

The venire of the Grand Jury being called the following persons answered to their names & now sworn:

1 John A. WILLIAMS
2 Wm. McCORMIC
3 Joel DAWSON
4 ~~Wm. McCORM~~
Michael HORN Jr.
5 James CLARKE
6 Thos. JOHNSON Sr.
7 James S. IVEY
8 George WALKER
9 Jos. B. BRYAN
10 Jno. DEES
11 Hinchy WARREN
12 John B. PACKER
13 Wm. YARBOROUGH Senr.
14 Orandatus WATSON
15 Thos. MILLS
16 Thos. HOWELL
17 John GRINSTED
18 Furney F. GATLIN

Page 158

19 Richard H. THOMAS foreman
20 Joseph SESSIONS
21 Turner EVERETT
22 Ewd. BLACKSHEAR
23 Thomas McGRIFF

The following persons appeared and were sworn as Petit Jurors during the present term viz:

Jury No. 1
John ROZIER
John McCORMIC
Thomas WORSELY
Arthur TOOKE
John NELSON
William WHIGHAM
John PIERCE
Wiley WILLIAMS
Thomas CARDIN
Zion DAVIS
Dixon JELKS
Philip WHICHARD

Jury No. 2
Kinchen DAWSON
Jesse HARRELL
Nimrod PHILIPS
Moses GIDDINS
Amos WHEELER
John TAYLOR
John JONES
Lawrence FULSOM
Alexander VARNER
Frederic WOLF
John BRADSHAW
Henry MORRIS
~~John HAGAN~~

Page 159

The State)
vs.) Asst. & btty.
Young JOHNSTON &)
Alexr. JOHNSTON)

The State)
vs.)
Joel WALKER) Asst. & btty.
Joseph B. BRYAN)
& George WALKER) The parties in the above cases having attended regularly during this term & no prosecutor appearing, Ordered that they be discharged from their recognizance and any further attendance on or at this Court.

The State) Ind^{t}.
vs.) Petit Larceny
Ja^{s}. SALTER) No bill Rich^{d}. H. THOMAS foreman

The State)
vs.) Ind^{t}. Ass^{t}. & battery
Harbard TAYLOR) True bill Rich^{d}. H. THOMAS foreman

The State)
vs.) Ind^{t}. Assault & battery
Thomas MILLS) True bill against Moses SUTTON & Robert
Moses SUTTON) THOMPSON, No bill against Thomas MILLS
Robert THOMPSON) Rich^{d}. H. THOMAS foreman

Page 160

The State) Recogn^{ce}.
vs.) The passing counter money
W^{m}. NEIL) The party having attended on the above recognizance & the Solicitor General having stated that he cannot nor will not prefer a bill in said case, ordered that the said William NEAL be and he is hereby discharged.

John DOE Ex dem.)
Abner HOLLIDAY)
vs.) Ejectment
Rich^{d}. ROE)
Furney F. GATLIN) We the Jurors find for the defendant with cost of suit.
Tenant in possession) John BRADSHAW foreman

The Court adjourned till tomorrow morning nine oclock. Edward SMITH Clk.
Ex^{d}. Stephen W. HARRIS

October 28th. The Court met agreeable to adjournment. Edward SMITH Clk.

Page 161

Frederic FLOYD and Joseph REGAN were sworn as talisman in place of Henry MORRIS and John BRADSHAW.

William SLAIT)
vs.) Assumpsit
Jordan DEES) We find for the plaintiff five hundred dollars with interest & cost. Lawrence FOLSOM foreman

William CAWTHORN for)
the use of William TAYLOR)
vs.) Case
Murdoch M^{c}LEOD &)
Asa PIPKIN) I confess judgement for the plaintiff for twenty five dollars with interest and cost. Thomas W. HARRIS def^{ts}. atty.

James ALSTON Ex^{r}.)
of Drew ALSTON)
vs.) Case
Mitchell DORMAN &)
Nathan G. ROBINSON) We find for plaintiff ninety one dollars with interest & cost.
Thomas CARDIN foreman

Page 162

Charles WILLIAMSON)
vs.) Debt
James L. PERRY) We find for the plaintiff twenty five dollars interest & cost.
Thomas CARDIN fm.

William CURENTON)
vs.) Debt
Thomas SHEPPARD) We find for the plaintiff sixty six dollars with interest & cost.
Thomas CARDIN fm.

Rich^{d}. MAYO)
vs.) Spe. Case
Isham SHUFFIELD) We find for the plaintiff twenty five dollars with cost of suit.
R. H. THOMAS foreman

John W. BATTLE b^{r}.)
vs.) Case
Drew DEES otherwise)
called Drury DEES) I confess judgement to the plaintiff for two hundred and thirty eight dollars with interest & cost. Drew DEES

Ex^{rs}. Sol. A. HOPKINS)
vs.) Case
John PARRIS) We find for the plaintiff thirty seven dollars sixty two and one half cents with interest & cost. Thomas CARDIN for^{n}.

Page 163

Thomas RODGERS)
vs.) Debt
Isaac KIRKSEY) We find for the plaintiff seventy five dollars with interest & cost.
Thomas CARDIN for^{n}.

David CUMMINS for the)
use of Robt. CUMMINS) Debt
vs.) Octr. term 1816.
William HORNE) We find for the plaintiff thirty seven dollars & fifty cents with interest & cost.
Thomas CARDIN for^{n}.

Jos. WOOD)
vs.) Petition
Wm. McDANIEL) We find for the plaintiff twenty dollars with interest & cost.
R. H. THOMAS foreman

William SLAID) Assumpsit
vs.) Verdict for plff.
Jordan DEES) In this case the defendant being dissatisfied with the verdict of the jury comes forward pays all costs and prays an appeal in terms of the law and give John BRADSHAW for his security.

his
Jordan x DEES
mark
John BRADSHAW

Zachariah DAVIS was sworn as a juror in place of Philip WHICHARD.

Page 164

John DOE ex dem.)
Abner HOLLIDAY)
vs.) Ejectment
Richd. ROE)
Furney F. GATLIN) Verdict for defendt.
Tenant in possession) In this case the plaintiff being dissatisfied with the verdict of the jury comes forward pays all cost & gives Allen TOOKE security & prays an appeal in terms of the law.

Allen SCARBOROUGH [!]
Allen TOOKE Jr.

Mary RABSOM)
vs.)
William GARBETT) We find the property subject to the execution and fifteen percent of the amount due for false claim. Thomas CARDIN forn.

The Court adjourned till tomorrow morning half past eight o'clock.
Edward SMITH Clk. Exd. Stephen W. HARRIS

Page 165

October 30th 1816. The Sup. Court met agreeable to adjournment.

Robert HILL)
vs.) Fi fa
John McRAE) In this case the money having been raised by the Shff. and it appearing to the Court that the plaintiff has transferred the same to Thomas W. HARRIS in his own right, Ordered that the Shff. do pay over to him the said HARRIS the amount so collected.

Lodowick LARD)
vs.) Special Case
Allen TOOKE)

1 Richard H. THOMAS	7 William YARBORO Senr.
2 William McCORMIC	8 Thomas MILLS
3 Joel DAWSON	9 Thomas HOWELL
4 James S. IVEY	10 Jos. SESSIONS
5 George WALKER	11 Turner EVERETT
6 John B. PACKER	12 Thomas McGRIFF
We find for the defendant.	Richard H. THOMAS foreman

Page 166

John NELSON was sworn as talisman on Petit Jury No. 1.

Robert THOMPSON)
vs.) Fi fa
William WYNN) In this case it being made appear to the Court that the original fi fa is lost ordered that the Clerk do issue a new execution and deliver it to the plff. or Shff.

Wm. CAWTHORN for the)
use of Reuben HARGROVE)
vs.) Case
Murdock McLEOD &)
Asa PIPKIN) I confess judgement to the plaintiff for twenty five dollars with interest & cost.
M. McLEOD

United States of America)
vs.) Debt
Wheriat alias Wherry BUCK) We the jury find for the plaintiff one hundred dollars and cost of suit.
Amos WHEELER foreman

William CURETON)
vs.) Case
Thomas SHEPPARD) We the jury find for the plaintiff forty five dollars with interest & cost.
Thomas CARDIN forn.

Page 167

James M. TAYLOR)
vs.) Debt
Amos WHEELER) In open Court I confess judgement to the plaintiff for forty nine dollars & thirty three cents with interest & cost.
his
Test. Tho. W. HARRIS Amos x WHEELER
mark

Comssrs. of the Court house)
& Jail of Pulaski County) Debt
vs.)
Neal McALPIN) We find for the plaintiff seventy dollars with interest & cost.
Thomas CARDIN forn.

Hardy VICKERS &)
Jason BRINSON adm^{rs}.)
of Lester CRAFFORD)
vs.) Debt
Benjamin COLEMAN)
Jesse FULGHAM &)
Lewis HOLLAND) I confess judgement to the plaintiff for the sum of one hundred dollars with interest & cost reserving the right of appeal.
Lewis HOLLAND

John DOE ex dem.)
Abner HOLLIDAY)
vs.) Eject.
Richard ROE &)
Furney F. GATLIN) In this case it being stated to the Court that Stephen GATLIN has material papers in his possession for the plaintiff to wit the original plat and grant to Erastus PARKS for lot N°. 344 in the 21st dist. Wilkinson County now Pulaski which \is/ the subject matter of the above suit on motion it is ordered that the Clerk of this Court issue...

Page 168

a subpoena duces tecum directed to the said Stephen requiring him to produce said grant to be used as evidence on said trial.

Rightson DAVIS)
vs.)
Gideon KELLAM) Case
Thomas PHILLIPS)
& Daniel W. SHINE) In open Court we confess judgement to the plaintiff for the sum of two hundred & fifty seven dollars & fifty five cents with interest & cost reserving right of appeal. Rich^{d}. JONES def^{ts}. atto.

Commissioners of the)
Courthouse & Jail of)
Pulaski County)
vs.) Debt
Elizabeth SCOTT,)
Bailey ROBINSON)
& James L. PERRY) We find for the plaintiff thirty seven dollars & fifty cents with interest & cost of suit. Amos WHEELER

Jabaz LONGWORTH)
vs.) Fi fa
Arch^{d}. LASSITER) On motion of plff. atto. it is ordered that the Shff. shew cause why he should not pay over to plff. attorney the amount of the money in his hands by tomorrow morning.

United States of America)
vs.) Debt
Wheriat alias Wherry BUCK) In this case the defendant being dissatisfied with the verdict of the jury comes forward pays costs & gives Hardy BUCK as security and prays an appeal in terms of the law. Wherry BUCK
Test. Edw[d]. SMITH Clk. Hardy H. BUCK

The State)
vs.) Assault
Solomon FRANKLIN) The prosecutor being willing ~~willing~~ to have the case settled and the defendant having paid the cost and the bill being mislaid on motion of counsel it is ordered that a nole prosequi be entered and the defendant discharged.

Alexander HODGES)
vs.) Trespass for mean profits
Elisha FARNELL) We the Juror find for the defendant.
Thomas CARDIN for[n].

The State) Ind[t].
vs.) Asst. & battery
Thomas MILLS) True bill Rich[d]. H. THOMAS foreman

Page 170

The State) Ind[t].
vs.) Assault & battery
William MUSGROVE) True bill Rich[d]. H. THOMAS foreman

The State) Ind[t].
vs.) Perjury
Mary SHURLY) True bill Richard H. THOMAS foreman

The State) Ind[t].
vs.) Cattle stealing
Murdoch M[c]LEOD) No bill Richard H. THOMAS foreman

The State)
vs.) Ind[t].
James SALTER) Adultery & fornication
Mary SHIRLY) No bill Rich[d]. H. THOMAS foreman

The State)
vs.) Ind[t].
Sam[l]. FAIRBANK) Misdemeanor
Christopher EDWARDS) No bill Rich[d]. H. THOMAS foreman

The State) Ind[t].
vs.) Cattle stealing
James SALTER) No bill Rich[d]. H. THOMAS

The State)
vs.) Asst. batty.
Robt. THOMPSON) The defendant and James S. IVEY acknowledge themselves held and bound unto his Excellency the Governor in the sum of four \hundred/ dollars conditioned to be void if the said Robert THOMPSON do appear at the next Superior Court to be held on the fourth Monday in April next & not depart from thence without leave of said Court, otherwise to be and remain in full force and virtue.

Robert THOMPSON
Jas. S. IVEY

The State) Indt.
vs.) Asst. & batty.
Herbert TAYLOR) Herbert TAYLOR acknowledges himself bound to his Excellency the Governor in the sum of two hundred dollars and Moses HOLLAND in the sum of two hundred dollars and Lewis HOLLAND in the like sum of two hundred dollars conditioned be void if the aforesaid Herbert TAYLOR and Moses HOLLAND does appear at the next \Supr./ Court in this County and not depart from thence without leave of said Court.

his
Herbert x TAYLOR {Seal}
mark
his
Moses x HOLLAND {Seal}
mark
Lewis HOLLAND {Seal}

Page 172

The following persons were drawn to serve as Grand Jurors at next term viz:

1 Nath. MERCER
2 Benj. HARRISON
3 Jas. ROACH
4 Wm. HANEY
5 Ezekiel TAYLOR
6 Sanders COALSON
7 Charles DANIEL
8 Jas. M. TAYLOR
9 Jos. WOOD
10 Ralph KIRKLAND
11 Wm. WMS.
12 Jno. WILLCOX
13 Drury MAYO
14 Jas. POWELL
15 John SHERROD
16 Josiah EVERETT
17 Christopher RHODES
18 Wm. JOHNSON
19 Allen TOOKE
20 Aaron SCARBORO
21 Jos. BARRON
22 Clem. LANIER
23 Benj. BRUTON
24 Coalson ADAMS
25 Daniel RHODES
26 Wm. HALL
27 Ephm. PHILIPS
28 Saml. JONES Senr.
29 Jno. LEE Junr.
30 Jesse POWELL
31 Henry HAGAN
[32] Needham BRYAN

The following persons were drawn to serve as Petit Jurors during next term viz:

1 Etheld^{d}. HARRELL
2 Danl. SPARROW
3 Henry EVANS
4 Jno. BURNETT
5 Thos. ROGERS Senr.
6 Edm^{d}. HERRING
7 Thos. COLE
8 Athael PULLING
9 Benjn. WEEKS
10 Shad^{k}. SUTTON
11 Ab^{m}. NIPPER
12 Shad^{k}. LEE
13 Isaac BROUNT [*Blount?*]
14 John SPARROW
15 Ithurriom HAWKINS
16 John BRYANT
17 Jesse LIVELY
18 John VARNER
19 Mitchell DORMAN
20 Alex^{r}. SMITH
21 John M^{c}CORMIC
22 Robert LEE
23 Silas MERCER
24 W^{m}. BRYANT
25 Evin SCARBORO
26 Thos. GIDDENS
27 Zachariah CLAXTON
28 Ja^{s}. HOLLY
29 John CARDIN
30 John COFIELD
31 William TERRELL
32 Jordan DYKES

Page 173

33 Nehemiah POSEY
34 W^{m}. SMITH
35 John TINSLY
36 Jos. B. COALSON
37 Ab^{m}. BUSH
38 W^{m}. ALLEN
39 Benj. DANIL
40 Ja^{s}. BROWN
41 Chappel BOND
42 Danl. M^{c}NAIR
43 Rich^{d}. BATSON
44 Benjn. STEGALL
45 Robt. HODGES
46 Sherod PHILIPS
47 Isham DANIL
48 Ja^{s}. TRULL
49 Jesse LEE
50 Jno. BUSH
51 W^{m}. SMITH [#2]
52 Thos. PIERCE

The State) Ind^{t}.
vs.) Misdemeanor
Sands STANLY) No bill — Rich^{d}. H. THOMAS foreman

The State) Ind^{t}.
vs.) Misdemeanor
Saml. FOWL) No bill — Richard H. THOMAS foreman

The State) Ind^{t}.
vs.) Cattle stealing
William PIPKIN) No bill — Richard H. THOMAS foreman

Thomas BUTLER)
vs.) Bill for specific performance
Washington LANCASTER et [al.])
heirs of W^{m}. S. LANCASTER) Settled at plffs. cost.

John DOE ex dem.)
Bartholomew GAINEY)
natural guardian of)
William GAINEY)
vs.)
Richard ROE)
William JOHNSON) Settled at plffs. costs.

Page 174

Bartholomew GAINEY)
natural guardian of)
William GAINEY) Trespass quare clausum fregit
vs.)
William JOHNSON) Settled at plffs. costs.

Bartholomew GAINEY)
vs.) Case
William & Patsy JOHNSON) Settled at plffs. cost.

Mary SHURLY)
vs.) Slander
Benj[n]. JOHNSON) Dismiss[d].

Gideon KELLAM)
vs.) Case
John MOSES) Settled at pffs. costs.

John M[c]RAE)
vs.) Trespass quare clausum fregit
Hugh TAYLOR) Settled at plffs. costs.

Mason KIMMING for)
the use of Allen CARR)
vs.)
Henry SHEPARD) Settled at def[ts]. cost.

Page 175

Daniel RHODES adm[r].)
vs.) Case
Wilson BASS and)
W[m]. GARBITT) Settled & cost paid.

Daniel RHODES adm[r].)
vs.) Case
Wilson BASS and)
Thomas FRANKLIN) Settled & cost paid.

William LESTER)
vs.) Debt
William CURETON) Settled & cost paid.

Thomas MATHEWS)
vs.) Case
Henry FULGHAM) Settled

Tuttle H. MORELAND)
vs.) Case
Thomas BUTLER) Settled at mutual costs.

Commss^{rs}. &c)
vs.) Debt
Needham STEPHENS) Settled & cost paid.

Commss^{rs}. &c)
vs.) Debt
Thomas MILLS &)
Joseph WOOD) Settled at def^{ts}. cost.

Page 176

Comss^{rs}. &c)
vs.) Debt
Saml. FOWL &)
Elijah WALLACE) Settled at defd^{ts}. cost.

John GILLSTRAP)
vs.) Case
Gideon KELLAM) Settled & cost paid.

Commss^{rs}. &c &c)
vs.) Debt
John GILLSTRAP)
& John COFIELD) Settled & cost paid.

Blakely EDINS ap^{t}.)
vs.)
Aaron SCARBOROUGH resp^{t}.) Settled & cost paid.

Aaron SCARBOROUGH app^{t}.)
vs.)
Blakely EDINS resp^{t}.) Settled & cost paid.

The Court then adjourned till tomorrow morning half past 9 o'clock.
Edward SMITH Clk. Ex^{d}. S. W HARRIS

Court met agreeable to adjournment October 31st 1816.

Rich^{d}. MOYA resp^{t}.)
vs.) Case & verdict for plff.
Isham SHUFFIELD) On motion of counsel for the defendant it is ordered that plaintiffs counsel shew cause why the verdict should not be set aside & a new trial ordered grounded on the following ground: 1st For that the declaration set forth among other things that plaintiff was prevented from performing his part of the contract by defendant and driven away and no proof adduced that the plaintiff was prevented or was driven away by defendant; 2nd For that there was no evidence that plaintiff had finished the crop and the evidence was positive that he went away some time in June and of his own accord declaring that he could not perform his part of the contract; 3rd For that the finding was contrary to evidence the law and the justice & equity of the case.

Joseph SESSIONS)
vs.) Fi fa
John J. FORD) In the above case the Shff. having raised the sum of sixty five dollars ninety seven & three fourth cents & it appearing that several small executions in favor of Jonathan TAYLOR, Sias TAYLOR & SPRIGHT & POWELL have been placed in his hand with an order to retain the money & it appearing to the Court thairs are of an older date than the one under which the money was raised & it being stated by the Shff. that the said SESSIONS has relinquished his claim to said money ordered that the Shff. pay over said am^{t}. collected to said small executions.

Page 178

Jabez LONGWORTH) Fi fa
vs.) Rule nisi
Arch^{d}. LASSETER) Ordered that the Sheriff pay the am^{t}. of the money in his hands to the plff. atto.

John O. GRANT was sworn as a Petit Juror in place of Zachariah DAVIS, & Thomas SMITH in place of Arthur TOOKE.

The State)
vs.) Ind^{t}. murder
Joseph REED) True bill Rich^{d}. H. THOMAS foreman

The State)
vs.) Assault & battery
William MUSGRAVE) True bill Richard H. THOMAS foreman

The State) Ind^{t}.
vs.) Assault & battery
Eli LESTER) True bill Richard H. THOMAS foreman

The State) Ind^{t}.
vs.) Perjury
Samuel FOWL) No bill Richard H. THOMAS foreman

The State)
vs.) Fornication & adultery
Stephen MITCHELL)
& Mourning GRIFFIN) No bill Richard H. THOMAS foreman

The State)
vs.) Ind^{t}. Asst. & battery
William MUSGRAVE) William MUSGRAVE & Burrell [*blank*]

The State) Ind^{t}.
vs.) Assault & battery
Eli LESTER) Arraigned & plead gilty whereupon it is ordered by the Court that Eli LESTER be fined in the sum of ten dollars. ~~Fined \$10.00~~

The State)
vs.) Ind^{t}. Asst. & battery
William MUSGRAVE) William MUSGRAVE and Christopher EDWARDS acknowledge themselves bound each of them in the sum of two hundred dollars to his Excellency the Gover. of this State conditioned to be void if the said William MUSGRAVE does appear at the next Superior of Pulaski County & not depart from thence without leave of said Court. William MUSGRAVE {Seal}
Test. Edwd. SMITH Clk. Christopher EDWARDS {Seal}

Page 180

Georgia) Superior Court October term 1816.
Pulasi County) The Grand Jurors for the County aforesaid having examined the books of William KINCHEN tax collector for said county for the year 1815 recommend that he be allowed the sum of forty three \dollars/ 34$^{1}/_{2}$ [cents] on account of his insolvent list. We feel gratified that nothing worthy of presentment has come under our observation during the present term and in taking our leave of his honor Judge HARRIS we cannot refrain expressing our entire approbation of his administration of the law and should be well pleased for him to be continued in office. We further recommend that Richard H. THOMAS, Furney F. GATLIN & Joseph B. BRYAN be appointed as a committee to inquire into the situation of the County funds and report to the next session of the Superior Court of said County. And request that these presentments be published in the Georgia Journal.

Richard H. THOMAS for^{n}.	W^{m}. YARBOROUGH S^{r}.
John A. WILLIAMS	Orandatis WATSON
W^{m}. M^{c}CORMIC	Thos. MILLS
Joel DAWSON	Thos. HOWELL
James CLARKE	John GRINSTED
James S. IVEY	Furney F. GATLIN
George WALKER	Joseph SESSIONS
Jos. B. BRYAN	Turner EVERETT
John DEES	Edwards BLACKSHEAR
John B. PACKER	Thomas M^{c}GRIFF

Executors of Philip JONES)
vs.) Case
Thomas BUTLER) We find for the plaintiffs four hundred & seventy nine dollars & seventy nine & one fourth cents. Thomas CARDIN foreman

Executors of Philip JONES)
vs.) Case
Thomas BUTLER) In this case the defendants attorney being dissatisfied with the verdict of the Jury comes forward pays costs and gives Eli LESTER as his security & claims an appeal in terms of the law which is granted.

Thomas FITCH def^{ts}. atto.
Test. Edwd. SMITH Clk. Eli LESTER

Saml. FOWLE) Case
vs.) In the Sup^{r}. Court Octr. Term 1816
Peter J. HARVY) The parties in the above case having agreed to submit all matters of controversy between them to the arbitrament & award of James M. TAYLOR & Stephen GATLIN \on motion/ it is ordered that said Ja^{s}. M. & Stephen shall and they are hereby authorised to arbitrate all matters in dispute in the premises & make up their award and return it to the next Superior Court to be held in & for Pulaski County & if said arbitrators shall not agree in their award, it shall be lawful for them to call in a third man.

It appearing to the Court that the Grand Jury have recommended the appointment of Richard H. THOMAS, Furney F. GATLIN & Joseph B. BRYAN a committee to inquire into the funds of this County, ordered therefore that the said Richard H. THOMAS, Furney F. GATLIN & Joseph B. BRYAN be and they are hereby appointed a committee for said purpose and required to report their proceedings to the next Superior Court to be held in & for the County of Pulaski.

Court adjourned till Court in course. October 31st 1816.
Edwd. SMITH Clk. Ex^{d}. Stephen W. HARRIS

Page 182

William CURETON) In 2 cases
vs.) Verdict for plff.
Thomas SHEPHERD) In this case Thomas SHEPHERD comes ____ forward and gives William YARBOROUGH Senr. as his security and claims stay of execution sixty days which is granted. October 31st 1816.

Thomas SHEPPARD {LS}
Edwd. SMITH Clk. William YARBROUGH {LS}

[*end of book*]

INFERIOR COURT

MINUTES 1810-1816

Pages 1-4 and an undetermined number of pages at the end are missing from the original; even more pages are missing from the microfilm copy in the Georgia Archives.

...the road according to order number 2, [a]nd all hands ~~from~~ on the Milledgeville Road shall clear [t]hat? out except Turner AVERIT, James JOHNSON and DESHAZO. The Court say that they both shall be one unto the head of Denerts Branch and then to run their own courses and then [o]verseers are to clear them out.

The Court agrees with the report of the commissioners of the road from Hartford to the new garrison and the hands between the River Road and the river are to open the River Road from Hartford to the run of Bever Dam Creek and all hands that the road goes through his land shall work on this road allso.

Ordatus WATSON

Page 6

1. Agreed by the Court that the overse[er] Lewis HOLLAND are to turn the road round Mark MASONs plantation so as not to inger it.

2. Agreed by the Court that Orend[atus] WATSON shall turn the road round his plantation so as not to inger it.

Page 7

Georgia) ~~Ordered that William JOHNSON~~
Pulaski County) Pulaski Inferior Court the 20th August 1810.

Ordered that William GOODSON be and he is hereby appointed overseer of the River Road from Hartford down to where Hard[y] VICCERS begins and all the hands belonging thereto are subject to work under him.

Georgia) Pulaski Inferior Court the 20th of August 1810.
Pulaski County) Ordered that Hardy VICCERS be and he is hereby appointed overseer of the River Road from Muskete[r] Creek Run down opposet Lester CRAFFORDs mill and the hands subject to that part are to clear and open the same.

Georgia) Pulaski Inferior Court the 20th of August 1810.
Pulaski County) Ordered that Lawrence FOULSOM be and he is hereby appointed overseer of the River Road from opposet CRAWFORD mill down to the County line and all the hands belonging thereto are subject to work thereon.

Page 8

Ordered that William GOODSON and Stephen MITCHELL Senr. and Lester CRAWFORD are hereby appointed commissioners of a River Road from Hartford down to the County line as near the river as is convenient.

Ordered that [*blank*] Blakely EDINS are appointed Justice of the Pease in the fourth district of malitia Pulaski County commanded by Nathanial MERCER.

Ordered that William BRACKEN and Demsey DARITY be and they are hereby appointed Justices of the Peace for the fifth company of malisha commanded by said DORETY Pulaski County.

Ordered that Cristopher EDWARD be and are hereby appointed Constable for Captain MERCERs district.

Ordered that Thomas ROGERS be and he is hereby appointed Constables for Capt[t]. FIVEASH district.

Ordered that John TEMPLES be and he is hereby appointed Constable for Demsey DORITY district.

Page 9

Edmund HOGAN J.I.C.
James T. THOMAS J.I.C.
Sam[l]. JONES J.I.C.

Adjorned untill court in course. August the 20th 1810.

HARRIS)	Ri[t]eson DAVIS)		
)	vs. indorse)		
)	Sampson BRASWELL)	Case &c	
CROCKER)	James BRASWELL)		

Dismissed at the plantiffs cost the cost five dollars and fifty cents. Paid by the plantiff five dollars and fifty cents his cost this 29th October 1811.

D. GARTMAN Clk.

Page 10, February 1811

February Term met according to adjournment jud<u>e</u>s present February 18th 1811.

William A. HARPER)
Samuel JONES)
James T. THOMAS)

Ordered that David GARTMAN are authorised to issue lis<u>e</u>nce to all applicants.

1st Georgia Pulaski County) February the 18th 1811 This is to sertify that Allen TUKEs C[o]. is authorised to sell and retail spiritous liquors untill the first Monday in November 1811.

By order of the Court. D. GARTMAN Clk.

2nd Georgia Pulaski County) February the 18th 1811. This is to certify that Thompson BIRD is authorised to sell and retail spiritous liquors untill the first Monday in November 1811.

By order of the Court. D. GARTMAN Clk. I.C.P.C.

Page 11

3rd Georgia) February the 23rd 1811.
Pulaski County) This is to certify that Richard H. THOMAS is authorised to sell and retail spiritous liquors untill the first Monday in January 1812.

By order of the Court. D. GARTMAN Clk. I.C.P.C.

4th Georgia) February the 23rd 1811.
Pulaski County) This is to certify that William JELKS is authorised to sell and retail spiritous liquors untill the 1 day of December next.
By order of the Court. D. GARTMAN Clk. I.C.P.C.

5th Georgia) February the 23rd 1811.
Pulaski County) This is to certify that S. HOPKINS & PHILIPS is authorised to sell and retail spiritous liquors untill the 23rd day of February 1812.
By order of the Court. D. GARTMAN Clk. I.C.P.C.

6th Georgia) February the 23rd 1811.
Pulaski County) This is to certify that Theodk. MONTFORT is atherised to sell and retail spiritous liquors untill the 23rd of February 1812.
By order of the Court. D. GARTMAN Clk. I.C.P.C.

Page 12

Georgia) February the 23rd 1811.
Pulaski County) This is to certify that Joseph WOOD is authorised to sell and retail spiritous liquors untill the first day of December 1811.
By order of the Court. D. GARTMAN Clk. I.C.P.C.

6th Georgia) February the 23rd 1811.
Pulaski County) This is to certify that William JELKS & Neal McALPERN & Isham SHUFFIELD be and they are hereby appointed commissioners to lay out a road from the Uche shoal on the Oakmulga River the nearest and the best way through the Town of Hartford from thence the nearest & best way for Berony Mill Bluff to the County line.

~~7th Georgia) February the 23rd 1811.~~
~~Pulaski County) Ordered that Joseph SESSIONS be and he is hereby appointed overseer of the Savanah Road from the said shoal to the run of Musketer Creek and all persons liable to do road duty within five miles of said road shall be liable to do work on the said road.~~

Page 13

8th Georgia) February the 23rd 1811.
Pulaski County) Ordered that Jael? HARRELL be and he is hereby appointed overseer of the Savannah Road from the run of Musketer Creek to the County line and all hands liable to do road duty within five miles of said road shall be liable to work on said road under the directions of said overseer.

9th Georgia) February the 23rd 1811.
Pulaski County) Ordered that James McNORTON, John LEE & William BRIAN be and they are hereby appointed commissioners of a road beginning at the north corner of Pulaski County on Rocky Creek & [running] the best & nearest directest way from thence to intersect the Uche Road leading from Hartford to the Cars Bluff on the Ocone.

10th Georgia) February the 23rd 1811.
Pulaski County) Ordered that Daniel REGAN be and he is hereby appointed overseer [*end of sentence*]

James T. THOMAS J.I.C.
Adjourned untill court in course
Wm. A. HARPER J.I.C.
S. JONES J.I.C.

Page 14, August 1811

Georgia) On the application of William SMITH for a licence to sell
Pulaski County) sell spiritous liquors in small quantities and agreeable to an act of the Legislature passed at Milledgeville on the 13th day of December 1809 and an order of the Inferior Court of said County dated the 18th of February last I do hereby authorise the said William SMITH to sell spirituous liquors in small quantities for the term of six months to commence from the date herein.
Given under my hand this 19th of August 1811. D. GARTMAN Clk.

Georgia) On the application of Samuel HART for a licence to sell
Pulaski County) spirituous liquors in small quantities and agreeable to an act of the Legislature passed at Milledgeville on the 13th day of December 1809 and an order of the Inferior Court of said County dated the 18th of February last I do hereby authorise the said Samuel HART to sell spirituous liquors in small quantys for the term of twelve months to commence from this date hereof.
Given under my hand this 19th of August 1811. D. GARTMAN Clk.

Page 15

Georgia) April the 30th 1811.
Pulaski County) Returned this day by Archibald LASETER a magestrate for this County an inventory of estrays hogs told _____ before him by Charles CARDEN ten head of hogs two old sows and six pigs and too year olds of the same one a white & the other a spotted sow marked with a swolow fork under bit and over bit in the right [ear] and a crop & underbit & overbit in the left and appraised by James M. TAYLOR and James JONSON to elevan dollars.
Entered by - - Dd. GARTMAN Clk.

This not complied with.

Georgia)
Pulaski County) On the application of Samuel COLEMAN for a licence to sell spirituous liquors in small quntities and agreeable to an act of the Legislature passed at Milledgeville on the 13th day of December 1809 and an order of the Inferior Court of said County dated the 18th of February last I do hereby authorise the said Samuel COLEMAN to sell spirituous liquors in small quantyes for the term of twelve months to commence from the date hereof.
Given under my hands this 20th day of August 1811. D. GARTMAN Clk.

Page 16

Met according to adjournment. August Term 1811. Judges present.

Resolved that Gedion MAYO, James DEAS & Bolen SWARENGAME be and are hereby appointed commissioners to inspect the Milledgeville Road from the south branch of the Bever Dam up to the County \line/ & report what alteration are nesary & resolved further that the overseer on said part of road be and is hereby authorised immediately to execute such alteration if any agreeable to the report.

1st Ordered that John GINSTEAD be and he is hereby appointed overseer on the Milledgeville Road from Hartford to the run of Jordans Creek and all hands living between the two & on three miles of the east side of Millidgeville Road up to the said Jordans Creek are subject to work on the same. All extracted

2nd Ordered that Charles MAYO be and he is hereby appointed overseer of the Milledgeville Road from the run of Jordans Creek to the north fork of Bever Dam Creek Run and all hands living between the two rodes & on three miles of the east side of Millidgeville Road up to the Bever Dam from Hogans trail up to the Bever Dam.

3rd Ordered that Wm. H. GROSS be and he is hereby appointed overseer of the Milledgeville Road from the run of the north fork of Bever Dam Creek to the County and all hands between a line west of Thos. McGRIFF thence east of Messr. ROADS & MOSES & also by the hands in three miles east of side of said road up to the County line.

Page 17

4th Resolved that 12 dollars be and is hereby apropated to the support of Elizabeth BARNES out of any County funds unappropated untill the 1st of January 1812.

Received October the 12th 1811 - the above appropated sum of twelve dollars from the clerk. Biggars SINGLETON for Elizabeth BARNES

5th Ordered that Orain WATSON be and he is hereby appointed overseer of the River Road from Hartford to Bever Dam Creek Run and all hands on and between said road on the river are subject to said overseer and to work under his direction &c. Extracted

6th Ordered that Luwis HOLLAND be and he is hereby appointed overseer of the River Road from Bever Dam Creek to the County line and all hands liveing between the river & a line runing between William ISLER & Thomas McGRIFF thence east of Msrs. ROADS & MOSES &c. Extracted

7th Ordered that James JONES be and he is hereby appointed overseer of the Uche Road from the fork to Hogan Springs and all hands east of the Milledgeville Road from the fork to where it crosses Hogan trail are subject to work on the same Uche road.

Page 18

8th) Ordered that Moses KIRTLAND, Mark WHELER & Blakely EDWINS be and they are hereby appointed commissioners to lay out a road intersecting with a road leading from the Sand Bed Ford on Big Sandy the straightest best way that conveniency will admit of to the Town of Hartford.

9th) Ordered that John LEE be and he is hereby appointed overseer of the road intersecting with the Sand Bed Road and Abraham YARTA be and they are hereby appointed overseers and they are to divide as they think proper all the hands nearer said road then the middle road is liable to work on said road.

10th) Ordered that Nathaniel MERCER, Archibald ODOM Senr. & Christopher EDWARDS be and they are hereby appointed commissioners to lay out a road from said EDWARDS by Major ADAMS & Capt. MERCERs the straitest way to Nins Ford on Turky Creek on to the County line. Extracted

11th) Ordered that Robert HOGES be and he is hereby appointed overseer of said road from EDWARDS to Nins Ford on Turky Creek and all hands above said road that live nearest the said road then the upper be hereby obliged to help open the same & all persons that lives within five miles below said road shal be liable to help open the same.

Page 19

12th Ordered that William GOODSON be and he is hereby appointed overseer of the lower River Road from Hartford to Stanlys Creek and all the hands on three miles each side of the lower River Road shall work on said road.

13th Ordered that Shadarack ADKINS be and he is hereby appointed overseer of the lower River Road from Stanlys Creek to Sutton TRUELUCKs and all hands on three miles each side said of said road shall work on said road.

14th Ordered that Thomas ADAMS be and he is hereby appointed overseer of the lower River Road from TRUELUCKs to CRAWFORDs mill & all hands on three miles each side of said road shall work on the same.

15th Ordered that Lawence FOULSOM be and he is hereby appointed overseer of the lower River Road from CRAWFORDs mill to the County line and all hands on three miles each side of said road shall work on the same.

16th Ordered that Joab HORN, Samuel HART, Haywood JONES be and they are hereby appointed commissioners to lay out a road from Coulsons Bluf to Samuel HARTs agreeable to the requesions of the petion in the most convenient maner. All Extracted

17th Ordered that Joseph BARRON, Avon SCARBORROUGH & Nathl. MERCER be and are hereby appointed commissioners to mark out a road agreeable as Johnstons Trail run through this County and report the same to the next Cort.

Page 20

18th Ordered that Joseph SESSIONS be and he is hereby appointed overseer of the Savannah Road from said \Uche/ Shoal to the run of Musketer Creek and all the hands above the mount of Limestone to the head of Stanlys Creek & all the hands below Dewits Creek and still across from the head said creek to the head of Limestone shall be lyable to the order of Joseph SESSIONS to assist in opening said Savannah Road laid off.

19th Ordered that Stephen MICHEL, John LESTER & Lester CRAWFORD be and they are hereby appointed commissioners to lay out a road leaving the River Road at the Musketer Creek and the best way so as to intersect the Telfair Road at the County line.

20th Ordered that Sutton TRUELUCK be and he is hereby \appointed/ Marmaduke KENT, James ROUNDTREE appointed overseers of the Savannah Road to \cross at/ Bells Ferry and all hands within five miles are subject to work on the same as the overseers direct.

21st Resolved that Wil^{m}. WOOD of Hartford Silversmith be autherised to fix his shop on one corner of the publick square removeable at the option of the commissioners of said town.

22nd Ordered that Nedham STEPHENS, Henry SENTERFIT & Thomas HOWEL be and are hereby appointed commissioners to lay out a road begining at Stephens Bluff and runing the best way so as to intersect the River Road on the south side of Thomas HOWELLs plantation.

Page 21

23rd Ordered that William MAHAFFEE & Zion DAVIS be and they are hereby appointed Justices of the Peace for the fifth district of malitia for the County Pulaski commanded by Capt. SHUFFIELD in the room of William BRACKEN & Demsey DORETY who refused to quallify.

24th Ordered that Lewis LEE & Mikel HORN be and they are hereby appointed Justices of the Peace in the third district of malitia of Pulaski County commanded by said LEE in the room of Nedham STEPENS & Gedion MAYO Esquires resigned.

25th Ordered that John VASS be and he is hereby appointed Constable for Capt. FIVEASH district.

Georgia) On the application of Thomas M^{c}DANIEL for a licence to
Pulaski County) sell spirituous liquors in small quantys and agreeably to an act of the Legislature passed at Milledgeville on the 13th day of December 1809 and an order of the Inferior Court of said County dates the 18th of February last I do hereby autherise the said Thomas M^{c}DANIEL to sell spirituous liquors in small quantys for the term of twelve months to cemmence from the date hereof.
Given under my hand this 20th August 1811. D. GARTMAN Clk.

Page 22

H. FULGHAM
James T. THOMAS J.I.C.
W. A. HARPER J.I.C.
Edmund HOGAN J. I.C. [*rest of page blank*]

Page 23, February 1812

Georgia) On the application of Gideon KELLUM for licens to sell
Pulaski County) spirituous liquors in small measures and agreeable to an act of the general assembly passed at Milledgeville on the 13 December 1809 and an order of the Inferior Court of the said County dated March 1812 - I do hereby authorize Gideon KELLUM to sell spirituous liquors for the term of twelve months which was commenced on 29th November 1811.
Given under by hand this 17 February 1812. J. WOOD C.I.C.

February the 24th 1812 - Rec^{d}. of David GIRTMAN former clerk thirty five dollars and fifty cts. being all the money belonging to the office when given up to myself. J. WOOD C.I.C.

2nd March 1812. Ordered that Joseph WOOD Clk. be permitted to grant licen<u>s</u> to retailers of spirits &c.

Present Edmund HOGAN)
Henry FULGHAM)
James T. THOMAS)
Murdoc M^{c}CLOUD)
James M. TAYLOR) J.I.C.

Page 24

Georgia) 1 February 1812
Pulaski County) This is to certify that Joseph WOOD for Thomas BUTLER is authorised to sell and retail spirituous liquors in small measures for the term of six months commencing on the first day of December 1811. $2.50

By order of the court. Joseph WOOD Clk.

April 1812

~~Georgia)~~
~~Pulaski County) This is to certify that Solomon A. HOPKINS is authorised to sell and retail spirituous liquors in small measures for twelve months commencing 23rd February 1812.~~

~~By order of the court April the 22 1812. Joseph WOOD Clk.~~

Page 25

Georgia)
Pulaski County) This is to certify that Solomon A. HOPKINS is authorised to sell and retail spirituous liquors in small measures for the term of twelve months which was commenced the 23 February 1812 by order of the Court Given under by hand at office this 22nd April 1812. $5.00

Joseph WOOD Clk.

Rec^{d}. of Lewis LEE Esqr. a bond given by Abigail TAYLOR & Orandatis WATSON for the maintanance of an illegitemate begotten child this 28 April 1812. Jos. WOOD Clk.

Page 26-27 blank; Page 28

Jos WOOD Clk. Inferior Court

It is hereby ordered that you do pay David GIRTMAN the sum of fifty dollars for his servises as Clerk two years out of any moneys now in hands or may hereafter be in hand this 17th Jan. 1813.

James M. TAYLOR
Henry FULGHAM
Stephen GATLIN
James T. THOMAS J^{s}.I.C.

Inferior Court July 20th 1812. The Court met agreeable to law present the Honorable James M. TAYLOR, James T. THOMAS, Henry FULGHAM and Murdoch McLEOD.

The Court proceeded to the nomination of majistrates in the several districts in said County. In Capt. ATKINSONs district Hardy VICKERS Justice of the Peace, John BROWN and Stephen MITCHELL Jnr. Constables. For Capt. MEWBORNs district E[l]ijah WALLIS Justice of the Peace, John McRAE and William HILLIARD Constables. Capt. CLARKs district Furney F. GATLIN Justice of the Peace, William YARBROUGH Junr. and James JONES Constables. Capt. JOHNSONs district James ROACH and David GIRTMAN Justices of the Peace, Michael HORN Junr. & Joseph COLESON Constables. Capt. KELLUMs district Ezekiel TAYLOR & Hinchey WARREN Justices of the Peace, Patrick McGRIFF and John DECHAZO Constables. Capt. DYKESs district Abraham YERTY, Zachariah DAVIS Constables. Capt. MERCERs district Archibald ODOM Magistrate, Robert HART & Asa PIPKIN Constables.

Page 30

Petition No. 1. On the petition of sundry inhabitants praying an alteration in a road leading from the Town of Hartford to Milledgeville ordered that the same be granted and that Jacob SNELL, George G. GAINS & Furney F. GATLIN Esqr. be the commissioners.

Petition No. 2. On the petition of sundry inhabitants praying a road to be opened commencing at the Nest Egg Bluff and to continue up to the Milledgeville Road, granted under restrictions prayed for by the inhabitants and that James ROACH, Michael HORN Junr. and David SNELL be the commisioners.

Petition No. 3. On the petition of a number of inhabitants praying a road to be opened commencing in Hartford and running as directed a way as the nature and situation of the country will admit of so as to intersect the Savannah Road at PURKINSes on Sugar Creek ordered that said road be granted and Benjamin BRUTON, Benjn. BROWN & Elijah WALLIS be the commissioners thereof.

Petition No. 4. On the petition of a number of inhabitants praying a road to be laid off commencing at one corner of the County so as to intercect...

Page 31

the Sand Bead Road running as near to the sand district line as convenient to intersect the Milledgeville Road at or near James DEIKES. Ordered that the said petition be granted and Joseph BARRON, John LEE & Blakely EDDINGS be the commissioners thereof.

Petition No. 5. On the petition of a number of inhabitants praying a road to be laid off commencing at Lester CRAWFORD mill crossing the river road and intercecting the Savannah Road at or near the big lime sink, ordered that the petition be granted provided the inhabitants do open the said road at their private expense and labour and Lester CRAWFORD, John SILVESTER & Hardy VICKERS Esqr. be the commissioners.

It is ordered that William GOODSON, James BRACEWELL and William S. LANCASTER be and they are hereby appointed commissioners to let to the lowest bidder the building of bridg across Limestone Creek on the lower River Road.

It is hereby ordered that William HALL be a commissioner on the road leading town the river in looou of Stephen MITCHELL who is a commissioner on another road.

Page 32

It is ordered that Asa PIPKIN, William PHILIPS & Murdoch M^{c}LEOD be commissioner on the road leading from Gum Swamp to the County line - and William LITLE, William DONALDSON and Archibald LASITTER be the commissioners of the road leading from the other side Gum Swamp to Hartford.

It is ordered Hinchey WARREN, Mark MASON and Simon BARDEN be commissioners as far down as Beaver Dam - that James ROACH, John ISLER and Thomas HOWELL from the other side Beaver Dam Swamp to Thomas JOHNSONs from thence Josiah EVERETT, Stephen GATLIN & Furney F. GATLIN Esqr. to the Town of Hartford.

It is ordered that George WALKER, Ezekiel TAYLOR, Henery FULGHAM be commissioners on the Milledgeville Road from the to the creek on this side James DEIKES including said creek from thence to Hartford Jessey POWELL, John B. PACKER and James T. THOMAS on the Savannah Road.

It is ordered that Thomas SHEPHERD...

Page 33

Niel M^{c}COLPIN and William S. LANCASTER Esqr. be the commissioners on the road leading from Hartford to Godwins Ferry on the Oconey River as far as the County line and he appoint overseers & proportion the hands to cut it out.

It is ordered that the Tax Collector proceed to collect one twelfth of the general tax to defray County expences and that one twelfth of the general tax be levied in addition to the other for the support of the poor of the County.

M. M^{c}CLEOD)
Ja^{s}. M. TAYLOR)
James T. THOMAS) Justices of the
Jos. WOOD Clk. H. FULGHAM) Inferior Court

Page 34

This is to certify that William HILLIARD has taken the necessary oath as Constable & the oath to support the constitution of United States and given his bond for performance &c &c.

It is ordered that William YARBROUGH Senr. do receive thirteen dollars for his services as Coroner in the care of Moses OGLESBY and the Clerk is directed to pay the same out of any money now in fund or that may be here after July 20th 1812.

Henry FULGHAM)
James M. TAYLOR) Justices of the
M. M^{c}LEOD) Inferior Court

Capt. Shadrack ATKINSON, Capt. James CLARK, Capt. Thomas JOHNSON, Liut. Etheldred HOWELL, Ensign James CARDIN, Ensign Thomas COLE, Ensign William TAYLOR, Doctor Micajah H. POWELL Surgeon, & Henery F. SIMMONS Paymaster. I do certify that the above commissioned leveled? and staff officers have come forward and taken the necessary oath and oath to support the constitution of the State and of the United States, given under my hand this 8 day of August 1812. James T. THOMAS J.I.C.

Page 35, September 1812

Sep^{t}. 22nd 1812. This day payd William YARBROUGH Coroner thirteen dollars for his services in attending to Moses OGLESBY dec^{d}. By order of the Court. $13.00 paid J. WOOD Clk.

October 1812

Georgia) This is to certify that Thomas BUTLER is authorised to sell
Pulaski County) and retail spirituous liquors in small measures for the term of twelve months commencing the date under written by order of the Court. Given under my hand this 1st October 1812.
$5.00 J. WOOD Clk.

Georgia) This is to certify that ~~Thomas BUTLER~~ \John M^{c}CRAY/ is
Pulaski County) authorised to sell and retail spirituous liquors in small measures for the term of twelve months commencing the date under written by order of the Court. Given under my hand this 5 Oct. 1812.
$5.00 J. WOOD Clk.

Page 36

Georgia) This is to certify that that MONTFORD & EVERETT are
Pulaski County) authorised to sell and retail spirituous liquors in small measures for the term of twelve months commencing the date under written by order of the Court. Given under my hand this 29 October 1812.
$5.00 J. WOOD Clk.

I do certify that Capt. Benjamin MEWBORN hath taken the necessary oath to support the constitution of the State of Georgia & the United States this 1st October 1812. E. WALLIS J.P.

December 1812

Georgia) This is to certify that Thomas M^{c}CARTEAN is authorised
Pulaski County) to sell and retail spirituous liquors in small measures for the term of twelve months commencing the day and ~~day~~ \year/ under written by order of the Court. Given under my hand this 29 December 1812.
$5.00 J. WOOD Clk.

Pulaski Inferior Court January 18th 1813. Present the Honorable James T. THOMAS, Henry FULGHAM, Jas. M. TAYLOR & Stephen GATLIN.

The Court proceeded to appoint Constables in the several districts in said County - In Capt. MEWBORNs district William HILLIARD & William T. REANAU - In Capt. CLARKs district Wm. YARBROUGH Jnr. & Robert THOMPSON - In Capt. JOHNSONs district Joseph COALSON & Michael HORNE - In Capt. KELLUMs district Mark MASON & Daniel W. SHINE - In Capt. DIKESes district Abraham YERTY & William LONG - In Capt. PHILIPSes district David PIPKIN & John ROGERS - In Capt. BRUTONs district Chapel BONDS & Conrod AUGLY - In Capt. ATKINSes district Stephen MITCHELL Jnr. & John BROWN.

Petition No. 1st. Ordered that a road be granted commencing where TAYLORs line & EVERETTs intercets the River Road thence along said TAYLORs line upt to the corner of his field from thence to the south side of Edward BLACKSHERs plantation thence along said BLACKSHERs line till it intercects CARDINs line thence along said line untill it passes his shop...

Page 38

and from thence the most convenient way till it intercects with a road leading from Coleson's Bluff to the River Road the same to intercect at or near the said bluff - provided that said road be kept up without interfereing with any other road or the hands of any other road.

It is ordered that Joseph WOOD present Clerk detain twenty five dollars for his services as Clerk last year 1812 and the same amount for his services the present year 1813.

It is ordered that Bartlett McDANIEL Esqr. be a commissioner in loou of Benjamin BROWN to serve with Elijah WALLIS & Benjamin BRUTON.

It is ordered that James BRACEWELL, William GOODSON & David BROOM Esqr. be commissioners on the lower River Road.

Court adjourns till tomorrow morning 10 oclock.

Stephen GATLIN J.I.C.
H. FULGHAM J.I.C.
James T. THOMAS J.I.C.
Jas. M. TAYLOR J.I.C.P.C.

Jos. WOOD Clk.

Page 39

Inferior Court Tuesday 19 Jany. 1813. Proceeded to draw Jurors for the trial of slaves in the County aforesaid.

	No.		No.
Charles CARDIN	1	Dempsey TAYLOR	9
Jesse BRYANT	2	Archibald JONES	10
Jonathan MILLER	3	William WARD	11
Jacob McCOLLOM	4	Conrod OGLEY	12
Richard GAINEY	5	John VASS	13
Christopher EDWARDS	6	John HAWTHORN	14
Etheldred HOWELL	7	John CLARK	15
Jordan DEESE	8	William BARRON	16

Daniel HENDERSON	17	Meredith MERCER	23
Amos WHEELER	18	William HAGAN	24
Briant SHEFFIELD	19	Andrew FAUCK	25
John SMITH	20	Benjamin SMITH	26
Fredrick TEMPLES	21	Jacob HARRALE	27
Jessey JUMP	22		

It is ordered that a ferry shall be established at the end of Liberty Street in the Town of Hartford County of Pulaski for the benefit of said County.

Ja^{s}. T. THOMAS J.I.C.
Ja^{s}. M. TAYLOR J.I.C.
Jos. WOOD Clk. Stephen GATLIN J.I.C.

Page 40

Georgia Pulaski County. By order of the Inferior Court I have paid Jacb SPICKARD three dollars & fifty cents for making irons for jail &c this 25 Jany. 1812. [*1813?*]
$3 50 Jos. WOOD C.I.C.

February 1813

Rec^{d}. this 10 of February 1813 of W^{m}. JELKS Tax Collector one hundred & ten dollars which was laid on the general tax for to defray County expences.
Jos. WOOD Clk.

Paid over to the order of the Court to Hardy VICKERS & William PHELPS one hundred dollars for building a bridge across Limestone Creek this 10 February 1813. Jos. WOOD Clk.

After a correct examination I find with what I have this day rec^{d}. the Tax Collector one hundred sixty six dollars & 50 cents belonging to the County & after reducting the orders of Court as paid & entered this day, look to the next page ~~page~~ for a full statement.

Page 41

Amount on hand this 10 February 1813:		$166.50
Jos. WOOD)	Clerks pr. cent on receiving) and paying out @ 5 prct.	8.31 1/4
		$158.18 3/4
Jos. WOOD)	Order of Court for services in 1812	25. –
		$133.18 3/4
	Order of Court for compensating former Clerk D. GIRTMAN	33.18 3/4
		$100.00
	Order p^{d}. VICKERS & PHELPS for building bridge	100. –
		000.00

County this day in arrears with D. GIRTMAN for order part to him $16.81 1/4 for which there is no fund.

The above is a true statement this 10 February 1813. Jos. WOOD Clk.

By a return made to me and fild away in bundle markd B, you may see that the following names have taken the following oath to support the constitution of the United States according to the grade they hold–James DYKES, Blakley EDDINGS, Evan THOMAS, David PIPKIN...

Page 42

this 31 March 1813. Jos. WOOD C.I.C.

By return made me and fild away in bundle markt B you may see that Major Jos. B. BRYAN & Lieutenant Edward BRYAN have taken the oath to support the constitution of the United States this 1st April 1813.

Jos. WOOD C.I.C.

~~Georgia) This is to certify that GOOLSBY & IVEY are permitted to~~
~~Pulaski County) retail in spirituous liquors in small measures this [*blank*]~~
~~1813.~~ ~~J. WOOD C.I.C.~~

May 1813

Georgia) This is to certify that GOOLSBY & IVEY are permitted to
Pulaski County) retail spirituous liquors in small measures for the term of six
months commencing 1st May 1813. Jos. WOOD Clk.

Page 43, July 1813

Inferior Court July Term 1813 - Present the Honorable
James M. TAYLOR
James T. THOMAS
Henry FULGHAM
Stephen GATLIN

Ordered that William DESHAZO be a commissioner on the River Road from the County line separating this County from Twiggs to Beaver Dam Creek.

Ordered that Murdock McLEOD, Ebenezer ELLIS & Wm. BRACKIN be appointed commissioners of the Cotcher Road from Laurens County line to a hill on this side of Gum Swamp, where a hut was built by BRACKEN.

Ordered that Drury MAY, Daniel DYX J.P. & Wm. LITTLE be appointed commissioners of the sd. road from sd. BRACKENs hut to where it intersects the Milledgeville Road.

Ordered that James SHATTIEN, John BENNETT & John SNELLING be appointed commissioners of the Milledgeville Road from Hartford to where the Cotcher Road commences.

Page 44

Ordered that George G. GAINS, James T. THOMAS & John B. PACKER be appointed commissioners of the Milledgeville Road from ~~where the~~ John BENNETTs to Dee's Creek.

Ordered that James BRACEWELL, David BROOM J.P. & Jesse PEACE be appointed commissioners of the lower River Road from Hartford down to the dividing line between the County & Telfair.

" that Christian RHODES be appointed commissioner of the upper River Road in the place of Mark MASON resigned.

The commissioners appointed to lay off a road commencing at one corner of the County so as to intersect the Sand Bead Road &c &c reported that they had laid off s^{d}. road agreeably to the order of the Court. - which report was received &c.

Ordered that John SMITH J.P., Thomas RODGERS & Blakely EDDINS be appointed commissioners of s^{d}. road.

No. 1

Ordered, on the petition of Co^{l}. TOOKE that the Clerk pay over to him six dollars which he has expended in cleaning the arms diposited in this place for the safety of this part of the frontiers.

And further that the Co^{l}. for the future be authorized to bid out to the lowest bidder the keeping &c...

Page 45

of s^{d}. arms, the expenses of which'll be guaranteed by the Court.

No. 2

On the petition of W^{m}. S. LANCASTER praying for the privilege of establishing a ferry on an acre lot lyinging on the river & bounded on one side by Liberty Street - which s^{d}. lot was reserved to him for the sale of the fraction? to the commissioners - It is ordered, the petition be granted.

On the exhibition of the a/c of John A. WILLIAMS, John W. SUTLINE, John SHAW, Sha. ROGERS, Thos. A. HILL & W^{m}. JELKS for services performed in guarding the jail - It is ordered that the Clerk pay over to the s^{d}. men (out of any money now in his hands or may henceforth come & not otherwise appropriated) the sums which they may may be respectively due which is as follows viz

John A. WILLIAMS	$31.50 - a due bill given for same				
John W. SUTLINE	21. –	do	do	do	do
John SHAW	18 "	do	do	do	do
Sha. ROGERS	1 "				
Thomas A. HILL	2 "	do	do	do	do
W^{m}. JELKS	1 "				
Jonathan VICKERS	7 "				

Page 46

On the presenment of the a/c of Cap. MEWBORN & privates for services performed &c - It is ordered that the s^{d}. Cap. MEWBORN be allowed one dollar & fifty cents a day & each of the men who served under him one dollar also a day for the time they were respectively employed in guarding the jail.

Ordered further that the Clerk of the Inferior Court pay over to s^{d}. MEWBORN & men the sums to which they may be respectively entitled, out of any monies now or which may hereafter be in his hands & not otherwise appropriated - provided the s^{d}. MEWBORN 'll, before payment is made, render to the Clerk on oath a true & ample statement or account of the times he & each of the men was engaged in guarding the jail.

On application of the following defaulters of tax returns - it is ordered that the fourfold tax assessed on their property be remitted.

Philemon BRYANT, Labon KENT, John K. MONTFORD & James EVERETT.

Page 47

On hand two dollars & fifty cents which the Clerk may retain for services in part for the year 1813.

Joseph WOOD the present Clerk handed in his resignation - which was accepted & ordered that an election be held to supply the vacancy.

Stephen GATLIN J.I.C.
James T. THOMAS J.I.C.
Ja^{s}. M. TAYLOR J.I.C.
H. FULGHAM J.I.C.

February/March 1814

Ordered that the Clerk of the Inferior Court do pay to Patrick ROBINSON the sum of ten dollars out of any money that is now in the County funds or that may hereafter be in not otherwise appropriated this 7 March 1814.

A. ODOM
N. STEPHENS
Jas. BRACEWELL J.I.C.

Page 48

February 21st day 1814. the Honourable the Inferior Court of Pulaski County have met agreeable to law. Present their Honors:

James BRACEWELL
Stephen GATLIN
Josiah EVRETT
Archibald ODOM

Ordered that Elijah WALLACE, Ezekiel TAYLOR, Gideon KELLUM and Jourdain DEASE be and are appointed commissioners of the road from the north side of the Bevrdam Creek, to the upper line of this County. Commissions issued this 5th March 1814. Washington LANCASTER Clk.

Ordered that James ROACH, John ISLEAR and Thomas HOWELL be and are appointed commissioners of the line road from the which divids the 21st and 24th districts to the north bank of the run of the Bevrdam Creek. Commissions issued this 5th March 1814.

Adjourned untill 8 oclock tomorrow. Washington LANCASTER Clk.

February 22nd 1814. The Honourable the Inferior Court for the County of Pulaski have met according to adjournment.

We Turner EVERETT, Elijah WALLACE and Washington LANCASTER do somanlly swear, that we will have true faith and allegiance to the State of Georgia, to the utmost of our power and ability, observe, conform to, support and defend, the constitution of this State and that of the United States, to the best of our understanding so help us God.

Ordered that James ROACH, John ISLEAR and Thomas HOWELL be and are appointed commissioners of the road, commencing at Samuel HARTs, and running as near as most convenient, to Hogans Spring.
Commissions issued 5th March 1814. Washington LANCASTER Clk.

Ordered that Sanders COLESTON, David GIRTMAN, and Samuel HART be and are appointed commissioners to view the groond of the within petion and report to the Court the advantage or disadvantage of said road. Commissions issued this 5th March 1814. Washington LANCASTER Clk.

Page 50

Farrm? Rates

Dinner 25 cts. Brakefast 25 cts. Supper 25 cts. Stablage and feeding a horse for night 62 1/2 cts. Single feed corn and fodder 25 cts. Spirrits 12 1/2 cts. per half pt. brandy or whiskey West India or Jimaca rum 18 3/4 cts. Lodging 6 1/4 cts. pr. night.

The Court adjourned untill court in course.

Stephen GATLIN J.I.C.
Josiah EVERITT J.I.C.
Archibld. ODOM J.I.C.
James BRACEWELL J.I.C.

Attest
W. LANCASTER Clk.

Paid to the County funds by Edward SMITH, Daniel MAGEE, Thomas BUTLER and Theodrick MONTFORD twenty dollars for licence to retail spirrits the 26th February 1814.

Paid to Patrick ROBINSON agreeable to an order of Court to me directed ten dollars out of said funds this 8th March 1814.

Washington LANCASTER Clk.

Page 51

Ordered that Murdock McCLEOD, Wm. MORE and A. H. ODOM be and are appointed commissioners of the road leading from Ebinezer ELISes to intercect the road leading to Belles Ferry on the Oconee River. Commissions issued this 5th March 1814.

Ordered that James M. TAYLOR, Edward BLACKSHEAR and Richard H. THOMAS be and are appointed commissioners to view the ground, and report to the Court the public utility of said road from the corner of Orren D. WATSONs fence to the Milledgeville Road. Commissions issued this 5th March 1814.

Washington LANCASTER Clk.

Thomas BUTLER)
Theodric MONTFORD &C^{o}.)
Thomas MACARTAN)
Daniel MAGEE) Whereas the above petioners have applied for a
Thomas M^{c}DANIEL) licence to retail spirrits it is therefore ordered that
the Clerk do grant said persons licence and take bonds in terms of the law. Bonds taken and licence granted. Washington LANCASTER Clk.

Page 52

Ordered that Murdock M^{c}LEOD, W^{m}. BRACKEN & Robert THOMPSON be and are appointed commissn^{rs}. of the road leading from Hartford to intercect with Dublin Road at Asa PIPKINSes. Commissions issued 5 March 1814.
Washington LANCASTER Clk.

Ordered that David BROOM Esqr. be and hereby is appointed commissioner of the road leading from Hartford to intercect the road leading from McCULLOUs cowpen to Bells Ferry on the Oconee.
Commissions issued 5th March 1814. Washington LANCASTER Clk.

Ordered that William HALL Esqr., Hardy VICKERS and Stephen MITCHEL Jun. be and are appointed commissioners of the lower River Road leading from Hartford to the County line dividing Pulaski and Tailfaire Counties. Commissions issued the 5th March 1814. Washington LANCASTER Clk.

Page 53

On the petion of rodes - Ordered that Daniel DYKES, Benjamin ~~MOOR~~ HARRISON, W^{m}. MOOR be and are appoint commissioners of the Line Road leading from Hogans Spring to Intersect the new road at W^{m}. MOORs on a direct line. Commissions issued the 5th March 1814. Washington LANCASTER Clk.

Ordered that John BRACKIN, Jesse POWELL, James DEES be and are appointed commissioners of the road leading from Hartford to Milledgeville to where it strike the Dublin Road. Commissions issued the 5th March 1814.
Washington LANCASTER Clk.

Georgia)
Pulaski County) Personally appeared before me James BRACEWELL one of the Justices of the Inferior Court for said County, William HANEY, and after being duly sworn sayeth on oath that rason why he did not give in his taxable property for the year 1813, was that he did not know of the law in that case in time, sworn to and subscribed before me this March 1814.
James BRACEWELL J.I.C. William HANEY
Examined and approved by the Court.

Page 54, April 1814

Georgia) Personally appeared before me William MACOMMIC and
Pulaski County) after being duly sworn sayeth that he was taken sick about the
last of 1813 in February in the service of the United States, and did note get home

untill ~~after the time of givin in taxable property~~ ~~expence sworn to before me~~ the 26 of April and remained unable to do any kind of business untill after the time given tax returns expired sworn to before me this 6th April 1814.
Examined and approved by the Court. David GARTMAN

I do solemnly swear that I will duly and faithfully perform all and singular the duties required of me as Constable of Pulaski County, according to the best of my abilities and understanding so help me God.
Attest Washington LANCASTER Clk. Christopher EDWARDS

Page 55

I William YARBOROUGH do solemnly swear that I will duly and faithfully perform all and singular the duties required of me as Constable of Pulaski County, according to the best of my abilities and understanding so help me God.
Test Washington LANCASTER Clk. Wm. YARBOROUGH

Paid out of the County funds to David GEARTMAN fourteen dollars the 26th April 1814.
Agreeable to an order of) Washington LANCASTER Clk.

Paid into the County funds by Thomas McDANIEL for a retailing licence five dollars this 23rd April 1814. Washington LANCASTER Clk.

Hartford 24th October 1814. Ordered that the Clerk do issue a licence to Samuel RIGGINS to retail spirrits by the small measure for the term of twelve months at his house in said town. Stephen GATLIN J.I.C.
Test. W. LANCASTER Clk. N. STEPHENS J.I.C.
James BRACEWELL J.I.C.

Page 56, October 1814

Hartford 24th October 1814. Ordered that the Clerk do issue a licence to Zelah PULLAM to retail spirrits by the small measure at ~~his house~~ the house of Jacob SNELLS on the Beaver Dam Creek for the term of twelve months from the the above date.

Ordered that the Clerk do issue a licence to to Willson BASS to retail spirrits at \his house/ on Gum Swamp for the term of twelve months by the small measure this 15th February 1814. Stephen GATLIN
Needham STEPHENS
James BRACEWELL J.I.C.

Paid into the County funds by Samuel RIGGANS for retailing licence five dollars this 24th October 1814. W. LANCASTER Clk.

Paid into the County funds by Zelah PULLIN five dollars for retailing licence this 24th April 1814. W. LANCASTER Clk.

Paid out of the County funds to an order of the Court to John W. SUTLIN for his servises garding the jail ten dollars in part of the order this 3rd November 1814. Washington LANCASTER Clk.

Georgia) We Elizabeth STEWART and William BUMBLY acknow-
Pulaski County) ledge bound and held unto the Justices of the Inferior Court in the sum of five hundred dollars, conditioned to pay all charges that may accrue in the midwifes expences attend the the delivry of a child which the said Elizabeth is delivred of and further to keep the County harmless from every charge that may accrue untill the said child arives to the age of fourteen years old.

Signed & sealed January 18th 1815.

her
Elizabeth x STEWART {Seal}
mark

True Copy by
W. LANCASTER Clk.

William BUMBLY {Seal}

Page 58

Georgia) We Mary TAYLOR and Evans ANDROUS acknowledge
Pulaski County) ourselves bound and firmly held his Excellency the Govenor and to the Judes of the Inferior Court of the County of Pulaski in the sum of five hundred dollars conditioned to pay all the charges and expence that may accrue on the delivry, midwifes and attendance of Mary TAYLOR that is now pregnant, and further acknowledge ourselves bound to keep the ~~County~~ County aforesaid and every other County in the \sd./ State harmless from all and every expence of the expected child which the said Mary is now pregnant with untill it arives to the full age of fourteen years in witness wherof the parties have hereunto set their hands and affixed their seales.

affixed their seales.) her
January 12th 1815.) Mary x TAYLOR {Seal}
Test M. McLEOD J.P.) mark
True copy W. LANCASTER Clk.) Evans ANDROSS {Seal}

Page 59, June/July 1814

Georgia)
Pulaski County) This is to certify that Ensign John SPARROW has this day taken the constitutional oath before me this 10th June 1814.

David GARTMAN J.P.

Georgia)
Pulaski County) This is to certify that Ensign Arthor PHILLIPS has this day taken the constitutional oath required this 10th June 1814.

David GARTMAN J.P.

Georgia)
Pulaski County) This is to certify that Zion DAVIS has this day taken the constitutional oath required this 10th June 1814.

David GARTMAN J.P.

The above certificates recorded at this office the 15 July 1814.

Washington LANCASTER Clk.

G e o r g i a) To the Clerk of the Inferior Court of s^{d}. County.
Pulaski County) This is to certify that Richard H. THOMAS Capt. of the cavelry of the 4th squad 82nd regiment and ~~Furney F. GATLIN~~ James L. PERRY 1st Lieutenant of the cavelry 4th Squad 82nd regiment, and Theophilus SUTTON Cor\uh/net of the 4th squadron and 2nd regiment all have been duly qualified agreeable to law sworn to before me this the fifth November 1814.

Stephen GATLIN J.I.C.

Page 61 blank; Page 62, February 1815

February 20th 1815. the honourable the the Inferior Court of Pulaski County have met agreeable to law Present their Honours:

A. H. ODOM
N. STEPHENS
Jas. BRACEWELL J.I.C.

Ordered that Ezekiel TAYLOR, Gidean KELLIM and James TOMLINSON be and are appointed commissioners of the road from the north side of Beaver Dam Creek, to the upper line of this County - Copy sent out this 22nd February 1815.

W. LANCASTER Clk.

Ordered that James ROACH, Thomas HOWELL and Sanders COLESTON be and are appointed commissioners of the road from the line that divides the 21st and 24th districts to the north bank of the Beaver Dam Creek - Copy sent out 22nd February 1815. W. LANCASTER Clk.

Ordered that Joel DAWSON, William BRACKEN, Robert THOMPSON and Daniel DYKES Esqr. be and are appointed commissioners of the road leading from Hartford, to intersect the Dublin Road at Asa PIPKINSes. Copy sent out 22nd February 1815. Washington LANCASTER Clk.

Page 63

Ordered that William JOHNSON, Benjamin BROOTON and Archibald THOMPSON be and are appointed to view the ground from Hartford to MAHAFFEs cowpin the neares best way and report to the Court the public utility of a road running as above directed. Copy sent out 22nd February 1815.

Washington LANCASTER Clk.

Ordered that Stephen MITCHELL, Hardy VICKERS and William HALL Esqr. be and are appointed commissioners of the lower River Road to the County line. Copy sent out 22nd February 1815. Washington LANCASTER Clk.

Ordered that John BRADSHAW, Jessey POWELL and James DEES be and are appointed commissioners of the Milledgeville Road from the Dublin Road to the County line on the Milledgeville Road. Copy sent out 22nd February 1815.

Washington LANCASTER Clk.

Ordered that John LEE, Moses KIRTLIN and Joseph BARRON Esqr. be and are appointed commissioners of the road commencing at the North corner of Pulaski and runing the direct line untill it intersects the Milledgeville Road. Copy sent out this 22nd February 1815. Washington LANCASTER Clk.

On the petition of John O. GRANT praying an alteration on the road leading from the Nest Egg Bluff, Ordered that Wm. HORN, Thomas SMITH and Joel REAVES be and are appointed commissioners to view the ground of of said petioner and report [to] the Court.

Ordered that the Clerk do grant William BRACKEN a licence to retail spirrits by the small measure untill the 6th of December next this 20th February 1815. Licence ~~granted~~ issued by ~~Washington LANCASTER~~ Clk.

Ordered that the Clerk do grant Kinchen DAWSON a licence to retail spirrits by the small measure untill the 6th December next licence issued by ~~Washington LANCASTER~~ Clk.

I William MOOR do solemnly swear that I will faithfully perform all and singular the duties required of me as Constable of Pulaski County according to the best of my ability and understanding so help me God.

Attest W. LANCASTER Clk. William MOOR

Page 65

Ordered that William MOOR be and hereby is appointed Constable for this County.

Ordered that the Clerk do grant Edward SMITH, Thomas SHEPHERD, Theodrick MONTFORD, Daniel MAGEE and Thomas McDANIEL a licence to retail by the small measure at there respective houses. Licence issued to the above named accept McDANIEL. W. LANCASTER Clk.

Ordered that William HILLIARD) be and hereby ~~is~~ are appointed
William YARBOROUGH) Constables for the districts of
Frederick FLOYD) ALFRD, CLARK and DYKES

You and each of you do solemnly swear that you will truly and faithfully perform all and singular the duties required of you as Constables in your different districts according to the best of your abilities and understanding so help you God.

Attest W. LANCASTER Clk.
William HILLIARD
William YARBOROUGH
Frederick FLOYD

Page 66

Ordered that Samuel FOWLE have privaledge of improving five lots lying between his possesion and BUTLERs tan? yard.

The Court then adjourned untill tomorrow nine oclock.

Attest) Josiah EVERETTE
Washington LANCASTER Clk.) Stephen GATLIN
) Needham STEPHENS J.I.C.

February 21st day 1815. The Court have met according to to adjournment and proceeded to business.

No. 1. On petition of Allen TOOKE praying rent of his house which he deposited arms and ammunition in for the public the Court took Court took up the petion and for the want of a full Court it was laid over till August term.

~~W. LANCASTER Clk.~~

Ordered that the accoun[t] of William LYON for $141.43 1/2 cents brought in against the estate of Micajah H. POWELL be granted.

~~Washington LANCASTER Clk.~~

No. 2. On the petion of Samuel HART praying relief on instructions how to act on the property of Mr. ANDROES decd. laid over for consideration.

~~W. LANCASTER Clk.~~

Ordered that Charles CARDEN be and hereby is appointed Constable for Capt. CLARKs Dist.

You Charles CARDEN do solemnly swear that you will truly and faithfully perform all and singular the duties required of you as Constable for Capt. CLARKs Dist. according to the best of your abilitys and understanding so help you God.

God.	) Charles CARDEN
Test W. LANCASTER Clk.	) Steph. GATLIN J.I.C.
	) Josiah EVERITT J.I.C.
Adjourned till court in course.	) N. STEPHENS J.I.C.

Page 68, March 1815

~~7th March 1815 Called Court~~

Ordered that Christopher EDWARDS be and hereby is appointed Constable for Capt. ALFORDs Dist.

You Christopher EDWARDS do solemnly swear that you will duly and truly perform all and singular the duties required of you as Constable of Pulaski County to the best of your abilities and understanding so help you God.

Test W. LANCASTER Clk. Christopher EDWARDS

A Court called \and passed the above/ Present their Honors:

7th March 1815	)	James BRACEWELL
Test W. LANCASTER	)	Stephen GATLIN
Clk.	)	Josiah EVERETTE J.I.C.

Georgia) Ordered that the Clerk of the Inferior Court grant commis-
Pulaski County) sions to Edward SMITH, Samuel RIGGINS and William LYON as commissioners of the Town of Hartford.

This 1st May 1815	)	Josiah EVERETTE J.I.C.
Order filed in the office	)	Stephen GATLIN J.I.C.
this 5 May 1815	)	Needham STEPHENS J.I.C.

Page 69 blank; Page 70

March 1815. Received of William BRACKEN, Thomas SHEPHERD, Joshua HARRIS, Edward SMITH and Daniel MAGEE five dollars each for retailing licence. ~~my fees taken~~ $25.00 Washington LANCASTER Clk.

Paid to David GARTMAN Esqr. five dollars the balance of an order by the Inferior Court this 25th April 1815. W. LANCASTER Clk.

Georgia) I do certify that Henry HAGAN Capt. and Thomas W.
Pulaski County) HARRIS Esqr. have taken the oath to support the constitution which is required by the laws of this state this 23rd June 1815.

John A. WILLIAMS J.P.

Received of Thomas McDANIEL for retailing licence five dollars the [blank] October 1815. Washington LANCASTER C.I.C.

Page 71, September 1815

Inferior Court extary term September 4th 1815. Presents their Honors:

Stephen GATLIN)
Josiah EVERETTE) Esqrs.
A. H. ODOM)
Needham STEPHENS)

Ordered that Mark MASON, Wm. DESHAZO & Simon BARDIN be and are appointed commissioners of the River Road commencing at the North side of Beaver Dam Creek in liew of Ezekiel TAYLOR and others.

Order that Jas. DYKES be and is appointed Constable in Esquire DYKES District.

On the petion of sundry of the inhabitants of Pulaski praying a road to commence to Mark MASONs or near there and intersect with the Uchee tract at Gum Swamp (petion granted) and Joseph B. BRYAN, Henry FULGHAM, Gideon MAYO be and are appointed commissioners.

Page 72

Georgia) You Jas. DYKES do solomanly swear that you will and
Pulaski County) truly and faithfully perform all and singular the duties required of you as Constable of Esquire DYKES District according to the best of your abilities and understanding so help you God.

Test W. LANCASTER Clk. James DYKES

Ordered that the Clerk do ~~pay Jas. L.~~ cause a stamp to be made for the us of stamping weights and measures throughout this County and that the said stamp be a single letter **H**.

Josiah EVERETTE J.I.C.
James BRACEWELL J.I.C.
Stephen GATLIN J.I.C.

Page 73, November 1815

~~Georgia) Christopher BOND of Capt. DYKES district in this County~~
~~Pulaski County) tells before me a chesnut sorral mare about fourteen and a half [hands] high about twelve years old a blaze in her face very much marked the gear branded on the mounting shoulder thus S A a sore on her back, appraised by John SWERINGIN and James MILLER at fifty dollars this 3rd November 1815.~~

~~Daniel DYKES J.P.~~

~~State of Georgia) This day personally appeared before me Ebenezar FOALSOM~~
~~Pulaski County) makes oath and saith that a certain chesnut sorrel mare about twelve or thirteen years old a blaze in her face very much marke with the gear about fourteen and a half hands high branded on the mounting thus S.A. a sore on her back tolde by Christopher BOND of Capt. DYKES dist. before Danl. DYKES Esqr. for this County appraised by John SWEARINGAN and Jas. MILLER on the third day of November 1815 at fifty dollars he knows to be the property of Edward SHERMON and that the above described mare did either brake out of a lot or was stolen out on the night of the twentyfirst of October in the Town of Dubling in the County of Laurence.~~ ~~(turn over)~~

Page 74

~~Sworn and subscribed to before me this 7th December 1815.~~
~~Daniel DYKES J.P.~~ ~~Ebenezer FOLSOM~~

~~Description and valuation of an estray~~
~~Georgia) John WILCOX of the County aforesaid tells before me one~~
~~Pulaski County) certain darke bay filly she of four years old next spring appraised by Wm. LESTER and Hardy VICKERS at thirty dollars December the 25th day 1815.~~ ~~Jason BRINSON J.P.~~

Page 75 blank; Page 76, January 1816

January 15th 1816 The Honourable the Inferior Court hath met agreeable to law Present their Honours:
A. H. ODOM)
Stephen GATLIN)
Needham STEPHENS)
Josiah EVERETTE)
Jas. BRACEWELL) J.I.C.

Ordered that W^{m}. HILLIARD be and hereby is appointed Constable of Capt. WILLIAMS dist.

Ordered that W^{m}. YARBOROUGH Jn^{r}. and Daniel M^{c}NEAR be and hereby are appointed Constables of Capt. CLARKs dist.

Ordered that Joseph COLESON be and hereby is appointed Constable of Capt. HORNs dist., and Benjamin HOWELL.

Ordered that Luis HOLLAND and Ja^{s}. DYKES be and are hereby appointed Constables in Capt. DYKES dist.

Page 77

Ordered that Josiah ELISS be and [*blank*] be and hereby are appointed Constables of Capt. HARDESONs dist.

Ordered that Ja^{s}. DOWIT be and hereby is appointed Constable of Capt. LESTERs dist.

Ordered that John MAYO be and hereby is appointed Constable of Capt. SHINEs dist.

On the petion of Abraham VICKERS praying an alteration on the lower River Road from ALFORDs to the upper ford on Leggits Creek – granted.

Ordered that Wm. HALL, William GOODSON and Jas. POWELL be and are appointed commissioners to view the ground affoursaid and report to the next Court.

Ordered that Isaac KIRKSEY be granted a licence to retail spirrits by the small measure.

Ordered that ~~Washington~~ LANCASTER \& WILLIAMS/, Joseph WOOD \& Co./ and Edward SMITH be granted a licence to retail spirrits by the small measure.

Page 78

Ordered that Jordan ANDERSON be and is appointed Commissioner in place of Mark MASON on the upper River Road from the Beaver Dam to the County line.

Ordered that Ebenezer ELIS be and is appointed commissioner in place of Wm. MOOR decd. and for all the other commissioners stand good as commissioners for three? months longer on all other roads.

Ordered that John A. WILLIAMS, William GOODSON be and are appointed commissioners to view the ground from Hartford to intersect the Beall Ferry Road at the County line and report to the Court the utility of said road that the above named men be and hereby are appointed on said road and proceed as the law directs.

Adjourned untill tomorrow morning ten oclock.

Thursday the 16th. The Honourable the Inferior Court have met according to adjournment. Present their Honors:

Jas. BRACEWELL)
Josiah EVERETTE)
Stephen GATLIN) J.I.C.

[*End of book - pages missing*]

COURT OF ORDINARY
MINUTES 1810-1817

Microfilm copy in Georgia Archives identifies this book as:
Superior Court Minutes, 2nd book 1810-1817

Georgia) On application of Martha SPEIGHT (a minor) praying that
Pulaski County) Sands STANDLY may be appointed as guardian to her person and property; It is therefore ordered that the said Sands STANDLY be appointed accordingly & that the clerk take bond & security in the sum of six thousand dollars for the faithfull performance of his duty.

Given under our hands this 22nd Octr. 1810.

Edmund HOGAN J.I.C.
Jas. T. THOMAS J.I.C.
Henry FULGHAM J.I.C.

November 1810

At a Court of Ordinary on the first Monday in November 1810 the court failing to attend Court then adjourned till tomorrow ten oclock.

5th Novr. 1810 Turner EVERETT Clk.

Page 2

Georgia) On application of Peter WILLIAMS and Sophia WILLIAMS
Pulaski County) and Isaac WILLIAMS and Mariah WILLIAMS orphans of Bowery WILLIAMS for Leonard STRINGER to be appointed their guardian; Therefore it is ordered that the aforesaid Leonard STRINGER be hereby appointed guardian for said orphans by his giving bond and security to the clerk according to law made and provided for that purpose.

Given under our hands Nov. 6th 1810.
An order of the court.

Edmund HOGAN J.I.C.
S. JONES J.I.C.
Wm. A. HARPER J.I.C.

Page 3, January 1812

Georgia) ~~Jessee POWELL Wm. Is~~
Pulaski County) In chambers 6th January 1812, Present their honors:

Edmond HOGAN
Henry FULGHAM
James T. THOMAS
James M. TAYLOR
Mordock McLOED

On the application of Drury MAY praying that he may be appointed as guardian to the persons & property of David, Nancy & Hiram MOSES; It is therefore ordered that the said Drury MAY be appointed accordingly.

An order of the Court of Ordinary on January term authorising the county surveyor to lay off 222 acres of land as her dower - out of the lands of John MOSES land and laid out as may be directed by Mrs. Ann MOSES (widow) to said decd.

Georgia) Jessee POWELL, Wm. ISLER, Reubin FITZGERRALD,
Pulaski County) Micajah H. POWELL, David SNELL

It is ordered that the above named persons or any three of them proceed to appraise...

the personal estate of Wm. A. HARPER decd. and render a scedule of the same to this Court on or before the first Monday in March being the next term in course.

Henry FULGHAM J.I.C.
Test 6th January 1812 Mordock McLOUD J.I.C.
Turner EVERETT Clk. Edmond HOGAN J.I.C.

Leonard STRINGER having made application to the Justices of the Court of Ordinary of Pulaski County for leave to sell a tract of land containing two hundred two & a half acres situate lying & being in the fourteenth district Baldwin and known in the plans of said district by No. two hundred and twenty eight; It is therefore ordered that the said Leonard STRINGER have leave to sell the aforesaid tract of land in terms of the law of the General Assembly in such cases made and provided. 6th January 1812 Edmond HOGAN J.I.C.
Test M. McLOED J.I.C.
Turner EVERETT Clk. Henry FULGHAM J.I.C.

Page 5, May 1812

Monday 4th May 1812. Present their Honors
James M. TAYLOR &) Court being called and
James T. THOMAS) not a Court made -
Court was then adjourned till court in course. Turner EVERETT Clk.

July 1812

Monday 6th July 1812, Present their Honors
James M. TAYLOR &) The Court being called
James T. THOMAS) and not a Court made
Court was then adjourned till court in course. Turner EVERETT Clk.

November 1812

Georgia) Monday the Second day of November 1812
Pulaski County) The Honorable the court of ordinary having this day met agreeable to adjournment present their honors:
James M. TAYLOR)
James T. THOMAS)
Henry FULGHAM)

The Last Will and Testament of Solomon A. HOPKINS late of this county & state aforesaid decd. being this day produced in open court and proved of as being proven in Baldwin...

Page 6

County according to probate on the will and Nancy HOPKINS, James M. TAYLOR and Mordica HOWARD Executors named in said Last Will and Testament being qualified as the law directs in such cases made & provided; It is therefore ordered that Letters Testamentory and Warrant of Appraisement be granted;

Ordered that the following persons be appointed appraisers - Henry F. SIMMONS, Joseph WOOD, Daniel MAGEE, William JELKS and Elijah WALLACE.

Henry FULGHAM J.I.C.
Test James T. THOMAS J.I.C.
Turner EVERETT Clk. James M. TAYLOR J.I.C.P.C.

Monday 2nd Novr. 1812. The Honorable the Court of Ordinary then met agreeable to adjournment. Present their Honors:

James M. TAYLOR)
Henry FULGHAM)
James T. THOMAS)

Page 7, September 1812 (after November)

September Term 1812. The Court of Ordinary having met at the court house in the town of Hartford on the 8th Septr. 1812. The following gentlemen members of the Court were present (viz) James T. THOMAS)
Henry FULGHAM)
James M. TAYLOR)
Murdock McLOED)

Ordered by the court that Stephen GATLIN, William S. LANCASTER & George G. GAINS be appointed overseers of the poor.

Ordered that the Sheriff of the county be authorised to contract upon the most favorable terms for the building of the requested number of tables & seats.

Murdock McLOED J.I.C.P.C.
Test James M. TAYLOR J.I.C.P.C.
Turner EVERETT Clk. Henry FULGHAM J.I.C.
James T. THOMAS J.I.C.

January 1813

The honorable the Court of Ordinary for the county of Pulaski having met at the court house in the town of Hartford on the fourth day of January 1813. The following gentlemen members of the court were present (viz)

James M. TAYLOR)
Henry FULGHAM)
James T. THOMAS)

Page 8

The court then adjourned till tomorrow morning ten oclock.

January 5th 1813 - The court then met agreeable to adjournment. The court then adjourned till court in course.

Test James M. TAYLOR J.I.C.P.C.
Turner EVERETT Clk. Henry FULGHAM J.I.C.
James T. THOMAS J.I.C.

Monday 3 day of May 1813. The honorable the Court of Ordinary then met agreeable to law. Present their Honors James M. TAYLOR
James T. THOMAS
Stephen GATLIN

Ordered that Letters of Administration be granted to Daniel MAGEE provided he give bond with such security as the court may approve of and that Joseph WOOD, Elijah WALLACE, Danil CORNWALL, John RAMSEY, James RAMSEY & Edward SMITH be appraisors.

Whereas John RAMSEY applied to become the guardian to the persons and property of Harriot HARPER, ...

Page 9

Jefferson & Andrew Nox HARPER orphans of William A. HARPER late of the County of Pulaski (minors) It is hereby ordered that the said John RAMSEY be appointed accordingly.

ŧ The court then adjourned till Monday the 17th day of this instant.

Test	James T. THOMAS J.I.C.
Turner EVERETT Clk.	Stephen GATLIN J.I.C.
	James M. TAYLOR J.I.C.

Monday 17th May 1813. The Honorable the Court of Ordinary then met agreeable to adjournment. Present their Honors
James M. TAYLOR
James T. THOMAS
Henry FULGHAM
Stephen GATLIN

Ordered that Letters of Administration be granted to Dianna DUNN on the estate of Jacob DUNN decd. and that a warrant of appraisement be directed to Philip BRYAN, Neal McALPIN, Joseph SESSIONS, Jas. CHASTAIN & Archibald THOMPSON.

Ordered that Letters of Administration be granted to Prutia COLE on the estate of John COLE decd. and that a warrante of appraisement be ~~drect~~ directed to [*small tear, likely no text missing*] ...

Page 10

Thomas BUTLER, Isaac GOOLSBY, James A. EVERETT, Elijah WALLACE and Joseph WOOD.

The court then adjourned till Court in course.

Test	James T. THOMAS J.I.C.
Turner EVERETT Clk.	Stephen GATLIN J.I.C.
	Henry FULGHAM J.I.C.

July 1813

Monday 5th day of July 1813. The Honorable the Court of Ordinary for the County of Pulaski being the day in course for the meeting of said Court of

Ordinary – was duly called and an insufficient of Justices not appearing to constitute a quorum was adjourned till Court in course. Present their Honors

Test — James M. TAYLOR
Turner EVERETT Clk. — Stephen GATLIN

January 1814

Monday 3rd January 1814. The Honorable the Court of Ordinary for the County of Pulaski then met agreeable to law, Present their Honors –

Page 11

James BRACEWELL
Needham STEPHENS
Josiah EVERETT
Archibald ODAM

Ordered that Letters of Administration be granted to Joel SHERROD and Mary JONES on the estate of James JONES late of Pulaski County (decd.) and that a warrant of appraisement be directed to Samuel JONES, George G. GAINES, John BRADSHAW, Robert DEWITT and Robert THOMPSON.

Ordered that Letters of Administration be granted to Robert HILL on the estate of Thomas A. HILL late of Pulaski County decd. and that a warrant of appraisement be directed to Elijah WALLACE, William LYON, David BROOM, Thomas McDANIEL and Edward SMITH.

ORDERED that the proceedings of Simon BARDIN as guardian...

Page 12

to the persons and property of Nancy & Celia LOFTLY orphans of Jessee LOFTLY late of Jefferson County decd. be removed to the County of Pulaski.

Whereas Aron SCARBOROUGH has petitioned this court to be exonorated from his securityship in the guardianship of Drury MAY to the persons & propertys of David, Hiram & Nancy MOSES orphans of John MOSES; It is ordered that said SCARBOROUGH shall be exonerated from said securityship & that Wm. BRYAN become security in place thereof.

Test
Turner EVERETT Clk.

Stephen GATLIN J.I.C.
Josiah EVERETT J.I.C.
Jas. BRACEWELL J.I.C.
N. STEPHENS J.I.C.

Page 13, March 1814

Monday 7th March 1814. The Honorable the Court of Ordinary for the county of Pulaski then met agreeable to law — Present their Honors

Needham STEPHENS
Archibald ODOM
James BRACEWELL

Ordered that Letters of Administration be granted to Joel DAWSON and Danil RHODES on the estate of John REEVES dec^{d}. and that they be bound in the sum of two thousand dollars and that a warrant of appraisement be directed to Jacob SNELL, Lewis HOLLAND, James ROACH, Theophilus SUTTON and Michael HORN.

Ordered that Letters of Administration be granted to Washington LANCASTER & Haywood ALFORD on the estate of William S. LANCASTER dec^{d}. and that they be bound in the sum of ten thousand dollars and that a warrant of appraisement be directed to Joseph SESSIONS, Thomas SHEPHERD, ...

Page 14

Neel M^{c}ALPIN, William GOODSON, and James BRACEWELL.

Ordered that Letters of Administration be granted to Daniel RHODES on the Estate of Mary HARPER late of this county dec^{d}. and tha[t] he be bound in the sum of three thousand dollars and that a warrant of appraisement be directed to W^{m}. ISLER, John RHODES, David SNELL, Abner EVERITT and Jessee POWELL.

N. STEPHENS J.I.C.
A. ODOM J.I.C.
Ja^{s}. BRACEWELL J.I.C.

The Court then adjourned until Court in course — Turner EVERETT Clk.

Page 15, May 1814

Monday the second day of May 1814. The Honorable the Court of Ordinary for the County of Pulaski failing to attend the Court then adjourned till Court in course. Present their Honors — James BRACEWELL)
Turner EVERETT Clk. Josiah EVERETT)

July 1814

Georgia) The Honorable the Court of Ordinary for the said County
Pulaski County) met on Monday the fourth of July 1814 agreeable to adjournment, present their Honors Stephen GATLIN)
A. ODOM)
Josiah EVERETT)
James BRACEWELL)
Needham STEPHENS)

On application by Chas. CARDIN Administrator on the estate of Susannah M^{c}GILL deceased it is ordered that the proceedings on said estate be received, and bond with approved security be taken from said Charles CARDIN bond for $2000 securities James CLARK, Moses SUTTON — & that he be furnished with a certificate for the same.

An account brought by Rich^{d}. H. THOMAS against W^{m}. A. HARPER deceased ordered that said account be allowed.

Page 16

An account brought by Sanders COLSON against the estate of Solomon A. HOPKINS deceased — ordered that said account be allowed.

On the application of Diana DUNN Adm^{x}. on the estate of Jacob DUNN deceased for leave to sell lot N°. 271 in the 21st District of Wilkinson now Pulaski County it is ordered that she have leave to sell said lot of land.

On the application of James M. TAYLOR for letters of administration on the estate and effects of Micajah H. POWELL deceased it is ordered that letters be granted him by giving bond with approved security — Warrant of appraisement to be directed to Thos. M^{c}DANIEL, Elijah WALLACE, W^{m}. LYON, Edward SMITH, David KINDALL.

On application of Daniel RHODE administrator on the estate of Mary HARPER for her part of the estate also her part of one of the heirs estate;

Ordered that Jacob SNELL deliver that part of the estate to Daniel RHODE and that Henry FULGAM, Jesse POWELL, Thomas M^{c}GRIFF, W^{m}. ISLER & John RHODE esq^{r}. be and are hereby appointed to make a division of s^{d}. estates and that they make a return to the next court of their proceedings.

Page 17

On application of W^{m}. GARBET and Elizabeth KING for letters of administration on the estate and effects of Samuel KING deceased — It is ordered that letters of administration be granted them by their giving bond with approved security — Warrant of appraisement to be directed to W^{m}. H. GROSS, George WALKER, Ezekiel TAYLOR, Henry FULGAM and Thos. M^{c}GRIFF.

An account brought by W^{m}. LYON against the estate of Solomon A. HOPKINS, and ordered that the same be allowed.

An account brought by John JONES against the estate of Solomon A. HOPKINS, and approved by the Court.

The Honorable Court of Ordinary then adjourned untill the first Monday in Septem^{r}. next.

Stephen GATLIN
Ja^{s}. BRACEWELL
N. STEVENS
Josiah EVERITT
Ach^{d}. ODOM

Test. David KENDALL
Clk. Pro tem

Page 18, September 1814

Georgia)
Pulaski County)
The Honorable the Court of Ordinary for said County met on Monday 5th September 1814 agreeable to adjournment.
Present their Honors
Stephen GATLIN)
Josiah EVERITT)
Needham STEPHENS)

Ordered that Stephen PENNINGTONs will be recorded.

Ordered that Letters Testamentary be granted to Elizabeth PENNINGTON executrix and Joseph B. BRYAN executor on the estate of Stephen PENNINGTON dec^{d}. Elizabeth PENNINGTON and Joseph B. BRYAN qualified as the law directs. Ordered that a warrant of appraisement be directed to David DUHURT, Beggars SINGLETON, Robert THOMPSON, Dixon JELKS and John GRINSTEAD.

Ordered that George G. GAINES, Ezekiel TAYLOR, Thomas McGRIFF, Jacob SNELL and James ROACH be appointed overseers of the poor for the County of Pulaski. Ordered that the Clerk do make out certificates to give to the above named persons for the above purpose.

Stephen GATLIN) Justices of
N. STEPHENS) the Inferior
Josiah EVERITT) Court

Court adjourned till Court in course.
Test Tuttle H. MORELAND for Turner EVERITT Clk. C.O.

Page 19, December 1814

The Honorable the Inferior Court for the County of Pulaski convened for Ordinary purposes the 24th Decr. 1814 — Present their Honors

Stephen GATLIN)
Needham STEPHENS)
Josiah EVERETT)

On the the application of Prusia COLE admx. on the estate of John COLE of said County deceased praying an order authorising her as admx. as aforesaid to make titles to a certain lot of land in the County of Randolph now Jasper County and known by the number one hundred & twenty nine, in the nineteenth district then Baldwin County, in compliance with a contract made by the said John COLE in his lifetime; Ordered that the said Prusia COLE admx. as aforesaid have full power & authority to make titles to said lot of land. N. STEVENS J.I.C.

Attest Stephen GATLIN J.I.C.
Turner EVERETT Clk. Josiah EVERETT J.I.C.

Page 20, March 1815

Georgia) Monday the sixth of March 1815 the Honorable the Court
Pulaski County) of Ordinary for the County of Pulaski met agreeable to adjournment - Present their Honors

Josiah EVERETT)
Needham STEVENS)
James BRACEWELL)
& Stephen GATLIN)

The records of the Court of Ordinary of the County of Jefferson so far as relates to the property of Celia & Nancy LOFTLY and their guardian together with his proceedings having been removed to this County — Ordered that the Clerk do enter the same & they be a part of the records of this court.

Ordered that Wm. HORNE's claim to medicine found in the possession of Micaijah H. POWELL decd. admitted as just, and that the administrator be directed to deliver the same to Wm. HORNE or order.

~~Ordered that the return of Daniel~~ \Jacob/ ~~SNELL of the estate of Wm. HARPER decd.for 1814 be received.~~

Page 21

Ordered that the return of Daniel RHODES & Joel DAWSON of the estate of John REEVES be received — for 1814.

Ordered that the return of Jacob SNELL of the est. of W^{m}. A. HARPER dec^{d}. for 1814 be received by the court.

Personally appeared in open court Alexander WATSON [*McBride?*] & Christian M^{c}BRIDE, who being duly sworn saith that the account of Docter Micajah H. POWELL dec^{d}. against Dugald M^{c}BRIDE is overcharged by one visit, and that the said POWELL never gave but one visit to the wife of the said Dugald M^{c}BRIDE. Alexander M^{c}BRIDE [*Watson?*]

her
March 6th 1815 Christian x M^{c}BRIDE
mark

Upon the petition of Sias TAYLOR & William TAYLOR for letters of administration on the estate of Josiah TAYLOR late of this county deceased, It is ordered that permanent letters of administration be granted them upon their giving bond with approved security and that a warrant of appraisement be directed to Thos. ADAMS, Laurence FOLSOM, George FULSOM, John DANIEL and Dennis ADAMS.

On application of Elizabeth SMITH & John A. WILLIAMS for letters of administration on the estate of W^{m}. SMITH late of this county deceased, It is ordered that letters...

Page 22

of administration be granted them and a warrant of appraisement be granted them and that a warrant of appraisement be directed to Benjamin SMITH, W^{m}. JOHNSON, William GOODSON, Robert DANIEL & Neil M^{c}ALPIN.

Ordered that Charles CARDINs exhoneration from Jones County from the administration on the estate of Susannah M^{c}GILL be received and the certificate entered on the minutes of this Court.

Georgia) I do certify that Charles CARDIN is exhonerated from the
Jones County) administration of the estate of Susannah M^{c}GILL in the County aforesaid this 7th Nov. 1814. H. M. COMER? C.C.O.

A true copy of the certificate
David KENDALL for Turner EVERETT Clk.

Samuel JONES Senr. & Nancy JONES were qualified as executors to the will of Phillip JONES deceased and – Ordered that Allen TOOKE, Furny F. GATLIN, Sanders COLSON, Charles CARDIN & Arch^{d}. H. THOMAS be and are hereby appointed to appraise the said estate, and that letters testamentary be granted them.

Page 23

The court then adjourned till 10 oclock tomorrow morning.

Stephen GATLIN
Test David KENDALL for N. STEPHENS
Turner EVERITT Clk. James BRACEWELL

Court met agreeable to adjournment this 7th March 1815.

B. GARDNER for Turner EVERITT Clk.

On the petition of Washington LANCASTER, Sarah LANCASTER & Wright LANCASTER legatees of William S. LANCASTER deceased praying a partition of the estate of said deceased, It is ordered that James BRACEWELL Esqr., William GOODSON, Neal McCALPIN, Abraham VICKERS and Joseph SESSIONS be and they are hereby appointed to make said division.

The court adjourned till court in course this 7th March 1815.

	Josiah EVERITT J.I.C.
Test Bynum GARDNER for	S[t]ephen GATLIN J.I.C.
Turner EVERITT Clk.	Jas. BRACEWELL J.I.C.

Page 24, May 1815

Monday 1st day of May 1815. The Honorable the Court of Ordinary for the County of Pulaski has now met agreeably to law. Present their Honors—

Stephen GATLIN
Josiah EVERITT
Needham STEPHENS

On the petition of Henry JONES praying the court of Ordinary to appoint Allen TOOKE guardian to the person and property of the said Henry JONES orphan of Philip JONES late of Pulaski County decd.; Ordered that the said Allen TOOKE be appointed guardian as aforesaid and that he be bound in the sum of three thousand dollars with sufficient security.

On the petition of Daniel KIRKLIN praying to be appointed as guardian to the person & property of Elizabeth KIRKLIN orphan of John KIRKLIN late of Bullock County decd. Ordered that the said Daniel KIRKLIN be appointed guardian as aforesaid and that he be bound in the sum of two thousand dollars with sufficient security.

Page 25

Ordered that letters of administration be granted to Hardy VICKERS and Jason BRINSON on the estate of Lester CRAWFORD late of Pulaski County decd. and that they be bound in the sum of ten thousand dollars, and that a warrant of appraisement be directed to John WILCOX, James ROUNTREE, Thomas ADAMS, William TAYLOR & Mills TAYLOR.

Ordered that letters of administration be granted to Bolling SWEARINGAIN on the estate of John SNELLING late of Pulaski County decd. and that they be bound in the sum of five thousand dollars, and that a warrant of appraisement be directed to William YARBOROUGH, Samuel REGAN, Thomas MILLS, John A. WILLIAMS & James CLARK.

Ordered that letters of administration be granted to William GARBITT on the estate of Brokenberry ANDERS late of Pulaski County decd. and that he be bound in the sum of one thousand dollars and that a warrant of appraisement be directed to Samuel HART, Frederick WOLF, James ROACH, Thomas HARRELL & William WOTEN.

Georgia) Upon application it is ordered by the Court of Ordinary that
Pulaski County) letters of administration be granted to Josiah D. CAUTHORN & Mary SYLVESTER on the estate of John SYLVESTER, on their giving bond and security as the law is such cases requires — Appraisers George FOLSOM, Laurence FOLSOM, W^{m}. TAYLOR, Mills TAYLOR, Thomas ADAMS, Jason BRINSON.

Georgia) Ordered that Saml. JONES & Nancy JONES do give up to
Pulaski County) Arthur TOOKE & Allen TOOKE guardian of Mary JONES a certain bill of sale in the possession of s^{d}. Saml. JONES for a negro girl named Nanci.

On the petition of Elizabeth SMITH praying the dowery of the real estate to be laid off for her benefit; Ordered that the said Elizabeth SMITHs petition be granted and that James BRASWELL, William GOODSON & Benjamin SMITH be appointed with the County Surveyor to divide the same.

Ordered that Saml. JONES do be exhonorated from being security in behalf of Prutia COLE administratrix for the estate of John COLE and that said Saml. JONES has his name eraced off of the bond & Theod. MONTFORT & Joshua HARRIS be inserted in the lieu thereof.

Page 27

The Court then adjourned till court in course. Stephen GATLIN)
Test Josiah EVERITT)
Turner EVERETT Clk. N. STEVENS) J.I.C.

September 1815

Monday the 4th of September 1815. The Honorable the Court of Ordinary for the County of Pulaski has now met agreeably to law. Present their Honors

Stephen GATLIN)
A. ODOM)
Needham STEPHENS)
Josiah EVERETT)

Ordered that permanent letters of administration be granted to Mark MASON on the estate of John SMEDLY (dec^{d}.) and that a warrant of appraisement be directed to John DEES, Hardy GATLIN, William DESHAZO, Simon BARDIN and James TOMLINSON and that he be bound in the sum of five hundred dollars.

Ordered that letters of administration be granted to Bazel HARRIS and Allen TOOKE on the estate of Joshua HARRIS (dec^{d}.) and that they be bound in the sum of one thousand dollars, and that a warrant of appraisement...

Page 28

be directed to Elijah WALLACE, William LYON, Washington LANCASTER, John A. WILLIAMS and Tuttle H. MORELAND.

Ordered that the Clerk to the Commissioners of the ~~Town~~ County of Pulaski do pay unto Elias BALLARD the sum of thirty dollars out of any money now in his hands bilonging to the County for the support of the poor.

Ordered that the appraisors on the estate of W^{m}. S. LANCASTER dec^{d}. in Burke County do appraise a certain tract of land in said county, and give from under their hands the valuation of said land to the administrators on said estate.

Ordered that Lester CRAFFORDs note for one hundred & five dollars due the 21st Decr. 1812 be taken from Elijah WALLACE in lieu of Reuben FITZGERALD notes and the balance to be paid said WALLACE in any notes in the office — the above note on Lester CRAFFORD is received.

The Court then adjourned till court in course.

4th September 1815) Stephen GATLIN)
Tuttle H. MORELAND for) N. STEVENS)
Turner EVERETT Clk.) A. ODOM)
Josiah EVERITT) J.I.C.

Page 29

Ordered that Joel SHERROD and Mary JONES ad^{m}. & adm^{x}. on the estate of James JONES (dec^{d}.) have leave to sell one lot of land in Pulaski County whereon said Joel SHERROD now lives – 4th Septr. 1815.

Ordered that the Clerk to the Commissioners of the County of Pulaski do pay to Frederick WOOLF four dollars for guarding the jail.

Ordered that the Clerk to the Commissioners of the County of Pulaski do pay to Josiah EVERITT eight dollars for surveying the lots and laying off the streets in the town of Hartford.

Stephen GATLIN)
Josiah EVERITT)
Arch^{d}. ODOM)
N. STEVENS) Comm^{rs}.

The Court then adjourned till court in course 4th Septr. 1815.

Tuttle H. MORELAND for Turner EVERITT C.C.O.

Page 30

Georgia) Rec^{d}. of S. JONES and Nancy JONES executors to the Pulaski County) will of the late Phillip JONES (deceased) one negroe woman named Nanci and her four children Jude, Jack, George, and Ben he being willed to Henry JONES this 8th May 1815.

Arthur TOOKE guardian
for Henry JONES

Record 5th Septr. 1815

On proof satisfactory to the Court of a negroe girl deeded to Mary & Henry JONES by Samuel DAVIS 8th Septr. 1799; Ordered that the executors do deliver said negroe to Mary & Henry JONES or their legal representative and her increase.

Josiah EVERITT J.I.C.
Stephen GATLIN J.I.C.
N. STEPHENS J.I.C.

8th May 1815
Rec^{d}. 5th Septr. 1815

Page 31, December 1815

Tuesday 19th December 1815 - The Court of Ordinary then met agreeably ~~to law~~ to a called cession of the Court of Ordinary.

The will of Mark MASON being produced in Court & legally proved – Ordered that James ROACH, Michael HORN Jr., Jacob HORN, Thos. McGRIFF & Henry FULGHAM appraise.

Josiah EVERITT J.I.C.
N. STEPHENS J.I.C.
Stephen GATLIN J.C.

Page 32, January 1816

Monday 1st day of January 1816. The Court of Ordinary then met agreeable to law. Present their Honors—

Stephen GATLIN)
Needham STEPHENS)
Josiah EVERETT)
Archibald ODOM) Esquires

On the application of Hannah SNELLING praying this Court that she may be at liberty to keep two negro women to wit, Raney & Silvey and their children, provided she keeps four white children clear of expense to the estate schooling excepted — Ordered that the above be granted.

The Last Will and Testament of William ROBERTS produced in open Court and legally proven.

Ordered that letters testamentary be granted together with a warrant of appraisement directed to George WALKER, Thomas McGRIFF, Charles MAYO, Ezl. TAYLOR & William MAYO.

Allen TOOKE came into Court and was duly qualified as an administrator on the estate of Joshua HARRIS late of said County decd.

Page 33

On the application of Mary ODOM \& Archibald ODOM/ praying letters of administration on the estate of Archibald H. ODOM late of Pulaski County decd.; Ordered that letters of administration be granted them and that a warrant of appraisement be directed to Shadrach SUTTON, William MOORE, Benjamin STEGALL, Nathaniel MERCER & Nathan MADOX.

On the application of Milley CARDIN & John CARDIN for letters of administration on the estate of Charles CARDIN late of Pulaski County decd.; Ordered that letters of administration be granted to them together with a warrant of appraisement directed to Allen TOOKE, Allen SCARBOROUGH, Furney F. GATLIN, Arthur TOOKE & Haywood JONES.

On application of Thomas W. HARRIS stating that Elizabeth L. HARRIS is an orphan of Sampson HARRIS decd. and living within this County. Ordered that he do be & he is hereby appointed guardian for said Elizabeth L. HARRIS upon his giving the necessary bond & security in the sum of four thousand dollars.

On the application of John WILSON praying letters of administration on the estate of James WILSON late of said County decd. ordered that letters be granted & a warrant of appraisement be directed to Drury DEES, James DEES, Wm. MAY, Henry FULGHAM, Charles MAY, Ezl. TAYLOR.

The Court of Ordinary then adjourned until court in course.

Test. T. EVERETT Clk.

Josiah EVERITT
Stephen GATLIN
N. STEVENS
Ja[s]. BRACEWELL
A. ODOM

On the application of Stephen GATLIN praying that he may be appointed guardian to the persons and properties of Daniel & Robert STURGIS orphans, Ordered that letters of guardianship be granted.

Ordered that James M. TAYLOR be exempt and discharged from making his returns on the estate of S. A. HOPKINS & M. H. POWELL until the next Court of Ordinary.

Josiah EVERITT
A. ODOM
Stephen GATLIN

Page 35, March 1816

~~Court of Ordinary March Term~~ 1816 ~~4th March 1816~~

Monday 4th March 1816. The Court of Ordinary met agreeable to law.

Present their Honors

Stephen GATLIN)
Needham STEVENS)
Josiah EVERITT)
Arch[d]. ODOM &)
James BRACEWELL)

Ordered that the administrators of the estate of W[m]. SMITH dec[d]. have leave to sell four negroes bilonging to said estate of said dec[d]. for the benefit of the heirs and creditors.

Ordered that Robert MORELAND be appointed guardian to the persons and property of Robert M. INGRAM and Sally W. INGRAM and give bond and security in the sum of eight thousand dollars.

On application of Daniel RHODES stating that Peggey R. REEVES otherwise called Peggey R. SNELL, Clarrisay Isabella REEVES otherwise Clarrisay Issabella SNELL & General Jackson REEVES otherwise called General Jackson SNELL are orphans resident within this County;

Page 36

Ordered that said Daniel RHODES be & he is hereby appointed guardian for said three orphans on his giving bond & security according to law in the sum of ten thousand dollars.

Ordered that James M. TAYLORs papers as adm[r]. of S. A. HOBKINS & the estate of D[r]. M. H. POWEL dst. be laid over untill Court in course.

The Court then adjourned till the 5th Monday in April.

N. STEVENS J.I.C.
Arch[d]. ODOM J.I.C.
Stephen GATLIN J.I.C.

Ordered that W^{m}. YARBOROUGH Senr. be and he is hereby authorised fully to take in the debts and ~~make~~ property of John D. HARVEY late of this County deceased, and a due return make of the same to this Court, within the time prescribed by law.

Josiah EVERITT J.I.C.
Arch^{d}. ODOM J.I.C.
N. STEVENS J.I.C.

Page 37, April 1816

Monday 29th April 1816. The Court of Ordinary then met agreeable to adjournment. Present their Honors

Stephen GATLIN)
Josiah EVERITT)
Needham STEPHENS)
Arch^{d}. ODOM)
James BRACEWELL)

Ordered that letters of administration be granted to Theodrick MONTFORT on the estate of John K. MONTFORT late of the County dec^{d}. and that he be bound in the sum of four thousand dollars.

On the decission of the Court on the will of Joseph REEVES admitting the same to record in toto, Joel DAWSON the applicant for administration in said estate comes into Court pays all costs & prays an appeal which is granted & John LITTLE enters himself security in terms of the law.

April 29th 1816 Jno. LITTLE

Page 38

Georgia) Court of Ordinary
Pulaski County) Adjourned Term April 1816

Whereas Theodrick MONTFORT has obtained letters of administration in & upon on the estate of John K. MONTFORT deceased from this court & wishes to make his returns to the Court of Ordinary in Putnam County; On motion it is ordered that the proceedings of said estate be hereafter & forthwith returned unto Putnam County & that the Clerk of this Court do upon application make out certified copies of all proceedings touching said estate recorded in this Court & transmit them to the Clerk of the Court of Ordinary of Putnam County.

It appearing to the Court that William H. GROSS is security to a bond given by William GARBIT administrator & Elizabeth WORMACK formerly Elizabeth KING adm^{x}. of the estate of Samuel KING dec^{d}. to secure the perfect administration on & to said estate & he the said William H. GROSS having removed out of this County & wishing to be exonerated from said securityship.

Page 39

On motion of counsel it is ordered that he be forthwith exonerated & discharged from his said securityship upon William GARBITT & the other administrators giving such security as will or may be approved of by this Court.

Ordered that Thomas W. HARRIS be appointed administrator de bonis non on the estate of William A. HARPER late of this county deceased and that he be bound in the sum of ten thousand dollars.

The court then adjourned till court in course.

Test
Robert MORELAND C.C.O.

Josiah EVERITT J.I.C.
N. STEVENS J.I.C.
St. GATLIN J.I.C.
Arch[d]. ODOM J.I.C.

Page 40, May 1816

Monday 6th May 1816. The Court then met agreeable to adjournment

Present their Honors
Stephen GATLIN
N. STEVENS
James BRACEWELL

Ordered that Holden DUNN be appointed guardian to the persons & property of Elizabeth DUNN & Penelope DUNN and that he bound in the sum of five hundred dollars and that William GRINSTEAD and Rolin DUNN be his security.

Ordered that letters of administration be granted to John SHERROD and \on the estate of Josiah CASON decd./ that he be bound in the sum of seven hundred dollars and that a warrant of appraisement be directed to Simon BARDIN, Thomas M[c]GRIFF, Henry FULGHAM, Charles MAY, & W[m]. ISLER.

Ordered that Robert THOMPSON, John GRINSTEAD, Wiley WILLIAMS, John BRADSHAW & Dixon JELKS be appointed commissioners to partition the property of Dianna DUNN.

Page 41

Ordered that Redmond B. MASON appointed \administrator/ de bonis non on the estate of John SMEDLY (dec[d].) and that he be bound in the sum of five hundred dollars.

Ordered that James M. TAYLOR Ex[r]. on the estate of Solomon A. HOPKINS and Adm[r]. on the estate of Micajah H. POWELL make his returns on said estates to the Clerk of this Court — and that the Clerk is authorised to examine the papers together with said TAYLOR and make a statement of s[d]. proceedings at next Court.

Ordered that the Clerk do purchase an office for the use of this office at Fifteen Dollars.

Ordered that John A. WILLIAMS \Admr./ and Elizabeth SMITH \Admx. on the estate of Wm. SMITH/ be cited to appear at the next court to shew cause why W[m]. GOODSON & Elijah WALLACE be \not/ exonerated from their securityship.

The Court then adjourned till Saturday next.

Ja[s]. BRACEWELL J.I.C.
N. STEVENS J.I.C.
Stephen GATLIN J.I.C.

Tuttle MORELAND C.C.O.
Pro Tem

Saturday 11th May 1816. The Court then met agreeable to adjournment.

Present their Honors Stephen GATLIN)
James BRACEWELL)
Josiah EVERITT)

Ordered that a warrant of appraisement be directed to James CLARK, Moses SUTTON, Thomas MILLS, William JELKS and Daniel M^{c}MAN to appraise the property of Moses ROBINSON late of this County dec^{d}.

Ordered that letters of administration be granted Mary THARP on the estate of William A. THARP and that she be bound in the sum of fifteen hundred dollars.

Ordered that Joseph B. BRYAN, John JEAN, ~~Robert MATHEWS,~~ \Joseph ROUS/ Presley THARP & Charnick THARP be and they are hereby appointed appraisers on the estate of said William A. THARP.

Page 43

The Court then adjourned till court in course.

Tuttle H. MORELAND C.C.O. James BRACEWELL J.I.C.
Josiah EVERITT J.I.C.
Stephen GATLIN J.I.C.

July 1816

Monday 1st July 1816. The Court then met agreeable to adjournment.

Present their Honors Stephen GATLIN)
Josiah EVERITT)
Needham STEVENS)
James BRACEWELL)

Ordered that letters testamentory be granted to Anne SNELL, Daniel RHODES and Daniel KIRKLAND on the estate of Daniel P. SNELL dec^{d}.

Ordered that Elizabeth SMITH be appointed guardian to the persons & property of Sarah SMITH, Alexander SMITH, W^{m}. SMITH & Margaret SMITH and that she be bound in the sum of four thousand dollars.

Page 44

July Term 1816

Ordered that the within named W^{m}. A. THARP do hold the within mentioned twelve head of hogs which hogs was purchased by said W^{m}. A. THARP son of W^{m}. A. THARP dec^{d}. agreeable to the statement of the within affidavit; Ordered that the Clerk do record the aforesaid order and file this affadavit in his office.

Ordered that Joseph B. BRYAN be appointed guardian to the person & property of W^{m}. A. THARP and that he be bound in the sum of two hundred & fifty dollars.

Ordered that John CARDIN be appointed administrator de bonis non on the estate of Susannah M^{c}GILL of Jones County and that he be bound in the sum of six hundred dollars.

Ordered that John BRADSHAW Jordan DEES & Easter KENT be appointed Adm^{rs}. & Adm^{x}. on the estate of Stephen KENT and that they be bound in the sum of five...

Page 45

thousand dollars. Ordered that a warrant of appraisement be directed to Furney F. GATLIN, Richard H. THOMAS, Saml. JONES, James CLARK, & Thomas CLAYTON on the estate of Stephen KENT.

Ordered that W^{m}. YARBROUGH coroner be authorized to sell the property of Moses ROBINSON dec^{d}.

Ordered that W^{m}. GOODSON & Elijah WALLACE be exonerated from their securityship for the administration of W^{m}. SMITHs estate and that Elizabeth SMITHs letter of administration be revoked.

~~Georgia) Court of Ordinary July Term 1816~~
~~Pulaski County) Upon the petition of Ely RAMSEY guardian of the minors of W^{m}. A. HARPER decd. praying that the estate of said decd. be forthwith dividived & delivered over to him as the legal representative of said minors.~~

~~On motion it is ordered that Jas. M. TAYLOR, James ROACH & George WALKER also Needham STEPHENS...~~

Page 46

~~& Josiah EVERITT are appointed commissioners to superintend the distribution of said estate at any day after the 25th December next whose duty shale be to divide said estate subject to distribution into as many parts or shares as there are distributees.~~

Ordered that Thomas W. HARRIS Adm^{r}. de bo nis non on the estate of W^{m}. A. HARPER dec^{d}. be authorised & directed to pay over to & settle with Ely RAMSEY guardian of Harriet A. HARPER, Jefferson A. HARPER & Andrew Nox A. HARPER orphans of said W^{m}. A. HARPER, the proportionable parts due the said orphans of W^{m}. A. HARPER by the first of January next & that any recp^{t}. taken by said HARRIS as Adm^{r}. of said Ely RAMSEY be good for said HARRIS to settle with this Court.

Page 47

The court then adjourned till court in course.
Steph. GATLIN)
James BRACEWELL)
N. STEVENS)
Josiah EVERITT) J.I.C.

Page 48, September 1816

Monday 2nd September 1816. The Court met agreeable to adjournment.
Present the Honorable
Stephen GATLIN)
James BRACEWELL)
Josiah EVERITT)
Archibald ODAM) J.I.C.

~~On the petition of~~ On application of John B. PACKER stating that he is in possession of a bond given by William A. HARPER in his life time to said PACKER to make titles to three lots of land Nos. 194, 198 & 223 in the 21 District Wilkinson County but now Pulaski County upon said PACKERs paying up to said HARPER by the first of May eighteen hundred & twelve the sum of nine hundred dollars which bond is now filed in the office of the Court & it being stated that some money has been paid — ordered that the administrators on the estate of said HARPER be ordered & directed to make titles in compliance with said bond by the first Monday in January next unless cause be be shown to the contrary & that this rule be published once a month in one of the publick gazettes of this state untill sitting of said Court. ~~True extract from the minutes~~.

Page 49

~~Stephen GATLIN~~)
~~James BRACEWELL~~)
~~Josiah EVERITT~~)
~~Archibald ODAM~~) J.I.C.

Ordered that letters desmissary be granted to the administrators of William S. LANCASTER decd. – Washington LANCASTER, Haywood ALFORD adms. that they and their securities be exempt from said administration.

Georgia) On application of William H. GROSS the security the
Pulaski County) security of William GARBET & Elizabeth KING administrators on the estate of Samuel KING praying to be discharged from his securityship it is ordered that the said administrators do appear at the next term of the Court of Ordinary for Pulaski County to shew cause why he the said William H. GROSS should not be discharged from his said securityship otherwise the said letters of administration to the said William & Elizabeth will be revoked and other proceedings will be had according to law.

Page 50

Georgia) On application of William GRINSTEAD the security of
Pulaski County) Holden DUN administrator on the estate of Jacob DUN praying to be discharged from his securityship it is ordered that the said Holden DUN do appear at the next Court of Ordinary for Pulaski County to shew cause why he the said William GRINSTEAD should not be discharged from his said securityship otherwise the said letters of administration to the said Holden DUN will be revoked and other proceedings will be had according to law.

Georgia) On the application of Washington LANCASTER the security
Pulaski County) of John A. WILLIAMS the administrator on the estate of William SMITH praying to be discharged from his securityship it is ordered that the said John A. WILLIAMS do be and appear at the next term of the Court of Ordinary for Pulaski County to shew...

cause why the said Washington LANCASTER should not be discharged from his said securityship otherwise the said letters of administration to the said John A. WILLIAMS will be revoked and other proceedings will be had according to law.

The court adjourned untill court in course.

Josiah EVERITT J.I.C.
Archd. ODOM J.I.C.
St. GATLIN J.I.C.

November 1816

Monday 4th November 1816. The Court then met agreeable to adjournment. Present their Honors
Stephen GATLIN
Josiah EVERITT
Needham STEVENS
James BRACEWELL

Ordered that a warrant of appraisement on the estate of Johnathan FAIRCLOTH be directed to Jas. ROACH, Needham STEVENS, John GILSTRAP, Theophilus SUTTON and Henry SENTERFIT.

Page 52

Ordered that a warrant of appraisement on the estate of John K. MONTFORT be directed to Peter B. TERRILL, George SMITH, Isham BRANHAM, Joel ABBOTT and William BALWIN.

It appearing to the Court that D[r. Wm.?] GARBITT has an account against the estate of William A. HARPER decd. for forty two dollars & fifty cents on montion it is ordered that the administrator Thomas W. HARRIS is hereby authorized to pay the same & render it in his return of expenditures to this court.

Ordered that a warrant of appraisement on the estate of Jacob SNELL be directed to James ROACH, Jessee POWELL, Thos. McGRIFF, John SHERROD and James DEES.

Ordered that a warrant of appraisement on the estate of David SNELL be directed to James ROACH, Jessee POWELL, Thos. McGRIFF, John SHERROD and James DEES.

Ordered that a warrant of appraisement on the estate of Daniel P. SNELL be directed to James ROACH, Jessee POWELL, Thos. McGRIFF, John SHERROD and James DEES.

Page 53

Ordered that Wm. H. GROSS and the heirs of Jacob SNELL be exonerated from their securityship with Wm. GARBITT and Elizabeth KING now Elizabeth WAMMACK Admr. & Admx. on the estate of Samuel KING decd. and their letters of administration be revoked.

Ordered that letters of administration de bonis non with the will annexed on the estate of William ROBERTS decd. be granted to John SHERROD — and that he be bound in the sum of six thousand dollars and that Simon BARDIN be his security.

Ordered that Allen TOOKE, Edward BLACKSHEAR, Josiah EVERITT, Richard H. THOMAS and Sanders COALSON be appointed to divide & appotion the land of Charles CARDIN deceased into seven equal parts between the \heirs &/ distributees of said estate & an equal part paid of the land so divided & appotioned to the assigned to each of the said \heirs &/ distributees by lot or otherwise.

Ordered that Milly CARDIN be appointed guardian to the person and property of Jefferson CARDIN and that she be bound in the sum of five hundred dollars and that Allen TOOKE and James CLARK be her security.

Page 54

Ordered that the administrators on the estate of Lester CRAWFORD is authorized to sell the balance of the stock at privat sale or otherwise and make a return of the same to this Court.

Ordered that letters of administration be granted to Ely RAMSEY on the estate of John RAMSEY decd. and that he be bound in the sum of five hundred dollars and that Allen TOOKE & Wm. YARBROUGH & Peter J. HARVEY be his securities.

Ordered that letters of administration be granted to Ely RAMSEY on the estate of William RAMSEY decd. and that he be bound in the sum of five hundred dollars and that Allen TOOKE & Wm. YARBROUGH & Peter J. HARVEY be his securities.

Ordered that George WALKER, Ezekiel TAYLOR, Thomas McGRIFF, Wm. MAY and Thos. PHILIPS be appointed to divide the property of William ROBERTS decd. agreeable to the will.

The Court then adjourned till Court in course.

Josiah EVERITT J.I.C.
N. STEVINS J.I.C.
St. GATLIN J.I.C.
Jas. BRACEWELL J.I.C.

Page 55, January 1817

Monday 6th January 1817. The court then met agreeable to adjournment.

Present their Honors Josiah EVERITT)
Archibald ODOM)
James BRACEWELL)
Needham STEPHENS)

Ordered that letters of administration on the estate of Shadrack LEE be granted to John ROZAR & that he be bound in the sum of three thousand dollars and that Lewis HOLLAND and Joseph REGAN be his securities.

Ordered that a warrant of appraisement on the estate of Shadrack LEE be directed to Stephen PIPKIN, David PIPKIN, Thomas ROGERS, John LEE Senr. and Lewis PIPKIN.

Ordered that the return on the estate of John SYLVESTER for the year 1816 be recd.

Ordered that Mrs. Synthia CRAWFORD have the use of two negroes now in her hands belonging to the estate of Lester CRAWFORD to support the children both black & white.

Page 56

Ordered that Lemuel BOON the son of Polly BOON was born the 1st June 1811, Burkett the brother to the above was born the 17th August 1812, Tempy the sister to the above was born the 4th September 1813, be bound to Wm. McCORMACK & that he be bound in the sum of three thousand dollars and that Jessee POWELL & Theophilus SUTTON be his securities.
[*in margin:*] Fee paid 1.00

Ordered that the verbal will of Elizabeth ROBERTS be recorded and that John SHERROD & John WOMMACK be executors to the same & John SHERROD be appointed guardian for Henry ROBERTS & John WOMMACK guardian to Benjamin ROBERTS both sons of Wm. ROBERTS decd.

Ordered that Daniel \COLE/ be appointed guardian to the person & property of John SYLVESTER & be bound in the sum of one thousand dollars.

Ordered that Edward BRYAN be appointed guardian to the person & property of Harriot SYLVESTER & that he be bound in the sum of one thousand dollars.

Ordered that Thomas W. HARRIS do make title to Jno. B. PACKER for the squares of land Nos. 194, 198 & 223 in the 21st district Wilkinson now Pulaski County.

Page 57

Ordered that Thomas McGRIFF, Jessee POWELL, Bolin SWEARINGAIN, Jno. B. PACKER and Daniel RHODES be appointed to divide the estate of Daniel P. SNELL decd.

Ordered that a warrant of appraisement be directed to James PHILIPS, Simon BARDIN, Ezekiel TAYLOR, Daniel RHODES and Daniel KIRKLAND on the estate of Wm. ISLER decd.

Whereas the estate of Samuel KING decd. is unrepresented by reason of the original letters of administration being forfeited by the original administrators it is therefore ordered that the Clerk of this Court be appointed adminstrator de bonis non & that he file the usual bond & security in the office of this Court.

Ordered that letters of admn. be granted to Theophilus SUTTON on the estate of Solomon SUTTON & that he be bound in the sum of one thousand dollars Jno. B. PACKER secy. Ordered that a warrant of appraisement be directed to James CLARK, Elifilit KING, Thos. MILLS, Thomas HOWELL & James ROACH on the estate of Soloman SUTTON.

Page 58

Ordered that Hannah SNELLING of Pulaski County be guardian of the persons & properties of Grace SNELLING, William F. SNELLING, Richard J. SNELLING & Phibeana SNELLING and that she be bound in the sum of eight thousand dollars.

Ordered that the administrators of the estate of James JONES dec^{d}. come forward at March term 1817 and shew cause if any they have why John JONES Senr. as security shall not be discharged on failure whereof the administration shall be revoked.

Ordered that the guardian of the children of James JONES dec^{d}. come forward and shew cause if any why John JONES Senr. shall not be discharged on the securityship of s^{d}. guardian in failing to comply the guardianship will be revoked.

Ordered that a warrant of appriasement be directed to Edward SMITH, Allen TOOKE, Robert MORELAND, Thomas MILLS & Duncan RAY on estate of W^{m}. RAMSAY. ~~on the estate~~

Page 59

Ordered that a warrant of appriasement be directed to Edward SMITH, Allen TOOKE, Robt. MORELAND, Thomas MILLS & Duncan RAY on the estate of John RAMSEY.

The Court then adjourned till Monday next.

N. STEVENS
Robt. MORELAND C.C.O. Josiah EVERITT
Arch^{d}. ODOM

Monday 13th January 1817. The Court then met agreeable to adjournment Present their Honors

Josiah EVERITT)
James BRACEWELL)
Needham STEPHENS)

Ordered \that/ Thos. W. HARRISs return on the estate of W^{m}. A. HARPER be laid over till next Court.

Ordered that James M. TAYLOR's returns on the estates of Solo. A. HOPKINS & the estate of Micajah H. POWELL be laid over till next Court.

Ordered that Sands STANDLY be the guardian to a coloured man named Francis BRANHAM and that he give bond & security in terms of the law.

Page 60

Ordered that James BRACEWELL be appointed guardian to the persons & properties of Patsey STURDIVANT, Susannah STURDIVANT, & Mary STURDIVANT and he be bound in the sum of twenty five hundred dollars.

Ordered that Robt. MORELAND be appointed guardian to the persons & property of Robert M. INGRAM and that the bond which said MORELAND gave this Court shall still be in force in lew of a new one.

It appearing to the Court that a division of the estate of Doct^{r}. W^{m}. A. HARPER has been made of the personal property & that all the personal property of said ~~deceased~~ estate now in the hands of Thos. W. HARRIS the adm^{r}. de bonis non does belong to the three children of said W^{m}. A. HARPER for whom & which Eli RAMSEY is the guardian; Ordered that said adm^{r}. do pay & deliver over to said Eli RAMSEY the whole of the personal property now in his hands or possession belonging to said estate.

Ordered that the administrators of the estate of Stephen KENT (dec^{d}.) appropriate the incomes of said estate for the year 1816 to the support of the wife & children of said dec^{d}.

On application of Mary PHILIPS one of the orphans of Moses HORN ~~who is of sufficient~~ & widow & relict of Thos. PHILIPS who is of sufficient age to make choice of a guardian; Ordered that Thomas M^{c}GRIFF be & he is hereby appointed guardian of & to the property & person of the said Mary PHILLIPS and that he be bound in the ~~sum of~~ fourteen thousand dollars and that Daniel COLE, James PHILLIPS & Thomas W. HARRIS & Richard H. THOMAS be his securities.

Ordered that Edward BRYAN be & he is hereby appointed guardian of & to the persons & property of Serena SYLVESTER an orphan of John SYLVESTER late of this county dec^{d}. and that he be bound in the sum of one thousand dollars.

Ordered that the Clerk of this Court be authorised to purchase 4 books for the purpose of recording the papers of said office and draw on the Treasurer for payment.

Page 62

Ordered that W^{m}. J. MURRELL be appointed guardian to the person & property of Simon ROBERTS and that he [be] bound in the sum of twelve hundred dollars and John WOMMACK and John HODGES be his securities.

Ordered that Turner EVERITT former Clerk of this Court do deliver over to the present Clerk all the books & papers belonging to this office ~~within~~ by the first Monday in March next or he will be dealt with according to law.

The Court then adjourned till Court in course.

Josiah EVERITT
N. STEVENS
James BRACEWELL

Page 63, March 1817

Monday 3rd March 1817. The Court then met agreeable to adjournment.

Present their Honors
Stephen GATLIN)
Needham STEVENS)
Archibald ODOM)
Josiah EVERITT)
James BRACEWELL)

Ordered that Simon BARDIN be appointed administrator on the estate of James BALTHROP dec^{d}. and that he be bound in the sum of one thousand dollars & that Blakely EDINS be his security.

Ordered that Allen TOOKE & Bazel HARRIS adm^{rs}. of Joshua HARRIS dec^{d}. be authorised to dispose of one bed one pine table & one pair of smoothing irons in Elbert County for the benefit of the heirs & creditors of said dec^{d}.

Ordered that Elizabeth SMITHs a/c against the estate of W^{m}. SMITH for $120.00 for board of children be allowed.

Ordered that Isaac NICHOLS be appointed guardian to the person & property of Martha W. REEVES & that he be bound in the sum of one thousand dollars & that Joel DAWSON & Kinchen DAWSON be his securities.

Ordered that a warrant of appraisement on the estate of James BALTHROP dec^{d}. be directed to James ROACH, Hardy GATLIN, Redmon B. MASON, James PHILIPS and Thomas M^{c}GRIFF.

Ordered that William KINCHEN, Robert DANIEL, James BRACEWELL, Neal M^{c}ALPIN & Charles DANIEL be appointed to divide the estate of W^{m}. SMITH dec^{d}.

Ordered that the Clerk to this Court be authorised to grant letters testamentary to all executors.

Page 65

Ordered that ~~Josiah EVERITT~~ Joel WALKER, Joseph B. BRYAN, Moses BRYAN, Blakely EDINS and John LEE be appointed to lay off Elizabeth LEE's dower of the land belonging to the estate of Shadrack LEE dec^{d}.

Ordered that Josiah EVERITT be appointed guardian to the persons & property of Sarah SMITH, William J. SMITH, Alexander SMITH and Margaritt SMITH \orphans of Wm. SMITH decd./ and that he be bound in the sum of six thousand dollars & that James BRACEWELL be his security.

The Court then adjourned till court in course.

N. STEVENS)
Josiah EVERITT)
Arch^{d}. ODOM)
Stephen GATLIN)
James BRACEWELL) J.I.C.

Page 66, May 1817

Monday 5th May 1817. The Court then met agreable to adjournment. Present their Honors

Stephen GATLIN)
Josiah EVERITT)
Needham STEVENS)
James BRACEWELL)

Ordered that Robt. MORELAND guardian to the persons & properties of Robert M. INGRAM & Sarah W. INGRAM appear at the next Court & give new security in place of Theodrick MONTFORT.

Ordered the administrators on the estate of Stephen KENT dec^{d}. be authorized to sell one negroe fellow belonging to said estate named Abraham.

Ordered that a warrant of appraisement on the estate of Elizabeth ROBERTS dec^{d}. be directed to Blakely EDINS, Thomas M^{c}GRIFF, Simon BARDIN, Ezekiel TAYLOR & William MAYO & that the above named persons be appointed to divide said estate.

Page 67

Ordered that a warrant of appraisement on the estate of Neil ARD be directed to William LITTLE, John SWEARINGAIN, John DONALSON, W^{m}. DONALSON & Malaki KELLY.

Ordered that ~~that~~ the administrator on the estate of W^{m}. A. THARP \dec^{d}./ be authorised to sell the real estate of said dec^{d}.

Ordered that administrators be allowed 2½ percent on ~~all monies~~ the sales of estates and 2½ percent on all monies paid out except to legatees.

The court then adjourned till ~~Court the first Mon~~ Court in course.

N. STEVENS
James BRACEWELL
Stephen GATLIN J.I.C.
Josiah EVERITT J.I.C.

Page 68, July 1817

Monday 7th July 1817. The Court then met agreeable to adjournment.

Present their Honors Stephen GATLIN)
James BRACEWELL)
Josiah EVERITT)
Needham STEVENS)

Ordered that Thomas HOWELL be appointed guardian to the persons & properties of Rebeccah HOWELL, Sarah HOWELL and James HOWELL heirs of Robt. HOWELL and that he be bound in the sum of six thousand dollars & that Thomas JOHNSON Senr. be his security.

~~Ordered~~

The exceptions to the proceedings upon the estate of Shadrack LEE by John ROZAR adminstrator of said estate are as follows: 1st That said adminstrator never made an inventory of said estate as required by law; 2nd That he neglected to cause said estate to be appraised;...

Page 69

3rd That he disposed of and sold three negroes and other articles belonging to said estate contrary to law or the direction and order of this court; 4th The appraisors were not sworn; 5th The the adm^{r}. took the estate ~~estate~~ at the appraised value (if it was appraised at all); 6th That he has commited waste.

The defendant admits of the former notice as legal.

Ordered that letters of administration be granted to Lydia LOVIN on the estate of Adam LOVIN dec^{d}. and that she be bound in the sum of five thousand dollars and that George G. GAINS be her security.

Ordered that a warrant of appraisement on the estate of Adam LOVIN be directed to William LITTLE, William DONALSON, Wily HORN, Thos. M^{c}GRIFF & John LITTLE.

Ordered that a warrant of appraisement on the estate of John JONES dec^{d}. be directed to John BRADSHAW, Robt. DEWITT, James CLARK, Robt. THOMPSON & William PRATT.

Page 70

Ordered that William J. MORRELL appear at the next Court of Ordinary to give new security in place of John WOMMACK & John HODGES.

It appearing to the Court that a notice of the application of the administrators of John SYLVESTER late of this County dec^{d}. for leave to sell all the real estate of said dec^{d}. has been published nine monthly at least & it being made fully & plainly appear to be for the benefit of the heirs & creditors of said dec^{d}.;

On motion it is therefore ordered that said administrators proceed to sell a certain tract of land in the County of Laurens by publishing the sale & pursuing the law in such ~~such~~ cases made & provided.

It appearing to the Court that a notice of the application of the administrators of Stephen KENT dec^{d}. for leave to sell all the...

Page 71

lands and negroes of said deceased has been published nine monthly at least & it being fully & plainly made to appear to be for the benefit of the heirs & creditors of said dec^{d}.; On motion it is ordered that said administrators proceed to sell a certain tract of land in Emanuel County & one negroe fellow called Abraham by publishing the sale & pursuing the law in such cases made & provided.

Ordered that John SHERROD be appointed administrator on the estate of Elizabeth ROBERTS dec^{d}. and that he be bound in the sum of one hundred dollars.

Ordered that Tuttle H. MORELAND and Aaron B. PUCKETT be taken for security for Robt. MORELAND guardian for the orphans of William...

Page 72

INGRAM dec^{d}. & that Theodrick MONTFORT be exonerated from his securityship for said Robt. MORELAND.

Ordered that W^{m}. J. MURRELL be exonerated from the guardianship of Simon ROBERTS by his request.

The Court then adjourned till the 1st Monday in August next.

Stephen GATLIN
N. STEVENS
James BRACEWELL
Josiah EVERITT

Page 73, August 1817

Monday August 4, 1817. The Court then met agreeable to adjournment, Present their Honors:

Stephen GATLIN
Josiah EVERITT
Archabald ODOM

Heirs of Shad^{k}. LEE)
vs.)
John ROZIER Adm^{r}.)

In this case the Court having heard arguments on both sides a majority are of the opinion that from the grounds taken by the applicants this Court has no jurisdiction of said case in its present shape therefore that said rule be discharged.

Appeal entered & cost paid.

The court then adjourned till the 1st Monday in September next.
Arch^{d}. ODOM J.I.C.
Josiah EVERITT J.I.C.
St. GATLIN J.I.C.

Page 74, September 1817

Monday 1st September 1817. The Court then met agreeable to adjournment. Present their Honors:
Stephen GATLIN)
Needham STEVENS)
James BRACEWELL)
Archibald ODOM)

Ordered that a warrant of appraisement on the estate of Elizabeth ROBERTS dec^{d}. be directed to Thos. M^{c}GRIFF, W^{m}. MAY, Hinchey WARREN, Jno. WOMMACK and Blakely EDINS.

Ordered that letters of administration be granted to M^{rs}. Ann BENNETT on the estate of Jno. BENNETT late of Wayne County dec^{d}. and that she be bound in the sum of twelve hundred dollars & that W^{m}. YARBROUGH be her security.

Ordered that John SHERROD be appointed guardian to the person & property of Simon ROBERTS and that he be bound in the sum of twelve hundred dollars & that John WOMMACK be his security.

Page 75

Ordered that the administrators on the estate of John SYLVESTER \dec^{d}./ do proceed to sell the negroes belonging to said estate.

On application of W^{m}. TAYLOR administrator of Josiah TAYLOR dec^{d}.; Ordered that Thomas ADAMS, Dennis ADAMS, Michael HORN, Laurens FOLSOM & George FOLSOM be appointed to divide said estate. ~~of Josiah TAYLOR decd~~.

Ordered that Samuel JEMMERSON he be appointed guardian to the persons & properties of Eliza JONES & Artimesa JONES orphans of Philip JONES dec^{d}. & that he be bound in the sum of ten thousand dollars and that John SHERROD be his security.

Ordered that a warrant of appraisement be directed to James HAYS, William PRATT, John BRADSHAW, Daniel CORNWALL and Robert DEWITT on the estate of John BURNETT dec^{d}.

Page 76

The Court then adjourned till court in course
James BRACEWELL
N. STEVENS
Arch^{d}. ODOM
Stephen GATLIN

Robert MORELAND
C.C.O.

Monday the 3rd November 1817. The Court then met agreeable to adjournment Present their Honors:

Stephen GATLIN)
Josiah EVERITT)
Needham STEVENS &)
James BRACEWELL) J.I.C.

Ordered that the administrators on the estate of John SNELLING decd. do proceed to sell all the negroes belonging to said estate.

Ordered that the executors on the estate of Johnathan FAIRCLOTH do proceed to sell two tracts of land and two negroes Daniel & Cloey.

Page 77

Ordered that John SHERRARD executor of ~~Elizabeth~~ \William/ ROBERTS decd. do proceed to sell sixty acres of land No. 200 24th District Pulaski County & three negroes George, Hester & ~~Cloey~~ Prew?.

Ordered that a warrant of appraisement on the estate of Moses SUTTON decd. be directed to James ROACH, James CLARK, Wm. YARBROUGH Senr., James HAYS and Wm. YARBROUGH Junr.

Ordered that Allen TOOKE be appointed guardian to the person & property of Hannah TOOKE orphan of Harlon H. TOOKE decd. and that he be bound in the sum of fifteen thousand dollars & that James M. TAYLOR \& Arthur TOOKE/ be his securitys.

Agreeable to the petition of Arthur TOOKE & Allen TOOKE ordered that Stephen GATLIN, Josiah EVERITT, Sanders COLSON, Richard H. THOMAS and Needham STEPHENS be appointed to divide the estate of Philip JONES decd. among the heirs of said decd.

Page 78

Ordered that Jane W. CRUTCHFIELD be appointed guardian to the persons & properties of James Dabney CRUTCHFIELD and Martha Anderson CRUTCHFIELD heirs of John CRUTCHFIELD decd. and that she be bound in the sum of fifteen thousand dollars and that William JELKS, Jas. S. IVEY ~~and~~ Rookins JELKS and Dixon JELKS be her securities.

Ordered that Lemuel BOON the son of Polly BOON \who/ was born the 1st June 1811, Burkett the brother to the above was born the 17th August 1812, Tempy the sister to the above was born the 4th September 1813 be bound to John McCORMACK & that he be bound in the sum of three thousand dollars and that Needham STEVENS be his security.

The Court then adjourned till court in course.

Stephen GATLIN J.I.C.
Josiah EVERITT J.I.C.
N. STEVENS J.I.C.

[*end of book - index omitted*]

LETTERS OF ADMINISTRATION
1813-1816

microfilm copy in Georgia Archives
identifies this book as:
Court of Ordinary Minutes
1813-1816

Georgia) By their Honors the Judges of the Court of Ordinary for
Pulaski County) said County.

To Mary HARPER & Jacob SNELL Greeting
Whereas William A. HARPER late of the County aforesaid died intestate as it is said, we do therefore give & grant unto you the said Mary HARPER & Jacob SNELL full power and authority to administer all and singular the goods, chattels & credits which were of the said deceased at the time of his death, and to demand, collect and buy, & in legal manner require and receive, all, & all manner of debt and debts, due and owing to the said deceased, and mete and well and faithfully to dispose of the same, and out of the goods, chattels and credits of the said deceased, which have, may or shall come to your hands or possessions, well and truly to pay the debts due by the said deceased, so far forth as the same will extend and the law will charge you, according to the true value of the sum thereof, you having first taken your oath will and truly to administer the same, and to make or cause to be made, a true & perfect inventory of all and singular the goods, chattels and credits of the said deceased, which have, may or shall come to your hands, possession or knowledge, appraised in dollars and cents; as also to render a true and just account of and upon your administration therein and to exhibit both into the ordinary's office for the said County, touching which inventory you are presently assigned to perform, or at furthest within three months from this date, and an account on the first term of the Court of Ordinary for the County aforesaid, in every year until you have completed your said administration. And lastly we do hereby nominate, constitute and appoint you the said Mary HARPER & Jacob SNELL administrators of all and singular the goods, chattels and credits of the said deceased.

Witness the honorable [*blank*] one of the judges of the Court of Ordinary for said county this [*no date*]

Turner EVERETT Clk.

Pages 2-3

Georgia) By their Honors the Judges of the Court of Ordinary for
Pulaski County) said County.

To Daniel MAGEE — Greeting
Whereas John M. MORAN late of the County aforesaid, died intestate... [*continues exactly as above*] Witness...this 3rd May 1813.

Turner EVERETT Clk.

Pages 4-5

Georgia) By their Honors the Judges of the Court of Ordinary for
Pulaski County) said County.

To Diana DUNN — Greeting
Whereas Jacob DUNN late of the County aforesaid, died intestate... Witness...this 17th May 1813.

Georgia) By their Honors the Judges of the Court of Ordinary for
Pulaski County) said County.

To Prutia COLE — Greeting
Whereas John COLE late of the County aforesaid, died intestate.... [*continues exactly as before*] Witness...this 17th May 1813.

Pages 7-8

Georgia) By their Honors the Judges of the Court of Ordinary for
Pulaski County) said County.

To Joel SHERRARD & Mary JONES — Greeting
Whereas James JONES late of the County aforesaid, died intestate.... Witness... this 3rd January 1814.

Pages 8-9

Georgia) By their Honors the Judges of the Court of Ordinary for
Pulaski County) said County.

To Robert HILL — Greeting
Whereas Thomas A. HILL late of the County aforesaid, died intestate.... Witness... this 3rd January 1814.

Pages 10-11

Georgia) By their Honors the Judges of the Court of Ordinary for
Pulaski County) said County.

To Joel DAWSON & Daniel RHODES — Greeting
Whereas John REEVES late of the County aforesaid, died intestate.... Witness... 7th ~~May~~ March 1814.

Pages 11-12

Georgia) By their Honors the Judges of the Court of Ordinary for
Pulaski County) said County.

To Washington LANCASTER & Haywood ALFORD — Greeting
Whereas William S. LANCASTER late of the County aforesaid, died intestate.... Witness...this 7th March 1814.

Pages 13-14

Georgia) By their Honors the Judges of the Court of Ordinary for
Pulaski County) said County.

To Daniel RHODES — Greeting
Whereas Mary HARPER late of the County aforesaid, died intestate.... Witness... this 7th March 1814.

Georgia) By their Honors the Judges of the Court of Ordinary for
Pulaski County) said County.

To James M. TAYLOR — Greeting
Whereas Micajah H. POWELL late of the County aforesaid, died intestate.... Witness...this 4th July 1814.

Pages 16-17

Georgia) By their Honors the Judges of the Court of Ordinary for
Pulaski County) said County.

To William GARBET and Elizabeth KING — Greeting
Whereas Samuel KING late of the County aforesaid, died intestate.... Witness... this 4th July 1814.

Pages 17-18

Georgia) By their Honors the Judges of the Court of Ordinary for
Pulaski County) said County.

To Sias TAYLOR and William TAYLOR — Greeting
Whereas Josiah TAYLOR late of the County aforesaid, died intestate.... Witness... this 24th December 1814.

Pages 19-20

Georgia) By their Honors the Judges of the Court of Ordinary for
Pulaski County) said County.

To Elizabeth SMITH & John A. WILLIAMS — Greeting
Whereas William SMITH late of the County aforesaid, died intestate.... Witness... this 24th December 1814.

Pages 20-21

Georgia) By their Honors the Judges of the Court of Ordinary for
Pulaski County) said County.

To Hardy VICKERS & Jason BRINSON — Greeting
Whereas Lester CRAWFORD late of the County aforesaid, died intestate.... Witness...1st May 1815.

Pages 22-23

Georgia) By their Honors the Judges of the Court of Ordinary for
Pulaski County) said County.

To Bolling SWEARINGAIN & [*blank*] — Greeting
Whereas John SNELLING late of the County aforesaid, died intestate.... Witness... this 1st May 1815.

Georgia) By their Honors the Judges of the Court of Ordinary for
Pulaski County) said County.

To William GARBETT — Greeting

Whereas Brockenberry ANDREWS late of the County aforesaid, died intestate.... [*same as before except:*] Witness the honorable Stephen GATLIN Esquire one of the judges of the court of Ordinary for said County this 1st May 1815.

Pages 25-26

Georgia) By their Honors the Judges of the Court of Ordinary for
Pulaski County) said County.

To Josiah D. CAUTHORN — Greeting

Whereas John SYLVESTER late of the County aforesaid, died intestate.... Witness... [*no judge listed*] this 1st May 1815.

Pages 26-27

Georgia) By their Honors the Judges of the Court of Ordinary for
Pulaski County) said County.

To Mark MASON — Greeting

Whereas John SMEDLY late of the County aforesaid, died intestate.... Witness... this 4th Septr. 1815.

Pages 28-29

Georgia) By their Honors the Judges of the Court of Ordinary for
Pulaski County) said County.

To Basil HARRIS & Allen TOOKE — Greeting

Whereas Joshua HARRIS late of the County aforesaid, died intestate.... Witness... this 4th Septr. 1815.

Pages 29-30

Georgia) By their Honors the Judges of the Court of Ordinary for
Pulaski County) said County.

To Archibald ODOM and [*blank*] — Greeting

Whereas Archibald H. ODOM late of the County aforesaid, died intestate.... Witness...this 1st January 1816.

Pages 31-32

Georgia) By their Honors the Judges of the Court of Ordinary for
Pulaski County) said County.

To Milly CARDIN and John CARDIN — Greeting

Whereas Charles CARDIN late of the County aforesaid, died intestate.... Witness... this 1st January 1815. [*probably should be 1816*]

G e o r g i a) By their Honors the Judges of the Court of Ordinary for
Pulaski County) said County.

To John WILSON — Greeting

Whereas James WILSON late of the County aforesaid, died intestate.... Witness... this 1st January 1816.

[*end of book*]

ADMINISTRATORS, EXECUTORS, AND GUARDIANS
1810-1825

Note: In some cases it is unclear whether certain orphan names are first or last names. For example, on page 12 the entry "Sarah Jourdan Elizabeth Dees" is believed to be three children with the last name of DEES, but it could be Sarah JOURDAN and Elizabeth DEES.

Pages 41-53 of the original book contain duplicate listings of earlier entries. Only information which differs from the first listing is included here, in brackets (non-italicized).

Names of Administrators & Guardians

Date	Admr. & Guard.	Securities	Amount	Names Orphans	Names Deceased
1810 Novr. 25	Leonard STRINGER Guardian	Joseph STRINGER	3,000.00	Peter WILLIAMS Sofiah WILLIAMS Isaac WILLIAMS Mariah WILLIAMS	Bowery WILLIAMS
1811 Decr. 12	Thomas HOWELL Tem. Admr.	Thomas JOHNSTON	2,000.00	~~Robert~~	Robert HOWELL
1812 Jany. 6	Drury MAY Guardian	William BRYAN Blakely EDINS [Aaron SCARBOROUGH]	3,000.00	David, Nancy, & Hiram MOSES	[John MOSES]
1812 Mar. 2	Thomas HOWELL Admr.	John B. PACKER	2,500.00		Robert HOWELL
1812 Mar. 2	Polly [Mary] A. HARPER Jacob SNELL Amrs.	David SNELL Danl. [P.] SNELL Jesse POWELL	10,000.00		William A. HARPER
1813 Feby. 20	John TROUTMAN Tempy. Adm.	James T. THOMAS	10,000.00		John MORAN
1813 May 3	John RAMSEY Guardian	William RAMSEY James L. PERRY & John B. PACKER	8,000.00	Harriet HARPER Jefferson HARPER Andrew Nox HARPER	[William A. HARPER]
1813 May 17	Daniel MAGEE Admr.	Elijah WALLACE Wm. RAMSEY James RAMSEY William LYON	3,000.00		John MORAN
1813 May 17	Dianna DUNN Admx.	Rollin DUNN Christopher EDWARDS	600.00		Jacob DUNN
1813 May 17	Prussia COLE Admx.	John K. MONTFORT Theodrick MONTFORT Joshua HARRIS	15,000.00		John COLE

Names of Administrators & Guardians

Date	Admr. & Guard.	Securities	Amount	Orphans	Names of the Deceased
1814 Jany. 4	Joel SHERARD & Mary JONES Admrs.	Henry FULGHAM John JONES Senr.	3,000.–		James JONES
1814 Jany. 4	Robert HILL Admr.	James L. PERRY Henry FULGHAM	3,000.–		Thomas A. HILL
1814 Jany. 4	Simon BARDIN Guardian	Henry FULGHAM	3,000.–	Nancy LOFTLY Cealia LOFTLY	Jesse LOFTLY
1814 Mar. 7	Daniel RHODES Admr.	Jacob SNELL John ISLER	3,000.–		Mary HARPER
1814 Mar.	Joel DAWSON & Daniel RHODES Admrs.	Jacob SNELL & John ISLER [Henry SMITH]	2,000.–		John REAVES
1814 Apl. 8	James M. TAYLOR Tempy. Admr.	William YARBOROUGH	10,000.–		Micajah H. POWELL
1814 July 4	William GARBETT & Elizabeth KING Admrs.	Jacob SNELL & William H. GROSS	3,000.–		Samuel KING
1814 July 4	Charles CARDIN Admr.	James CLARK & Moses SUTTON	2,000.–		Susannah McGILL
1814 July 9	James M. TAYLOR Admr.	Thomas McDANIEL & Elijah WALLACE	3,000.00		Micajah H. POWELL
1815 Jany. 4	Elizabeth SMITH Amx.	William GOODSON William JOHNSON	3,000.–		William SMITH
1815 Jany. 24	Sias TAYLOR Temp. Admr.	William TAYLOR	4,000.–		Josiah TAYLOR

Names of Administrators & Guardians

Date	Admr. & Guard.	Securities	Amount	Orphans	Names of the Deceased
1815 Jany. 1	Archibald ODOM & Mary ODOM	James ODOM & Nathan ~~ODOM~~ MADDOX	6,000.–		Archibald H. ODOM
1815 Feby. 22	Josiah D. CAUTHORN Admr.	Edward SMITH & Dennis POSEY	5,000.–		John SYLVESTER
1815 Mar. 6	Sias TAYLOR William TAYLOR Temp. Adm.	William HALL & Elisha EVANS	4,000.–		Josiah TAYLOR
1815 Mar. 6	Elizabeth SMITH & John A. WILLIAMS Temp. Adm.	Elijah WALLACE Wm. GOODSON	6,000.–		William SMITH
1815 May 1	Daniel KIRKLAND Guardian	Jacob SNELL	2,000.–		
1815 May 1	Allen TOOKE Guardian	Arthur TOOKE	3,000.– [300.]		
1815 May 1	Josiah D. CAUTHORN Mary SYLVESTER Admr. & Admx.	William GOODSON & Murdoch McDUFFEE	6,000.–		John SYLVESTER
1815 May 1	Hannah SNELLING & John SWEARINGEN Admx. & Admr.	Allen TOOKE & Jacob SNELL	10,000.–		John SNELLING
1815 May 1	Hardy VICKERS Jason BRINSON Admr.	William HALL & William GOODSON	15,000.–		Lester CRAWFORD
1815 May 1	William GARBITT Admr.	Samuel HART [HOLT]	10,000.–		Brokenberry ANDERS
1815 July 10	Bazil HARRIS Admr.	Elijah WALLACE	500.–		Joshua HARRIS

Names of Administrators & Guardians

Date	Admr. & Guard.	Securities	Amount	Orphans	Names of the Deceased
1815 July 3	Mark MASON Admr.	Jordan DEES	500.–		John SMILEY [SMEDLEY]
1815 Nov. 6	Mary JONES Guardian	John JONES Senr.	2,000.–	The orphans of	James JONES Deceased
1815 Nov. 20	Milley CARDIN & John CARDIN Admx. & Admr.	James CLARKE & Allen TOOKE	5,000.–		Charles CARDIN
1816 Jany. 1	John WILSON Admr.	John G. BARROW Reuben WARREN	500.–		James WILSON
1816 Jany. 1	Milley CARDIN & John CARDIN	James CLARK & Allen TOOKE	5,000.–		Charles CARDIN
1816 Jany.	Ely RAMSEY Admr.	Washington LANCASTER	3,000.–		John RAMSEY
1816 Mar. 4	Christopher EDWARDS Tempy. Admr.	Joseph WOOD	1,000.–		Dianna DUNN
1816 Mar. 4	Daniel RHODES Guardian	Daniel P. SNELL Daniel KIRKLAND	10,000.–	Peggy R. REEVES otherwise called Peggy R. SNELL, Clarissay Isabella REEVES, otherwise Clarisay Isabella SNELL & General Jackson REEVES otherwise General Jackson SNELL	Jacob SNELL
1816 Apl. 29	Thomas W. HARRIS Admr. on the unadm. part	Jesse POWELL	10,000.–		William A. HARPER
1816 Apl. 29	Theodrick MONTFORT	Robert MORELAND	4,000.–		John K. MONTFORD
1816 May 11	Mary THARP	Andrew SMITH & John SMITH	1,500.–		William A. THARP

Names of Administrators & Guardians

Date	Admr. & Guard.	Securities	Amount	Orphans	Names of the Deceased
1816 May 6	John SHERROD Admr.	Simon BARDIN	700.–		Josiah CASON
1816 May 6	Redman MASON Admr. [de bonis non]	James DEES	500.–		John SMEDLEY
1816 May 6	John A. WILLIAMS & Elizabeth SMITH Admr. & Admx.	William GOODSON Archibald THOMPSON	3,000.–		Wm. SMITH
1816 May 6	Holden DUNN Guardian	Robert [or Rolin] DUNN & William GRINSTEAD	500.–	Elizabeth DUNN Penelope DUNN	
1816 July 1	Joseph B. BRYAN Guardian	Joel WALKER	250.–	Wm. A. THARP	
1816 July 1	John A. WILLIAMS Admr.	Washington LANCASTER & Thomas W. HARRIS	5,000.–		Wm. SMITH
1816 July 1	John BRADSHAW Jordan DEES & Easter KENT Admrs. & Admx.	James DEES & Joseph BARROW [*BARRON*]	5,000.–		Stephen KENT
1816 July 1	John CARDIN Admr. de bonis non	James M. TAYLOR	600.–		Susannah McGILL
1816 Oct. 30	John RAZOR Tempy. Admr.	Samuel REGAN	3,000.–		Shadrack LEE
1816 Nov. 4	Ely RAMSY Admr.	Allen TOOKE William YARBROUGH Peter J. HARVEY	500.–		William RAMSY
1816 Nov. 4	Ely RAMSY	Allen TOOKE William YARBROUGH Peter J. HARVEY	500.–		John RAMSY

Names of Administrators & Guardians

Date	Admr. & Guard.	Securities	Amount	Orphans	Names Deceased
1816 Nov. 4	John SHERROD Administrator	Simon BARDIN	6,000.–		William ROBERTS
1816 Nov. 4	Milley CARDEN Guardian	Allen TOOKE James CLARK	500.–	Jefferson CARDIN	Charles CARDIN
1816 Decr. 19	Stephen GATLIN Guardian	George G. GAINES	7,000.–	Daniel [D.] & Robert STURGES	[Robt. STURGES]
1817 Jany. 13	Thomas McGRIFF Guardian	Daniel COLE Jas. PHILIPS Thos. W. HARRIS R. H. THOMAS	14,000.–	Mary PHILIPS	~~Mary~~ PHILIPS
1817 Jany. 13	William J. MURRELL Guardian	John WARMACK John HODGES	1,200.–	Simon ROBERTS	
1817 Jany. 13	Edward BRYAN Guardian	Daniel COLE	1,000.–	Serena SYLVESTER	John SYLVESTER
1817 Jany. 6	Edward BRYAN Guardian	Daniel COLE	7,000.–	Harriot SYLVESTER	"
1817 Jany. 6	Daniel COLE Guardian	Edward BRYAN	1,000.–	John SYLVESTER	"
1817 Jany. 13	John WARMACK Guardian	John HODGES	1,200.–	Benjamin ROBERTS	
1817 Jany. 6	Theophilus SUTTON Admr.	John B. PACKER	1,000.–		Solomon SUTTON
1817 Jany. 6	John RAZOR Admr.	Lewis HOLLAND Joseph REGAN	3,000.–		Shadrack LEE
1817 Feby. 6	Hannah SNELLING [Guardian]	George G. GAINES	8,000.–	Grace SNELLING William F. SNELLING Richard J. SNELLING Phebianna SNELLING	

Names of Administrators & Guardians

Date	Admr. & Guard.	Securities	Amount	Orphans	Names Deceased
1817 Mar. 3	Isaac NICHOLS Guardian	Joel DAWSON Kenchen DAWSON	1,000.–	Martha W. REEVES	
1817 Mar. 3	Simon BARDIN Admr.	Blakeley EDINS	1,000.–		James BELTHROP
1817 May 5	Josiah EVERITT Guardian	James BRACEWELL	6,000.–	Sarah SMITH William J. SMITH Alexander SMITH Margaret SMITH	Wm. SMITH
1817 July 7	Thomas HOWELL Guardian	Thomas JOHNSTON	6,000.–	Rebaccah HOWELL Sarah HOWELL & James HOWELL	Robt. HOWELL
1817 July 7	Lydia LOVIN Admx.	George G. GAINES	5,000.–		Adam LOVIN
1817 Sept. 1	John SHERARD Guardian	John WARMACK	1,200.–	Simon ROBERTS	
1817 Septr. 1	Samuel JAMISON Guardian	John SHERRARD	10,000.–	Eliza JONES & Artimisa JONES	Philip JONES
1817 Septr. 1	John SHERARD Admr.	John WARMACK	100.–		Elizabeth ROBERTS
1817 Septr. 1	Ann BENNET Admx.	William YARBROUGH	1,200.–		John BENNETT
1817 Octr. 30	Benjamin S. LANIER [Temp. Admr.]	Thomas SPEARS Charles CREECH & Jos. [Jas.?] SALTER	4,000.–		Clement LANIER
1817 Nov. 3	Jane W. CRUTCHFIELD Guardian	Rookins JELKS William JELKS James S. IVEY & Dixon JELKS	15,000.–	James Dabney CRUTCHFIELD Martha Anderson CRUTCHFIELD	John CRUTCHFIELD

Names of Administrators & Guardians

Date	Admr. & Guard.	Securities	Amount	Orphans	Names Deceased
1817 Nov. 3	Allen TOOKE Guardian	Jas. M. TAYLOR Arthur TOOKE	15,000.	Hannah TOOKE	Harlon H. TOOKE
1817 Nov. 18	Mary DEES Jordan DEES & John B. PACKER Tempy. Letters	William HORNE	15,000.		James DEES
1817 Nov. 28	Kinchen DAWSON Tempy. Admr.	Elisha FARNELL & Henry SMITH	4,000.		Joel DAWSON
1817 Nov. 22	Stephen HAGAN Admr.	John McCORMICK Mat McCORMICK	4,000.		Isham HAGAN
181~~7~~8 Jany 6	Stephen HAGAN Guardian	William HAGAN	500.	Mary HAGAN	Isham HAGAN
1818 Jany. 8	Benjamin S. LANIER Guardian	Bird LANIER Levi HARRILL Asa HARRELL [John HARRELL]	3,500.	John J. [S.] LANIER & Sarah M. LANIER	
1818 Jany. 8	John SPARROW Christian SPARROW Admrs.	Bolin SWEARINGEN	2,000.		Daniel SPARROW
1818 Jany. 6	John B. PACKER Jordan DEES & Mary DEES	Elisha FARNELL & Simon BARDIN	16,000.		James DEES
1818 Jany. 8	Benjamin S. LANIER Admr.	John HARREL Bird LANIER Levi HARRELL Asa HARRELL	2,500.		Clement LANIER
1818 Jany. 6	Stephen HAGAN Admr.	William YARBROUGH Daniel McNAIR	4,000.		Isham HAGAN

Names of Administrators & Guardians

Date	Admr. & Guard.	Securities	Amount	Orphans	Names of the Deceased
1818 Jany. 6	Kinchen DAWSON Admr.	Robert THOMPSON & Thomas HOWELL	4,000.		Joel DAWSON
1818 Feby. 2	John SHERRARD Guardian	Jospeh B. COLESON	1,500.	Benjamin ROBERTS	Wm. ROBERTS
1818 Feby. 5	James ROACH & Thomas JOHNSTON Temp. Admr.	William JELKS	20,000.		John B. PACKER
1818 Feby. 3	Josiah EVERITT & Washington LANCASTER Adm. de bonis non	Arthur TOOKE Thos. MILLS	10,000.		by John A. WILLIAMS administrator of William SMITH
1818 Mar. 18	Timothy BRUER Admr.	Joel SHERRARD	1,500.		Horace PEABODY
1818 May 4	John McRAE Master to	Richard MITCHELL James POWELL	400.	master to John STEPTOE who will be 16 years old the 16. Decr. 1818 & to Rick STEPTOE who is now thirteen	
1818 May 4	John DEES Admr.	Blakley EDINS John GILSTRAP	2,000.		Hillard DEES
1818 May 4	Mary BRYAN Admx.	Jesse BRYAN Jesse SUTTON & William HAWTHORN	12,000.		Needham BRYAN
1818 May 4	Timothy BRUER Admr.	James S. IVEY	1,500.		Horace PEABODY
1818 May 4	John SPARROW & Christian SAPRROW	Biggars SINGLETON Kinchen DAWSON	1,500.		Daniel SPARROW

Names of Administrators & Guardians

Date	Admr. & Guard.	Securities	Amount	Orphans	Deceased
1818 July 6	John GILSTRAP Guardian	John DEES	2,000.	Thomas GRAY Willoughby GRAY	Mathias GRAY
1818 July 6	James DYKES Henry DYKES Admrs.	William BRYAN Benjn. HARRISON William BOWLING Elias DYKES	25,000.		George DYKES
1818 July 6	James DYKES Admr.	Henry DYKES	600.		Daniel DYKES
1818 Septr. 7	Samuel JEMISON Guardian	Ezkl. TAYLOR	14,000.	Eliza JONES Artimisia JONES	Philip JONES
1818 Sept. 7	Josiah D. CAWTHORN Guardian	Jordan DEES	1,000.	John SYLVESTER	
1818 Sep. 7	Simon BARDIN Guardian	Jordan ANDERSON	2,600.	Henry ROBERTS	William ROBERTS
1818 Sept. 9	Benjamin COLLINS Guardian	Thomas SHEPHERD	400.	John COLLINS Mathew COLLINS & James COLLINS	his wife, children
1818 Sept. 9	Thomas SHEPPARD Admr.	Benjamin M. COLLINS	50.		Reuben BATES
1818 Sept. 7	John DEES Admr.	Ezekiel TAYLOR Jordan ANDERSON	4,000.		Hillard DEES
1818 Nov. 2	Nathaniel DYKES Guardian	William HAWTHORN Benjn. S. LANIER Conrad AUGLEY	600.	John E. DYKES	David DYKES

Names of Administrators & Guardians

Date	Admr. & Guard.	Securities	Amount	Orphans	Names of Deceased
1818 Octr. 5	James M. TAYLOR Admr.	James S. IVEY	500.		James L. PERRY
1818 Decr. 17	Stephen GATLIN Guardian	Samuel JONES Furney F. GATLIN	15,000.	Louissa TOOKE Joseph TOOKE Mary R. TOOKE Allinson TOOKE	William TOOKE
1818 Decr. 11	Dennis ADAMS Allen CARR Temp. Adm.	John RAWLS & William HILLIARD	6,000.		William WILLIAMS
1818 Decr. 7	Josiah STEWART Tempy. Admr.	Wright DAVIS Samuel CHERRY	50,000.		William DAVIS
1818 [*no date*]	James M. TAYLOR Temp. Adm.	Edward SMITH	1,000.		James L. PERRY
1819 Jany. 11	Dennis ADAMS [Allen CARR] Admr[s].	Allen CARR William HALL	1,000.		William WILLIAMS
1819 Jany. 11	Furney F. GATLIN Richard MITCHELL Admr.	Samuel JONES Arthur TOOKE	20,000.		Hardy GATLIN
1819 Jany. 11	Fanney DELAMAR Admx.	Thomas CLAYTON Senr. & Tuttle H. MORELAND	5,000.		Thomas DELAMAR
1819 Jany. 11	Rhoda HANKS Admx.	William YARBROUGH	500.		Joseph HANKS
1819 Jany. 11	Thomas W. HARRIS Admr. de bonis non	James DYKES Henry DYKES	20,000.		Needham BRYAN

Names of Administrators & Guardians

Date	Admr. & Guard.	Securities	Amount	Orphans	Deceased Persons
1819 Jany. 11	Thomas McGRIFF William MAYO Guardian	Blakely EDINS James ROEBUCK	11,000.	Sarah[,] Jourdan[,] Elizabeth DEES [*see note p. 239*]	James DEES
1819 May 3	Fanny DELAMAR Guardian	Thomas CLAYTON Tuttle H. MORELAND	3,000.	Sarah DELAMAR John DELAMAR Thomas DELAMAR	Thomas DELAMAR
1819 May 3	R. W. W. WYNNE Guardian	Kinchen DAWSON	1,200.	Harriet GILLAH & Mary GILLAH	
1819 May 3	Henry DYKES Admr. de bonis non	James DYKES	1,500.		David DYKES
1819 July 5	Stephen GATLIN Guardian	Joseph WOOD	10,000.	Elizabeth DUHART	David DUHART
1819 July 19	Thomas W. HARRIS Guardian	Josiah EVERITT	6,000.	Elizabeth L. HARRIS Catharine W. HARRIS	Sampson HARRIS
1819 July 5	John McRAE Guardian	Wm. HAWTHORN Duncan RAY	6,000.	Caroline JACKSON	Thos. JACKSON
1819 July 5	Burton H. PITTS Admr.	George G. GAINES	6,000.		John DUHART Junr.
1819 Sept. 6	Isaac KIRKSEY Temp. Adm.	William HALL	1,000.		Parham TUDER? alias Parham KIRKSEY
1819 Sept. 6	William FOLSOM & Edith FOLSOM Admr. & Admx.	Ashley CAWTHORN Reddin STRINGER	8,000.		George FOLSOM
1819 Sept. 7	Thomas BURNAM Admr.	Jas. M. TAYLOR	1,400.		Martha MANNING a minor

Names of Administrators & Guardians

Date	Admr. & Guard.	Securities	Amount	Names Orphans	Names Deceased
1819 Sept. 6	William HALL Admr. with the will annexed	Joseph WOOD Joel SHERRARD Isaac KIRKSEY	16,000.		Sutton TRULUCK
1819	Thomas BURNAM Admr. to a minor	James M. TAYLOR	1,000.		Martha MANNING a minor decd.
1819	Burton H. PITTS Admr.	George G. GAINES	5,000.		John DUHART
1820 Jany. 29	William MAYO & Rolley? ROEBUCK Temp. Adms.	Thomas JOHNSTON	3,000.		John ROEBUCK
1820 Jany. 12	John CARDIN Temp. Admr.	Daniel McNAIR	500.		Jesse CARDIN
1820 Jany. 12	Nancy GRAHAM Admx.	Joseph FLETCHER John FLETCHER Jesse KENT Benjn. MANNING D. McRAE	3,000.		James GRAHAM
1820 Jany. 1	Lewis HOLLAND Admr. with the will annexed	Kinchen DAWSON & Sherod ALLEN	4,000.		Thomas SMITH
1820 Jany. 3	Hardy VICKERS Admr.	William LESTER	2,000.		Soloma SHEPHERD
1820 Jany. 17	William HALL Admr. with the will annexed	William JELKS & Joel SHERRARD	10,000.		Sutton TRULUCK
1820 Feby. 5	Sherrod ALLEN Tabitha YERTA Temp. Admr. & Admx.	John LEE	5,000.		Abraham YERTA

Names of Administrators & Guardians

Date	Admr. & Guard.	Securities	Amount	Orphans	Names Deceased
1820 Mar. 6	John GILSTRAP Guardian	Josiah EVERITT	5,000.	Joolet, Betsey, Polly, & Evelina GILSTRAP	Jeremiah GILSTRAP
1820 Mar. 6	Hardy VICKERS Guardian	William LESTER	3,000.	Caisa SHEPHERD	Soloma SHEPHERD
1820 Mar. 6	Joel SHERRARD Guardian	William JELKS Hardy VICKERS	5,000.	Simon ROBERTS & Benjamin ROBERTS	William ROBERTS
1820 Mar. 22	Gray B. GARDNER & Henry KENT Tempy. Admrs.	Richard MITCHELL Edward SMITH Peter B. GREENE John RAWLS James A. EVERITT Jacob WATSON	60,000.		Samuel JONES Senr.
1820 Mar. 6	Stephen GATLIN Admr.	Furney F. GATLIN Allen TOOKE	30,000.		David DUHART
1820 Mar. 6	Rolley ROEBUCK William MAYO	James ROBUCK Thos. McGRIFF	3,000.		John ROBUCK
1820 May 11	Bray MAYO Admr.	John B. BUSH	3,000.		Mark MAYO
1820 July 3	Isaac NICHOLS Guardian	Fredk. FLOYD	600.	Martha W. REAVES	
1820 July 8	Jessee SUTTON Guardian	John LEE	1,000.	Zelpha BRYANT	
1820 July 3	Bray MAYO Admr.	John B. BUSH James ROBUCK	3,000.		Mark MAYO
1820 July 3	Shadrick ALLEN & Tabitha YERTA	Jesse SUTTON John LEE John POWELL	4,000.		Abraham YERTA

Names of Administrators & Guardians

Date	Admr. & Guard.	Securities	Amount	Orphans	Names Deceased
1820 Septr. 7	James BRACEWELL Tempo. Admr.	G. B. GARDNER James A. EVERITT	5,000.		Edward CLINCH
1820 Nov. 27	Joseph B. COALSON Guardian	John GILSTRAP Bartlett BARKER	6,000.	Mary Ann & James Madison PACKER	John B. PACKER
1820 Nov. 13	Stephen GATLIN Guardian	Furney F. GATLIN James M. TAYLOR	8,000.	Thomas GATLIN	
1820 Decr. 1	Benjamin MEWBERN Guardian	Edward SMITH Peter B. GREENE James S. IVEY	7,000.	William B. R. DAVIS	William DAVIS
1820 Decr. 5	Isaac FOREMAN Temp. Admr.	Edward SMITH	4,000.		David FOREMAN
1821 1st Jany.	John POWELL Guardian	Sherod ALLEN Louis HOLLAND	3,500.	George M. WILLIAMS	Samuel & Samuel [?] WILLIAMS
1821 Jany. 2	Furney F. GATLIN Guardian	R. W. W. WYNNE Josiah EVERITT	10,000.	Lincy? SNELL Willet SNELL & Henry SNELL	Daniel P. SNELL
1821 Jany. 1	Nelson CLAYTON Guardian	Thomas CLAYTON John CARUTHERS	12,000.	Delamar CLAYTON	Thomas CLAYTON
1821 Jany. 3	Thomas JOHNSTON Guardian	John GILSTRAP Jesse POWELL	2,500.	Dorcas PACKER an idiot	
1821 Jany. 2	Mary JONES Guardian	Peter B. GREENE Furney F. GATLIN Samuel JONES	20,000.	Haas JONES Lucinda JONES Newnan JONES Hartford JONES	Samuel JONES
1821 Jany. 3	Anna POSEY Umphrey POSEY Benjamin SMITH Benjamin POSEY admrs.	Amos WHEELER John McRAE Isaac KIRKSEY Benjamin MEWBERN	12,000.		Nehemiah POSEY

Names of Administrators & Guardians

Date	Admr. & Guard.	Securities	Amount	Orphans	Deceased Persons
1821 Mar. 5	Hardy VICKERS Guardain	William LESTER Joel SHERROD	9,000.	Silas M. LESTER Nathan M. LESTER Alfred J. LESTER	Nixon LESTER
1821 Mar. 5	Nancy GRAHAM Admx.	George G. GAINES	3,000.		James GRAHAM
1821 Apl. 28	John DESHAZO Admr.	Henry KING	500.		Martin B. HORNE
1821 Apl. 9	Jesse SENTERFIT Henry SENTERFIT Temp. Admrs.	Joel SHERRARD	5,000.		Jesse SENTERFIT Senr.
1821 July 2	Lewis WOOD Guardian	Abram WOOD William HALL	2,000.	Jane TRULUCK	
1821 July 2	John DESHAZO ~~Guardian~~ Admr.	Jordan DEES	500.		Martin B. HORNE
1821 July 2	William HALL Admr.	Wright LANCASTER & Henry KING	8,000.		Isaac KIRKSEY
1821 July 3	Mary JONES Admx.	Henry KING Edward SMITH	4,000.		Newnan JONES
1820† July 3	Mary JONES & Henry KING Admx. & Admr.	Elisha FARNELL James S. IVEY Duncan RAY	30,000.		Samuel JONES Senr.
1820 July 15	Hardy VICKERS Admr.	William LESTER	10,000.		Soloma SHEPHERD
1820 Aug. 1	Wright LANCASTER Aaron JOHNSTON Admrs.	Shadrack ATKINSON Wash. LANCASTER	4,000.		Charles DANIEL

Names of Administrators & Guardians

Date	Admr. & Guard.	Securities	Amount	Orphans	Deceased Persons
1820 Nov. 13	James BRACEWELL Elizabeth CLINCH Admr. & Admx.	William HALL Duncan RAY Richard MITCHELL Furney F. GATLIN Jas. M. TAYLOR Jacob WATSON	10,000.		Edward CLINCH
1820 Nov. 13	Josiah EVERITT Admr.	Duncan RAY	500.		Elizabeth SMITH
1820 Nov. 7	Wright LANCASTER Elizabeth DANIEL	Aaron JOHNSON Shadrack ATKINSON	2,000.		Charles DANIEL
1821 Sept. 3	Henry SENTERFIT Guardian	Jesse SENTERFIT Stephen SENTERFIT	2,000.	John SENTERFIT	Henry SENTERFIT Senr.
1821 Sept. 3	Jesse SENTERFIT Henry SENTERFIT	Stephen ROACH Gray B. GARDNER	12,000.		Henry SENTERFIT Senr.
1821 Nov. 5	Allen TOOKE Guardian	Arthur TOOKE	9,000.	Lawrence TOOKE Jesse Brett TOOKE	John TOOKE
1821 Nov. 26	Neal CULBREATH Temp. Adm.	Charles SEABERT Edward SMITH	1,000.		Daniel CULBREATH
1821 Nov. 5	Mary DEES Admx.	Thomas McGRIFF Hardy VICKERS	9,000.		James DEES
1822 Jany. 14	James BRACEWELL Guardian	William HALL William JELKS	8,000.	Edmund W. ODOM Martha J. H. ODOM Archibald H. ODOM	
1822 Jany. 14	William HALL Guardian	Thomas JOHNSTON John GILSTRAP	4,000.	James KIRKSEY John KIRKSEY Wm. KIRKSEY Mary KIRKSEY	Isaac KIRKSEY

Date	Admr. & Guard.	Securities	Amount	Orphans	Names of the Deceased
1821 Jany. 2	Hardy POWERS Admr. with will annexed	Thomas McGRIFF James ROBUCK	9,000.		Jacob SNELL
1822 Jany. 14	James TRULUCK Guardian	Lewis WOOD Sutton H. TRULUCK	2,000.	Elizabeth TRULUCK	Sutton TRULUCK
1822 Jany. 2	William COLE Temp. Admr.	Isaac W. MITCHELL John RAWLS Joshua R. WIMBERLEY	20,000.		Joseph WOOD
1822 Jany. 26	Levin GILSTRAP Guardian	Lewis M. LOPER John GILSTRAP	200.	Elizabeth GILSTRAP	James GILSTRAP
1822 Jany. 15	Richard WHITAKER Guardian	Thomas McGRIFF John B. BUSH	5,000.	Martha[,] Hamblin[,] Madison SNELL Alison SNELL Cornelia SNELL	[*see note p. 239*]
1822 Jany. 14	Hardy VICKERS Guardian	William LESTER Furney F. GATLIN	4,000.	Casandra SHEPHERD	Joseph SHEPHERD
1822 Jany. 14	Elizabeth DANIEL Guardian	Richard MITCHELL Wm. HAWTHORN	1,500.	Elizabeth DANIEL Martha DANIEL Charity DANIEL Andrew Jackson DANIEL	Charles DANIEL
1822 Jany. 14	William HALL Guardian	William JELKS James BRACEWELL	2,000.	Sarah TRULUCK	Sutton TRULUCK
1822 Jany. 14	Reddick BRYANT Exr. in right of his wife	Turner COLEY Jesse BRYANT	4,000.		Joseph REGAN [Joseph BRYANT?]
1822 Feby. 4	Joney SAVAGE Robert SAVAGE Tempo. Admrs.	Lewis HOLLAND Archd. ODOM	3,000.		Nathan L. SAVAGE

Names of Administrators & Guardians

Date	Admr. & Guard.	Securities	Amount	Orphans	Deceased
1822 Jany. 14	Lovey KIRKSEY Guardian	Richard BARLOW Hardy VICKERS	-	Susan KIRKSEY	Isaac KIRKSEY
1822 Feby. 11	John BRISCOE Temp. Admr.	Richard MITCHELL	6,000.		Abednigo WRIGHT
1822 Mar. 28	James S. IVEY Temp Admr.	Bartlett BARKER	1,000.		Epps IVEY
1822 Mar. 18	James McCORMICK Temp. Admr.	Mat[hias] McCORMICK Stephen ROACH	2,200.		Samuel HART
1822 Mar. 30	Wesley YARBROUGH Temp. Admr.	Bartlet BARKER	2,000.		Uriah YARBROUGH
1822 May 6	Alethea COALSON Furney F. GATLIN Admx. & Admr.	Allen TOOKE Stephen GATLIN Stephen ROACH	- [6,000.]		Joseph B. COALSON
1822 May 6	Benjamin HOWELL Admr.	N. STEVENS Thomas JOHNSTON	10,000.		Thomas HOWELL
1822 May 6	John HABMLETON Admr.	Washn. LANCASTER	4,000.		David FOREMAN
1822 May 6	Robert SAVAGE Admr.	Lewis HOLLAND Archd. ODOM	3,000.		Nathan L. SAVAGE
1822 May 6	Simon BARDIN Arthur BARDIN Admrs.	Thomas McGRIFF John DEES	6,000.		Redmon B. MASON

Names of Administrators & Guardians

Date	Admr & Guard.	Securities	Amount	Orphans	Deceased
1822 May 6	John BRISCOE Milton WRIGHT Admrs.	Richard MITCHELL Moses YARBROUGH	10,000.		Abednigo WRIGHT
1822 May 6	~~John HAMBLETON~~ Wm. McCORMICK Anne H. HART James McCORMICK Admrs.	~~Wm. McCORMICK~~ ~~Anne H. HART~~ ~~James McCORMICK~~ Needham STEVENS John GILSTRAP	4,000.		Samuel HART
1822 July 22	James S. IVEY Admr.	Bartlett BARKER Thomas McGRIFF	2,000.		Epps IVEY
1822 July 2	Wesley YARBROUGH Admr.	Bartlett BARKER Furney F. GATLIN	2,000.		Uriah YARBROUGH
1822 July 1	Seldon J. DELAMAR Thomas DELAMAR Admrs.	Nelson CLAYTON John CARRUTHERS Sen.	6,000.		Francis DELAMAR Sen.
1822 Sept. 2	William LOVELESS Guardian	Lewis HOLLAND Fredk. FLOYD	800.	Martha REAVES	John REAVES
1822 Sept. 16	Thomas J. JOHNSTON Barbara THOMAS Admr. & Admx.	James JOHNSTON Senr. Josiah EVERITT	15,000.		Richard H. THOMAS
1822 Octr. 31	Benjamin HOWELL Guardian	John B. BUSH Stephen ROACH David ROACH	2,000.	Turner HOWELL	
1822 Nov. 4	Duncan RAY Tempy. Admr.	James BACEWELL Josiah EVERITT Furney F. GATLIN Thomas JOHNSTON	60,000.		Allen TOOKE

Names of Administrators & Guardians

Date	Admr. & Guard.	Securities	Amount	Orphans	Deceased
1822 Nov. 18	Jacob WATSON Guardian	Seth G. WATSON Robert THOMPSON James S. IVEY	2,000.	Francis PUGH	Francis PUGH
1822 Nov. 18	Josiah EVERITT Guardian	Thomas JOHNSTON	2,000.	James PUGH	Francis [Thos.?] PUGH
1822 Nov. 18	Sherard ALLEN Guardian	Archd. ODOM Simon BARDEN	1,500.	Jacob BLOUNT	Isaac BLOUNT
1823 Jany. 13	Gidion KELLUM Temp. Admr.	Henry W. FENN	1,500.		Thomas W. BENSON
1823 Jany. 15	Archibald ODOM Temp. Admr.	William JELKS	2,000.		Henry HART
1823 Feby. 11	James NEWMAN & Elizabeth HADDOCK Temp. Adm.	Elisha FARNELL	3,000.		William HADDOCK
1823 Feby. 17	Nelson CLAYTON Temp. Admr.	Furney F. GATLIN	2,500.		William CLAYTON
1823 Mar. 4	Edith FOLSOM Guardian	Abraham WOOD F[r]ancis J. HOBBY	600.	Ebenezer G. FOLSOM Clary Ann FOLSOM	George FOLSOM
1823 Mar. 17	Thomas ADAMS Guardian	Wm. B. McGEHEE	750.	Eliza CRAWFORD	Lester CRAWFORD
1823 Mar. 17	Cintha CRAWFORD Guardian	John CRAWFORD James [H.] TRULUCK	1,500.	Cintha CRAWFORD Ezekiel CRAWFORD	["]

Names of Administrators & Guardians

Date	Admr. & Guard.	Securities	Amount	Names Orphans	Names Deceased
1823 Mar. 3	John CRAWFORD Guardian	William HALL William JELKS	600.	Nancy CRAWFORD Bird CRAWFORD	Lester CRAWFORD
1823 Mar. 3	Randal FOLSOM Guardian	John CRAWFORD	300.	Thomas FOLSOM	George FOLSOM
1823 Mar. 3	Alethea COALSON Guardian	Furney F. GATLIN	4,000.	Mary Ann PACKER	John B. PACKER
1823 Mar. 17	John RAWLS & William COLE Admrs.	Wm. B. McGEHEE Thomas McGRIFF Furney F. GATLIN	25,000.		Joseph WOOD
1823 Mar. 3	William FOLSOM Guardian	James ROUNTREE	600.	Israel FOLSOM Pernel FOLSOM	George FOLSOM
1823 Mar. 3	Hannah BENSON Joseph W. BRANTLEY	Robt. W. W. WYNNE Thomas McGRIFF	2,000.		Thomas W. BENSON
1823 Mar. 3	Robert HODGES Admr.	Robert GLINN William PACE Edward GIDDINS	20,000.		Ephraim PHILIPS
1823 Mar. 3	Archibald ODOM Admr.	Adon SCARBROUGH Robert SAVAGE	2,000.		Henry HART
1823 Mar. 3	Murdock McLEOD Admr.	Robert HODGES	100.		Asa PIPKIN
1823 May 6	Bartlett BARKER & William FARNELL Temp. Admrs.	Thomas McGRIFF James S. IVEY Nelson CLAYTON	30,000.		Elisha FARNELL

Names of Administrators & Guardians

Date	Admr. & Guard.	Securities	Amount	Names Orphans	Names Deceased
1823 May 5	Mary ANDERSON Admr. with the will annexed	Simon BARDIN Stephen GATLIN	12,000.		Jordan ANDERSON
1823 May 5	Nelson CLAYTON Admr.	George COOPER Furney F. GATLIN	5,000.		William CLAYTON
1823 May 5	Elizabeth HADDOCK James NEWMAN Admx. & Admr.	Furney F. GATLIN Samuel ROBISON	4,000.		William HADDOCK
1823 June 28	Mathias McCORMICK Tem. Admr.	David LEWIS	1,500.		William McCORMICK
1823 July 7	Hillory HENDERSON Temp. Admx.	Furney F. GATLIN	600.		Furney TRIPP
1823 Sept. 1	Nancy MASON Guardian	Stephen GATLIN	4,000.	Berril B. MASON Susanah MASON Arthur B. MASON	Redmon B. MASON
1823 Sept. 1	Nancy HART Guardian	Mathias McCORMICK George CHERRY	1,000.	Emanuel HART Elmira HART	Samuel HART
1823 Sept. 1	Mary CLAYTON Guardian	Jeffry MONTFORT James BRACEWELL	1,700. [700]	Thomas CLAYTON	William CLAYTON
1823 Sep. 1	Bazil KORNEGAY Guardian	Shadk. ATKINSON Kindred HALL	5,000.	Daniel KORNEGAY	George KORNEGAY
1823 Sept. 1	Bartlett BARKER William FARNELL Admrs.	Thomas McGRIFF James BRACEWELL	35,000.		Elisha FARNELL

Names of Administrators & Guardians

Date	Admr. & Guard.	Securities	Amount	Names Orphans	Names Deceased
1823 Sept. 1	Mathias McCORMICK Admr.	George CHERRY Jeffrey MONTFORT	1,600.		William McCORMICK
1823 Sept. 1	Hillary HENDERSON Admx.	Thomas McGRIFF	500.		Furney TRIPP
1823 Octr. 7	Amos BROWN Temp. dmr.	Bartlett BARKER John J. LANIER	3,000.		Robert L. CHURCH
1823 Octr. 10	William HOLLOMAN Guardian	Thomas JOHNSTON William MAYO	400.	Elizabeth, David, Fountain, Needham HOLLOMAN	William HOLLOMAN
1823 Nov. 3	William HADDOCK Temp. Admr.	Willis B. REEVES Thomas SUTTON	1,000.		Luke HADDOCK
1824 Jany. 20	Hardy VICKERS Nathan VICKERS Temp. Admrs.	William LESTER	3,000.		Abraham VICKERS
1824 Jany. 7	Bartlett BARKER Guardian	Thomas McGRIFF	2,300.	Henry SPARROW Biggars J. SPARROW	~~Henry~~ SPARROW
1824 Jany. 7	Robert HIGDON Guardian	William HALL	800.	William KIRKSEY	
1824 Jany. 7	Murdock McLEOD Guardian	Hardy POWERS	100.	Jesse PIPKIN	
1824 Jany. 5	Celia KELLUM & Robt. W. W. WYNNE Admx. & Admr.	Stephen ROACH Benja. HOWELL	2,400.		Gideon KELLUM

Names of Administrators & Guardians

Date	Admr. & Guard.	Securities	Amount	Names Orphans	Names Deceased
1824 Mar. 1	William HADDOCK Admr.	Willis B. REEVES Turney COLEY	600.		Luke HADDOCK
1824 Feby. 3	Wright HOWELL Temp. Admr.	David ROACH	800.		Frederick HOWELL
1824 Mar. 15	Sessims PERKINS Guardian	Furney F. GATLIN	5,000.	[Mary Ann PACKER]	[John B. PACKER]
1824 Mar. 1	Silas E. CRAWFORD Guardian	John CRAWFORD James H. TRULUCK	717.	Ezekiel CRAWFORD	Lester CRAWFORD
1824 Mar. 1	Hiram ATKINSON Guardian	James H. TRULUCK John CRAWFORD	1,800.	Cyring SYLVESTER	John SYLVESTER
1824 Mar. 1	Thomas JOHNSTON Admr.	William JELKS Hardy VICKERS	2,000.		Dorcas PACKER
1824 Mar. 1	Turner COLEY Admr. de bonis non	Moses BRYAN Furney F. GATLIN	4,000.		[*none listed*]
1824 Mar. 1	Hardy VICKERS Nathan VICKERS Admrs.	Thomas JOHNSTON Furney F. GATLIN	2,500.		Abraham VICKERS
1824* Mar. 7 [1814]	Washington LANCASTER Haywood ALFORD Admrs.	Robert THOMPSON P. BRYAN Jas. M. TAYLOR	10,000.	[**should be 1814* *see minutes p. 209*]	William S. LANCASTER
1824 May 3	Joel SHERROD Guardian	Stephen GATLIN Willis B. REEVES	5,000.	Simon ROBERTS Benjamin ROBERTS	William ROBERTS
1824 May 3	Wright HOWELL Admr.	David ROACH	800.		Fredk. HOWELL

Names of Administrators & Guardians

Date	Admr. & Guard.	Securities	Amount	Names Orphans	Names Deceased
1824 July 6	William F. SNELLING Guardian	James BRACEWELL James HAYES [Jeffry MONTFORD] [Bolen SWEARINGEN]	1,200.	Thomas CLAYTON	William CLAYTON
1824 July 6	Thomas JOHNSTON Admr.	James BRACEWELL	4,000.		Lewis M. LOPER
1824 July 6	Darling JONES Guardian	Mary JONES Haas JONES	3,000.	Andrew D. BEATY Thomas J. BEATY	Thomas BEATY
1824 Octr. 5	James P. CARUTHERS Temp. Admr.	Seldon J. DELAMAR Solomon NELSON	700.		Solomon SUTTON Junr.
1824 Octr.	Neal MOSES Guardian	Ezekiel TAYLOR Baker ADAMS James BROXTON	500. [2,000.]	James GRAYHAM	
1824 Octr. 5	Jason BRINSON Guardian	Hardy VICKERS	700.	Cloe Ann FOLSOM Ebenizer George FOLSOM	
1824 Octr. 5	Mary JONES Admx.	Samuel JONES Haas JONES	2,000.		Lucinda JONES
1824 Decr. 7	Robert HODGES Temp. Admr.	Stephen FULSOM Nathl. MERCER	20,000.		Exum PHILIPS
1825 Jany. 17	William SULLIVANT Guardian	Thomas McGRIFF	300.	Luami? KEITH	Elihu KEITH
1825 Jany. 17	William SULLIVAN Guardian	Thomas McGRIFF	300.	Ann KEITH	Elihu KEITH
1825 Jany. 3	Allen PERRY Guardian	William JELKS Furney F. GATLIN Stephen ROACH	2,500.	Warren SUTTON William H. SUTTON Moses Ann SUTTON	Moses SUTTON

Names of Administrators & Guardians

Date	Admr. & Guard.	Securities	Amount	Names Orphans	Names Deceased
1825 Jany. 29	Stephen FOLSOM Temp. Admr.	Robert HODGES Nathl. MERCER	15,000.		Burrel PHILIPS
1825 Jany. 4	Levin GILSTRAP Temp. Admr.	Henry DEWETT Wesley YARBROUGH Pinkney YARBROUGH Daniel CORNWALL	2,500.		Lewis DEWETT
1825 Jany. 3	James P. CARRUTHERS Tempo. Admr.	Seldon J. DELAMAR Soloman NELSON	2,000.		Solomon SUTTON
1825 Feby. 10	James BRACEWELL Washington LANCASTER Tempo. Admrs.	William JELKS Furney F. GATLIN James S. IVEY	35,000.		Gray B. GARDNER
1825 Mar. 7	Calvin PRATT Admr.	Joseph SIMMONS Daniel SPARROW Nelson CLAYTON	4,000.		William PRATT
1825 Mar. 7	Stephen FOLSOM Admr.	Robert HODGES Nathaniel MERCER	15,000.		Burwell PHILIPS
1825 Mar. 7	James HAYS Admr.	Lewis WOOD Samuel NOBLE Samuel JONES	4,000.		Lewis DEWETT
1825 Mar. 7	Mary MILLS Admx.	Stephen ROACH	1,000.		Spire MILLS
1825 Mar. 7	Richard J. SNELLING Admr.	Washington LANCASTER Wright LANCASTER	6,000.		Dempsey LEARY

Names of Executors &c

Date of Will	Name of Deceased	Name of Executors	When Qualified	Remarks
1809 Octr. 25	Sanders BUSH	Mary BUSH	1810 Feby. 19	
1812 Octr. 12	Solomon A. HOPKINS	Nancy HOPKINS James M. TAYLOR Doctor George PHILIPS Mordicai HOWARD		
1813 June 15	Stephen PENNINGTON	Elizabeth PENNINGTON George WALKER Joseph BRYAN		George WALKER did not qualify
1815 Jany. 15	Phillip JONES	Nancy JONES Edward BLACKSHEAR Samuel JONES	1815 March 6	Edwd. BLACKSHEAR did not qualify
1815 Decr. 6	Mark MASON	Sarah MASON Redman MASON James DEES	23rd Decr. 1815	
1815 Jany. 13	William ROBERTS	Ann ROBERTS Sherrod ROBERTS	1st Jany. 1816	
1816 April 18	Daniel P. SNELL	Anne SNELL Daniel RHODE Daniel KIRKLAND	4th Novem. 1816	KIRKLAND not qualified
1816 Aug. 20	Elizabeth ROBERTS verbal will proved 20th August 1816			
–	William ISLER	Thomas McGRIFF Nancy ISLER	6th Jany. 1817	

Names of Executors &c

Date of Will	Name of the Deceased	Name of Executors	When Qualified	Remarks
1816 Jany. 4	David SNELL	Franky SNELL Daniel RHODES	4th Nov. 1816	
1816 Septr. 26	Jonathan FAIRCLOTH	Thomas HOWELL Thomas JOHNSTON	4th Novr. 1816	JOHNSTON did not qualify
1816 May 9	Thomas PHILIPS	James PHILIPS	12th Jany. 1817	
1817 April 21	Neil ARD	Easter ARD Martha SINGLETARY Hugh CARR	May 5th 1817	Martha SINGLETARY did not qualify
1816 Aug 1	John JONES	Sarah JONES Samuel JONES	7th July 1817	Sarah JONES did not qualify
1817 July 13	Moses SUTTON	Theophilus SUTTON William HADDOCK	Novemr. 3rd 1817	Wm. HADDOCK did not qualify
1817 Nov. 20	Jeremiah GILSTRAP	Ann H. GILSTRAP John GILSTRAP	4th May 1818	
1816 28 Decr.	Daniel SPARROW			
1818 May 26	Mary BUSH	John BUSH William LITTLE		proved 6th July 1818

Names of Executors &c

Date of Will	Name of Deceased	Name of Executors	When Qualified	Remarks
1818 Septr. 23	Edwin VICKERS	Joseph VICKERS Nathaniel MERCER	2nd Novr. 1818	
1814 April 6	Joseph REEVES	his wife Willis B. REEVES		proved the [*blank*] day of [*blank*] 1818
1818 Mar 25	William DAVIS	Micajah DAVIS John ABBOTT Samuel RICHMOND		proved January the 11th 1819
1819 Apl. 1	David DUHART	Stephen GATLIN		provd. 5th July 1819
1819 June 22	Allen SCARBROUGH	Nancy SCARBROUGH		provd. 6th Septr. 1819
1818 Jany. 27	Sutton TRULUCK	Stephen MITCHELL Jr. Elisha EVANS		provd. 6th Septr. 1819
1818 Jany. 2	Jesse TRAYWICK	Francis TRAYWICK Moses TRAYWICK Betsey TRAYWICK	5th July 1819	The two first named Execrs. did not qualify
1820 June 4	Thomas CLAYTON	James CLAYTON Thomas CLAYTON Nelson CLAYTON		
1820 Decr. 18	James REGAN	Elizabeth S. REGAN	proved 1st Jany. 1821	

Names of Executors &c

Date of Will	Name of the Deceased	Name of Executors	When Qualified	Remarks
1820 Sept. 4	Charles HADDOCK	Furney F. GATLIN William HADDOCK	proved Nov. 13th 1820	
1820 Apl. 20	Raleigh ROEBUCK	James ROEBUCK	proved Nov. adjd. term 1830	
1820 Octr. 2	James ROACH	Joseph BLACKSHEAR Elijah BLACKSHEAR Stephen ROACH	proved Nov. adjd. term 1820	
1819 June 3	Thomas SMITH		proved 1st Jany. 1820	
182 † May 27	James M. TAYLOR	Duncan RAY Furney F. GATLIN Allen TOOKE	proved July 2nd 1821	
1821 July 17	George KORNEGAY	Bazzel KORNEGAY Needham STEPHENS	proved May 6 1822	
Agust 24	Arthur TOOKE	Allen TOOKE James TOOKE John TOOKE	proved the 2nd Septr. 1822	
1822 Decr. 6	Jordan ANDERSON		proved 3rd March 1823	
1823 Mar. 20	Needham STEPHENS	Kornegay STEPHENS Benjamin HOWELL	proved 7th Mar. 1825	
–	Allen TOOKE	Arthur TOOKE Gray B. GARDNER James ROACH	proved 6th Mar. 1823	

Names of Executors &c

Date	Admrs. & Guards.	Securities	Amt.	Names of Deceased Persons & Orphans
1825 April 4	Washington LANCASTER James BRACEWELL Admr.	James S. IVEY Furney F. GATLIN William JELKS	30,000.	Gray B. GARDNER
1825 April 4	James S. IVEY & Bertlett BARKER Admr.	William FARNELL Thomas JOHNSTON	3,000	Thomas HATTON
1825 May 2	Hiram ATKINSON Guardian	William JELKS	2,000	Guardian to Elizabeth LEARY orphans
1825 May 2	Penelope LEARRY Guardian	Hiram ATKINSON Richard J. SNELLING	4,000	Guardian to James & Cornelius LEARY orphans
1825 May 2	Robert HODGES Admr.	Nathan MADDOX Nathanl. MERCER	20,000	Axum PHILLIPS
1825 May 2	Richard J. SNELLING Admr.	William F. SNELLING	400.	Francis L. ARMSTRONG
1825 July 4	James TOOKE Admr. with the will annexed	Sterling TOOKE & John RAWLS	20,000.	Allen TOOKE
1825 Sept. 5th	Nelson CLAYTON Guardian	Wiley KENT	1,800.	John JONES & Sarah Ann JONES
1825 Novr. 7th	Sarah ARMSTRONG Admx.	Thomas SPEARS & James JONES	2,000.	Ludwell ARMSTRONG decd.
1825 Novr. 7th	Margaret STEVENS Guardian	K. STEVENS & B. HOWELL	1,000.	Marshall, Elizabeth, & George Kornegay GRIMES minors
1825 Octr. 3rd	Wm. B. POULAN Temporary Admr.	Daniel J. THOMAS	1,000.	Petoway MANN

The book continues with lists for the late 1820's and 1830's. On pages 41-53 many of the 1809-1825 entries are repeated.

The last page is Page 53:

State of Georgia) By the Court of Ordinary for said County
Pulaski County)

To William B. McGEHEE, Wm. LESTER, Hardy VICKERS, Lewis WOOD, Caswell BALL;

These are to authorize and empower you or any three of you to make a just and \true/ appraisement of all and singular the goods and chattels (ready mony only excepted) of James T. THOMAS late of said County deceased in dollars and cents as shall be produced by [*blank*] the Exec[utor] of the estate of the said [*blank*] you and each of you first taking the oath required by law before some Justice of the Peace for said County and you will return the same - Certified under your hands and also a certificate of your having taken the oath thereto annexed unto the said Executor [*blank*] within the time prescribed by law witness the honorable [*blank*] one of the Judges of the said Court of Ordinary this the [*blank*] day of [*blank*] one thousand eight hundred and twenty.

[*End of Book*]

INDEX

Since spelling variations are common, similar-sounding names (i.e. Dreadin/Dryden, McCloud/McLeod) are indexed together, except when evidence suggests that they are different families (as in Ford and Fort).

An asterisk (*) denotes that the entry appears on the indicated page in more than one location.

Anyone who finds what they believe to be an error in the transcribing or indexing of this book is encouraged to send the correction to the author in care of Southern Historical Press.